Higher Education in
Austerity Europe

Also available from Bloomsbury

Academic Identities in Higher Education, edited by Linda Evans and Jon Nixon
Academic Working Lives, edited by Lynne Gornall, Caryn Cook, Lyn Daunton, Jane Salisbury and Brychan Thomas
Identity and Pedagogy in Higher Education, Kalwant Bhopal and Patrick Alan Danaher

Higher Education in Austerity Europe

Edited by Jon Nixon

Bloomsbury Academic
An imprint of Bloomsbury Publishing Plc

BLOOMSBURY

LONDON · OXFORD · NEW YORK · NEW DELHI · SYDNEY

Bloomsbury Academic
An imprint of Bloomsbury Publishing Plc

50 Bedford Square   1385 Broadway
London   New York
WC1B 3DP   NY 10018
UK   USA

www.bloomsbury.com

BLOOMSBURY and the Diana logo are trademarks of Bloomsbury Publishing Plc

First published 2017

© Jon Nixon and Contributors, 2017

British Library Cataloguing-in-Publication Data
A catalogue record for this book is available from the British Library.

ISBN: HB: 978-1-4742-7726-6
ePDF: 978-1-4742-7727-3
ePub: 978-1-4742-7728-0

Library of Congress Cataloging-in-Publication Data
A catalog record for this book is available from the Library of Congress.

Typeset by Newgen Knowledge Works Pvt Ltd., Chennai, India
Printed and bound in Great Britain

In memoriam
Tony Judt
1948–2010

Contents

Illustrations

Figures

Tables

Contributors

Anne Corbett is an Associate of the London School of Economics and Political Science (LSE), UK. A professional journalist for many years in the UK and France, she was a Visiting Fellow at the European Institute of the LSE (2005–2013). Making a lifelong learning turn in the late 1990s, she earned a PhD in government from London University, UK (2002) on the foundational politics and policies of higher education within European Union (EU) institutions. Her research interests continue to be in the policymaking of higher education in European arenas. She has recently turned to the relationship between Britain and Europe, as exemplified by Brexit, and higher education and research. Recent publications include the LSE Commission report on the *Future of Britain in Europe* and *Higher Education and Research 2016*. Her books include *Universities and the Europe of Knowledge, Ideas, Institutions and Policy Entrepreneurship in European Union Higher Education, 1955–2005* (2005), and she has published scholarly articles in the field of European policy on higher education, Brexit and public management. Currently a team member on LSE Enterprise, a contract related to education, she also contributes regularly to *Times Higher Education* and *University World News*.

Dorota Dakowska is Professor of Political Science at the University of Lyon 2 (ENS Triangle), France and a member of the Institut Universitaire de France, France (since October 2015). She has published a book on German political foundations and their involvement in democratization processes (*Le pouvoir des fondations: Des acteurs de la politique étrangère allemande,* 2014) as well as several articles in journals and chapters in edited volumes on the post-communist transition, the European Union's Eastern enlargement, German foreign policy and the Europeanization of higher education in Poland in a regional, comparative perspective. She has coordinated two research projects and introduced two special issues on the transformations of Central and Eastern European academic fields (in the *Revue d'Études Comparatives Est Ouest*, with Ioana Cîrstocea and Carole Sigman, and in the *European Journal of Higher Education* (2015), with Robert Harmsen). Her current research focuses on the international dimension of higher education reforms.

Danijela Dolenec is Assistant Professor at the Faculty of Political Science, University of Zagreb, Croatia, and she teaches comparative politics, politics of contention and social science methodology. She received her master's from the LSE, UK (2005) and her doctorate from the ETH Zürich, Switzerland (2012). Danijela researches post-communist democratization trajectories and preconditions for sustainability reorientations as well as the political economy of higher education. She also serves as the President of the Board of the Institute for Political Ecology in Zagreb, Croatia.

Ourania Filippakou is Reader in Education at Brunel University London, UK. She did her first degree in Education at University of the Aegean, Greece and then obtained a scholarship from the Academy of Athens, Greece to do her postgraduate studies at the UCL Institute of Education, UK. Her main interest is in the theoretical condition of higher education, with particular reference to comparative historical analysis, a perspective that seeks to combine the methods of history with social sciences theories and concepts. She has published in a wide range of journals including *Discourse: Studies in the Cultural Politics of Education; Higher Education; Higher Education Policy; and Higher Education Quarterly,* and edited (with Gareth Williams) *Higher Education as a Public Good* (2014). She is a council member of the Society for Research into Higher Education (SRHE) and visiting fellow at the Oxford Centre for Higher Education Policy Studies (OxCHEPS), New College, University of Oxford, UK.

Tanya Fitzgerald is Professor of History of Education at La Trobe University, Australia, and Head of School, Humanities and Social Sciences. Her research interests span the fields of history of women's higher education, and higher education policy and leadership. She is currently working on an ARC-funded project: *Fostering Women Leaders through Educational Exchange 1930–1980.* Publications in progress include a major reference work, *International Handbook of Historical Studies in Education: Debates, Tensions and Directions* (forthcoming). Tanya has been the Chief Editor of *History of Education Review* (2002–2012), is currently co-editor of the *Journal of Educational Administration and History* (with Helen M. Gunter, 2007–17) and is one of the series editors of *Perspectives on Leadership in Higher Education* (with Jon Nixon and Camilla Erskine). She is the elected President of the Australian and New Zealand History of Education Society (2015–17).

Åse Gornitzka is Professor in the Department of Political Science, University of Oslo, Norway and affiliated Research Professor at Arena – Centre for European Studies, University of Oslo, Norway. She is also Adjunct Professor, Department of Administration and Organization Theory, University of Bergen, Norway and is currently Co-Editor in Chief of *Scandinavian Political Studies.* Her academic interests include the organization of political orders, European Union governance and decision-making, public reforms and organizational change, especially in knowledge systems. She has conducted studies on the role of experts in policymaking.

Esko Harni is a PhD candidate at the University of Tampere, Finland. His dissertation focuses on the ethos and politics of entrepreneurialism in late capitalism. He has also conducted research on political theory (especially on Michel Foucault's and Giorgio Agamben's political philosophy), the politics of psy-sciences and educational sociology. He teaches philosophy and writes book reviews. You can follow him on Academia.edu (https://jyu.academia.edu/EskoHarni).

Marnie Holborow, Associate Faculty member in the School of Applied Language and Intercultural Studies at Dublin City University, Ireland, has written widely on politics and language. Besides holding visiting scholar positions at Hunter College, New York, USA, and San Francisco State University, USA, she has been a guest lecturer at City University of New

York, USA. She is author of *The Politics of English,* and of chapters and articles on neo-liberalism and applied linguistics, on the legacy of Raymond Williams and, most recently, on conflicting interpretations of the political keyword Brexit. In 2016, she contributed the first entry of *Neoliberalism* for the *Encyclopaedia of Applied Linguistics.* Her most recent book is *Language and Neoliberalism* (2015). She is a long-standing trade union activist and has campaigned against austerity policies in Ireland and for the defence of the public university.

Ari-Elmeri Hyvönen is a PhD candidate at the University of Jyväskylä, Finland. His research focuses on contentious politics, international relations (world politics) and political theory (especially the thought of Hannah Arendt). He is currently finalizing his PhD dissertation on the notion of experience in Arendt's political thought. In 2014–15 he was a visiting fellow at the Hannah Arendt Center for Politics and Humanities at Bard College, New York, USA. You can follow him on Academia.edu (https://jyu.academia.edu/AriElmeriHyvönen) and Twitter (@AriElmeriHyvnen).

Manja Klemenčič is Lecturer in Sociology of Higher Education at Harvard University, USA. She researches, teaches, advises and consults in the area of international and comparative higher education, with particular interest in the implications of contemporary higher education reforms for students. Manja is also Editor-in-Chief of *European Journal of Higher Education*; Thematic Editor of the volume *Elite and Mass Higher Education in the 21st Century* of the *International Encyclopaedia of Higher Education Systems and Institutions*; and Co-editor of the book series *Understanding Student Experiences in Higher Education.* She is a member of the editorial boards of *Policy Reviews in Higher Education, Tertiary Education and Management, Higher Education in Russia and Beyond, Journal of Student Affairs in Africa* and *The Europa World of Learning.* She serves on the governing board of the Consortium of Higher Education Researchers (CHER) and on the advisory board of the Global Forum on Improving University Teaching (IUT). For her publications see, http://scholar.harvard.edu/manja_klemencic/ns

Marek Kwiek holds a UNESCO Chair in Institutional Research and Higher Education Policy and is a director of the Center for Public Policy Studies at the University of Poznan, Poland. His most recent monograph is *Knowledge Production in European Universities: States, Markets, and Academic Entrepreneurialism* (2013). His research interests include university governance, academic entrepreneurialism and the academic profession. He has published 170 papers and nine monographs, mostly internationally (*Higher Education, Studies in Higher Education, Science and Public Policy, Comparative Education Review, International Journal of Educational Development, Journal of Studies in International Education*). He is a Principal Investigator or country Team Leader in about fifty international higher education research and policy projects (global and European), funded by the European Commission (e.g. the 6th and 7th Framework Programs), the European Science Foundation (ESF) and the Fulbright, Ford, and Rockefeller Foundations. He is an editorial board member of *Higher Education Quarterly, European Educational Research Journal, British Educational Research Journal* and *European Journal of Higher Education.* Email: kwiekm@amu.edu.pl.

Daphne Kyriaki-Manessi is a Professor in the Department of Library Science and Information Systems, Technological Educational Institute (TEI) of Athens, Greece. She also teaches in the Graduate Program on Museum Studies of the University of Athens, Greece. She has a PhD from the Faculty of Information Science of the University of Toronto, Canada. She also holds a master's of library science from Dalhousie University, Halifax, Canada. She served as the Special Secretary of the Greek Ministry of Education for four years (2000–4) and was responsible for the country's Libraries, Archives, Educational Television and Educational Media. Recent publications include *Managing Digital Content* (2016). She has participated in or led various research/development projects, and she is currently team leader of the TEI of Athens Research Team participating in the Horizon2020 Crosscult Project: 'Empowering Reuse of Digital Cultural Heritage In Context-Aware Crosscuts of European History'. Her academic interests include knowledge management, structures of data and their description standards as well as their applications in repository environment. Web page: http://users.teiath.gr/dkmanessi/index.html

Paolo Landri is a Senior Researcher of the Institute of Research on Population and Social Policies at National Research Council in Italy (CNR-IRPPS). His main research interests concern educational organizations, professional learning and educational policies. He has edited with Tara Fenwick *Materialities, Textures and Pedagogies* (2014). Email: p.landri@irpps.cnr.it

Rosaria Lumino is a Postdoctoral Research Fellow in the Department of Political Science, University of Naples Federico II, Italy. Her main research interests are in the field of evaluation studies and social policies. Among her latest publications are *Evaluative Knowledge and Policy Making: Beyond the Intellectual Virtue of Téchne* (with D. Gambardella, 2016). Email: rosaria.lumino@unina.it

Jon Nixon is an independent scholar based in the United Kingdom. He is affiliated to the Education University of Hong Kong, Hong Kong as an Honorary Professor and as an Honorary Senior Research Fellow within the Centre for Lifelong Learning Research and Development. His most recent books are *Gadamer: The Hermeneutical Imagination* (2017) and *Hannah Arendt and the Politics of Friendship* (2015). His other books include *Interpretive Pedagogies for Higher Education: Arendt, Berger, Said, Nussbaum and Their Legacies* (2012); *Higher Education and the Public Good: Imagining the University* (2011); and *Towards the Virtuous University: The Moral Bases of Academic Practice* (2008). He has co-edited *Academic Identities in Higher Education: The Changing European Landscape* (with Linda Evans, 2015) and *The Reorientation of Higher Education: Challenging the East-West Dichotomy* (with Bob Adamson and Feng Su, 2012). He is a founding editor of the Bloomsbury Perspectives on Leadership in Higher Education Series. His full list of publications can be accessed via his website: www.jonnixon.com.

John O'Sullivan, MA, PhD, lectures in journalism, media and technology at the School of Communications, Dublin City University (DCU), Ireland where he is a researcher attached to the Institute for Future Media and Journalism. He is Research Fellow in the Faculty of Humanities and Social Sciences, 2016–17, and was a Visiting Researcher (2016) at the University of Udine, Italy. His research interests have centred on the interplay of professional journalism with digital technologies and on the use of media platforms. He is currently supervising research on social media in South East Asia, and on sourcing of online health news in Ireland. A former member of the DCU union committee, he was active in opposing austerity measures and in the establishment of recent campaigns to defend the public role of the university. His DCU web profile is available at http://www.dcu.ie/communications/people/john-osullivan.shtml.

Jae Park is an Assistant Professor at the Education University of Hong Kong, Hong Kong. His research interests are in sociology and philosophy of education. He recently published articles in *Educational Philosophy and Theory, International Studies in Sociology of Education, Comparative Education* and *Ethics & Behaviour.* Among his works on higher education are a co-edited volume, *Sociological and Philosophical Perspectives on Education in the Asia-Pacific Region.* He is the Past President of the Comparative Education Society of Hong Kong and serves as the Head of the International Education Research Unit in the Centre for Lifelong Learning Research and Development of the Education University of Hong Kong, Hong Kong. He is Editor-in-Chief of the *International Journal of Comparative Education and Development.*

Nicole Rege Colet is an independent consultant whose academic career has been involved in exploring educational development in higher education. She has actively taken part in the unfolding of the Bologna Process. Her work has focused on supporting academics in adapting to their new environments and engaging in professional and organizational development. Her most recent mission, at the University of Strasbourg, France, involved building up the teaching and learning capacities there, setting up a new structure exploring and evaluating innovative practices. Drawing on her interdisciplinary and intercultural experience, her current work looks at leadership development and change processes. She is committed to supporting people, communities and organizations to shift and engage collectively in meaningful and socially responsible projects, letting go of old paradigms of thought and action.

Almantas Samalavičius earned his PhD in architectural history and theory and is currently a Professor at the School of Architecture, Vilnius Gediminas Technical University, Lithuania, where he teaches architectural criticism, aesthetics of architecture, cultural theory and urban studies. Simultaneously he is professor of literary theory at Vilnius University, Lithuania. He is author of twelve books on architectural history, urbanism and literature (including two books focused on the history and present problems of higher education) and has edited ten volumes of collections of academic essays and literary anthologies and numerous essays and articles. He has taught as guest professor at various universities in Europe, the United States and Asia. He serves as the Editor-in-Chief of two international scholarly periodicals: *Journal of Architecture and Urbanism* and *Lituanus.* For more than a decade he has worked as an expert at the Lithuanian Center for Quality Assessment of Studies and Lithuanian National Research Council. His writings won him eight prizes in

Lithuania and were translated into fourteen languages. In addition he has previously served as president of Lithuanian PEN of PEN International.

Roberto Serpieri is Professor of Educational Policy and of Sociology of Education in the Department of Social Sciences, University of Naples Federico II, Italy. His interests are in the field of Foucauldian and governmentality studies. Among his latest publications is the co-edited *New Public Management and the Reform of Education: European Lessons for Policy and Practice* (with H. M. Gunter, E. Grimaldi and D. Hall, 2016). https://www.docenti.unina.it/roberto.serpieri

Acknowledgements

The editor would like to thank the editorial team at Bloomsbury – Alison Baker, Maria Giovanna Brauzzi and Camilla Erskine – for their encouragement, support, understanding and patience, and for overseeing the rigorous peer-review process involved in bringing this project to fruition. Thanks also to the anonymous reviewers whose comments on the original proposal and the submitted manuscript have been insightful, constructive and challenging. Finally, thanks to Marnie Holborow and Stewart Ranson for their comments on an early draft of the editorial introduction.

The book is dedicated to the memory of Tony Judt, the chronicler and interpreter of post–World War II Europe, who – through his work and by example – taught us what it means to be European.

Foreword

Anne Corbett

London School of Economics and Political Science, UK

There is a black joke at the start of this stimulating book on Europe and higher education in the wake of the financial crisis of 2007–8: 'Austerity ... downgrades all our deepest bonds to junk'.

I, for one, lock into that. I read the most disquieting legacy of the last ten years of austerity to be social. The massive public bailout of the banks, the adoption of austerity policies to reduce public debt and the economic recession that followed have produced divided societies. They are divided not simply for and against the European Union (EU) but by respect or scorn for reason. It is a societal problem and not just a sectoral problem that the intellectual and scholarly professions are hit from two directions. On the one hand they are devalued by governments impervious throughout the EU to critiques of austerity policies, however authoritative the source. On the other they are derided by a significant section of the population in the EU, along with the governing elites and experts, as responsible for their diminished quality of life.

The present book is a treat for this reader for stretching the conceptual boundaries of the interaction of austerity and the higher education sector in looking at the issue from three perspectives. It provides contextual understanding of the idea of austerity in terms of ideas and institutions. The second perspective opens up cross-European empirical evidence on government treatment of higher education as economic recession has set in. Third, and especially welcome, are reflections and evidence of what higher education actors might do by actively calling into play the epistemological values and the practices of the sector.

What do we learn about context? Difficult-to-change ideas such as austerity are the product of decades of interlocking thoughts and institutions, and existed long before globalization. The years since 2007 have not been the first time governments have struggled over how to stabilize an international economic order that is subject to a massive accumulation of public debt. It was John Maynard Keynes who first articulated the problem in *The Economic Consequences of the War*. The solutions have changed in the wake of events and the balance at the time between giving powers to strong political institutions and treating the issue as technocratic, allowing the market free rein subject to defined criteria. Bretton Woods, the Washington Consensus and the Maastricht Treaty are all part of this story.

What we should also register is that the EU is not quite such a unitary actor as it pretends to be and as it is treated by all who speak the word 'Brussels' through gritted teeth. Its economic role is as described in the introduction, one of the policemen of austerity. But the case of the education and culture branch of the Commission bureaucracy should be noted. It could so well have been swept away by the crisis. Instead, in the face of the exogenous shock it got its act together with sectoral support. It now negotiates a place at the crossroads of the EU's economic, cultural, democratic and social concerns.

A second lesson of the book, with implications for policy, is that austerity rules may be put in place through the EU and national governments, but on the ground there are radical differences as to how the rules should be interpreted in the higher education domain. At one extreme is the effect of a country heavily exposed to debt and the external and internal pressures that go with it. Greece is the classic example. At the other extreme is Poland, where domestic forces see external incentives for higher reform less in the evolution and more in the context of post-communist transformation and EU accession. In between are countries where path dependence seems to be the rule, here exemplified by Croatia. Lithuania and France, seeking to calm their publics, have tried to disguise their turn to austerity. But there is one linking factor: the choices are political, not mechanical.

The third lesson is that higher education scholars and higher education institutions can, and should, draw on their epistemic strengths, partly to understand why a disquieting number of citizens have directed their anger at democracy rather than at capitalism since recession set in, partly to show why in a competitive university world, there are alternatives to being ruthless.

There are illustrations in this book. One reaction of scholars working in Finland was to intellectualize their protest against austerity by going back to the thinking of Hannah Arendt on 'responding thoughtfully' and being prepared to disturb the status quo or what she termed the 'undisturbed maintenance of the social life process'. An ethnological account of how academics at the University of Strasbourg in France set about using their autonomy when they came into funds that had been won through competitive funding challenged the status quo in a different way. They chose to demonstrate that fairness and equity can be combined with excellence to the benefit of a university's interlocking roles in teaching, scholarship and research.

One author in this collection suggests that universities can best avoid an equation between the decline of the welfare state and the decline of the university by continuing to fight to be themselves. But for this reader there are even bigger issues than the fate of the sector at stake. If European societies are to meet the challenges set by the UK Brexit vote, the election of Donald Trump to the US presidency and the rise of populist parties on the Continent, then there is a much greater public role for universities across Europe to perform. It matters to everyone that there are strong social institutions which function on reason and evidence.

This book demonstrates why we should think beyond austerity – and on a European scale.

Introduction: Thinking *Within, Against* and *Beyond* Austerity

Jon Nixon

Austerity starves the more its maw is fed, and downgrades all our deepest bonds to junk.

(A. E. Stallings, 2016)

The reasons for the 2007/08 global economic crisis have been widely debated.[1] However, there is now a general consensus that one of the major contributory factors was ever-riskier lending by the banks employing ever-more unintelligible models and financial instruments. Indeed, none other than Mervyn King, the former governor of the Bank of England, has gone on record as condemning not only the banks themselves but the bankers for their complicity in a system that was clearly driven by greed and hubris (2016) .The immediate response was to stave off full-blown economic collapse through programmes of quantitative easing (the process whereby a central bank purchases government securities or other securities from the market in order to lower interest rates and increase the money supply). With this end in view the United Kingdom created £375 billion of new money in its quantitative easing programme between 2009 and 2012, while the eurozone began its programme in January 2015 with a view to creating 60 billion worth of euros each month till September 2016. (The programme was later extended to March 2017.)

With the central banks having printed enough currency to avoid the complete collapse of the financial system, governments were under less pressure to make the structural, regulatory and fiscal reforms necessary to avoid a recurrence of the crisis. As a result they held back from any serious attempt at financial regulation, while at the same time pushing forward with austerity measures that include cuts in public spending and welfare and the privatization of public assets and services. The claim underlying

---

[1] August 2007 is generally given as the start of the global crisis. However, it took a year for it to come to a head, a key point being the date on which the US government allowed the investment bank Lehman Brothers to go bankrupt: 15 September 2008. Contributors to this book vary in referring to the crisis as either the '2007/08 crisis' or the '2008 crisis'.

these measures – which are pursued with ever more vigour – is that reduced public spending will lead to overall economic expansion by increasing business confidence. Austerity – so it is claimed – sounds a loud and clear message to business that it will not be 'crowded out' of the marketplace; business – suitably reassured – will then respond with entrepreneurial zeal and increased investment; and – as day follows night – economic growth will thereby ensue and with it increased prosperity. With ten years having elapsed since the 2007/08 financial crisis it should be possible to make some provisional assessment of these claims and the challenges they present – and, on the basis of that assessment, to point to some of the ways in which practitioners, institutions and the higher education sector as a whole are responding to these challenges. This book sets about that task.

In this chapter I first outline the origins of austerity within post–World War II Europe. The institutional frameworks, economic mechanisms and ideological assumptions developed during that period created the conditions under which austerity became the automatic response to the 2007/08 crisis. Having outlined how economic austerity became institutionally and ideologically embedded within post–World War II Europe, I go on to review three significant lines of critical argument mounted against the policies and underlying assumptions of austerity. These focus on notions of fairness and effectiveness and on the presupposition that the economy is an autonomous or 'disembedded' sphere. I then highlight the legacy of austerity with reference to the democratic deficit among the citizenry as a whole, the generational stratification experienced most keenly by the millennial generation of those born between 1980 and 1999 and the divisions opening up within and across the continent of Europe. The final section outlines the structure of the book and relates individual chapters to some of the major themes touched on in this opening chapter. The purpose is to think through the impact of austerity in order to think beyond it.

Underlying the argument of the book is the claim that, as A. E. Stallings highlights in the quotation that heads this chapter, economic austerity downgrades the bonds of civil society and in so doing erodes the moral foundations of participative democracy.

The origins of austerity

The practices and underlying assumptions of economic austerity have a history. They did not simply appear from nowhere as a reaction to the 2007/08 crisis, but were already present as key determinants of how the response to that crisis would take shape and by what institutional mechanisms it would be delivered. They were also, as Alex Callinicos (2010) has argued, part of a much more protracted crisis of overaccumulation and profitability within the global economy as a whole. To understand the significance of austerity we need therefore to locate it within a broader institutional and geopolitical history: a history, that is, of how in an increasingly globalized world European governments have sought – and continue to seek – to establish an international monetary and financial order capable of sustaining individual nation states. The crucial question was and remains, what are the conditions necessary for maintaining social cohesion and political stability across nations while ensuring economic growth?

The Bretton Woods Agreement

That was – in general terms – the question addressed by the 730 delegates from all forty-four allied nations who attended the United Nations Monetary and Financial Conference held at Bretton Woods, New Hampshire, United States, between 1 and 22 July 1944.[2] Their answer was to establish one strong and seemingly sustainable currency as the anchor currency of the global exchange rate system with fixed but adjustable rates. It was agreed that the US dollar should serve as this anchor. Two institutions were established to support this exchange rate system: the International Monetary Fund (IMF) and the World Bank. The IMF consisted of a funding pool to which participating nations contributed through a quota system and from which countries with a payment imbalance could borrow. It was in effect the custodian of the system. The World Bank was responsible for encouraging economic development through private lending and sought to achieve greater economic stability worldwide. (Somewhat confusingly, the 'fund' was in effect a bank, and the 'bank' really a fund!) The Bretton Woods agreement – coupled with the Marshall Plan of 1947, by which the United States provided funds to rebuild Western European economies – formed the economic basis of the European post-war settlement which lasted until the early 1970s.

At the heart of that settlement was the notion of 'the welfare state'. This constituted a radical rethinking of the state according to social democratic principles. Tony Judt, in his magisterial history of post–World War II Europe, argued that 'the welfare states of western Europe were not politically divisive. They *were* socially re-distributive in general intent (some more than others) but not at all revolutionary ... Far from dividing the social classes against each other, the European welfare state bound them closer together than ever before, with a common interest in preservation and defense' (2005: 76; original emphasis). Judt continues, 'The post-war state all across Europe was a "social" state, with implicit (and often constitutionally explicit) responsibility for the well-being of its citizens' (77). Different governments interpreted 'welfarism' in different ways according to their histories and cultures. No 'welfare state' was identical to any other. Nevertheless, each was an expression – at the level of practice and policy – of the need for state intervention in the rebuilding of societies and polities in the aftermath of World War II.

From the outset controversy surrounded the IMF. John Maynard Keynes, author of the hugely influential 1935 *General Theory of Employment, Interest, and Money* and one of the main architects of the Bretton Woods Agreement, was desperate to persuade the American delegates not to place the headquarters in Washington, where he feared it would function more as an appendage of the American state than as an independent and international body. He argued vehemently for the IMF – and the World Bank – to be based in New York, but lost the crucial vote (see Skidelsky, 2004: 829–30.) Nevertheless, the Bretton Woods Agreement was a huge symbolic and practical achievement: its symbolic significance lay in its acknowledgement that

---

[2] For histories of Bretton Woods, see Gardner (1956); Steil (2013); and van Dormael (1978). Steil draws on relatively new material relating to Harry Dexter White – now known to have been a Soviet spy – who with Keynes was one of the major architects of the Bretton Woods Agreement.

lasting peace would be possible only if states cooperated in managing the world economy, while its practical importance lay in its establishment of a system of fixed but variable exchange rates that provided economic security across states while allowing individual states to pursue their own domestic policies.

This way of thinking about interstate relations was in marked contrast to the peace settlement negotiated after World War I, which had prioritized political and legal questions (such as settling territorial boundaries) over economic and moral questions (such as how to build a united Europe). For Keynes, the Bretton Woods Agreement was, for all its compromises, a riposte to what he had characterized in his 1919 *The Economic Consequences of the Peace* as the gross iniquities and sheer wrong-headedness of the Versailles Treaty. As Robert Skidelsky, an eminent economist in his own right and author of a major biography of Keynes, put it, 'We still live in the shadow of Keynes, not because his legacy has been assimilated, but because it is still disputed' (2004: 837).

The Washington Consensus

The Bretton Woods Agreement, a major part of Keynes's disputed legacy, began to fall apart when in August 1971 US president Richard Nixon announced the suspension of the dollar's convertibility into gold. The background to this decision was the huge military burden of the Vietnam War and a growing US Federal budget deficit, which between 1965 and 1968 increased from $1.6 billion to $25.2 billion (Judt, 2005: 454). By 1973 the major currencies were beginning to float against each other, maintaining semi-fixed ratios between their currencies and allowing a margin of 2.25 per cent movement either side of the approved rates. This interstate agreement – termed 'the snake' – was highly vulnerable given its exposure to the 1973–74 stock market downturn and the 1973 oil crisis.[3] The latter impacted particularly harshly on countries heavily reliant on oil imports, countries such as Italy, which relied on imported oil for 75 per cent of its energy requirements, and Portugal, which relied on it for 80 per cent of its requirements (Judt, 2005: 455). For such countries, the snake clearly had a sting in its tail. It is hardly surprising, therefore, that in 1978 it was recast into the more rigorous – and, as hoped, more reliable – European Monetary System (EMS), whereby exchange rates were linked by a purely notional unit of measure termed the European Currency Unit, or ecu, and underwritten by the German economy and the Bundesbank.

Although the system that was emerging – commonly referred to as the Washington Consensus – was the outcome of a series of pragmatic responses to largely unforeseen economic problems, it nevertheless represented a radical break with the previous regime. As Skidelsky points out,

> The two regimes were shaped by two different philosophies. The Bretton Woods system broadly reflected the Keynesian view that an international economy needed strong political and institutional supports if it was to be acceptably stable.

---

[3]   The 1973 oil crisis was occasioned by the Arab members of the Organization of Petroleum Exporting Countries (OPEC) imposing an oil embargo in response to the United States supplying arms to Israel during the Yom Kippur War. The embargo lasted from October 1973 to March 1974 by which time the price of oil had quadrupled.

> The Washington Consensus regime was shaped by the theory of the self-regulating market. (2009: 117)

The notion of 'the self-regulating market' to which Skidelsky here alludes is the economic cornerstone of what is now generally termed 'neo-liberalism'. Although something of an academic catchphrase – and used in the main pejoratively – the term does highlight the ideological emphasis within the dominant orthodoxy on trade liberalization with regard to economic boundaries and the liberalization of capital across global markets.[4] Both forms of liberalization denote a shift in the control of the economy from the public to the private sector – a shift that is managed through a monetary policy regime whereby central banks, currency boards or other regulatory bodies determine the size and rate of growth in the money supply. From a neo-liberal perspective, monetary policy renders all but the most minimal fiscal policy – whereby the state seeks to control the economy by adjusting tax rates and public spending – both unnecessary and counterproductive: fiscal expansionism, through either raised taxation or increased borrowing, can – so the neo-liberal argument runs – only serve to disturb the supposedly delicate equilibrium towards which the market naturally and inevitably aspires. According to this analysis 'the welfare state' is part of a problem to which 'the small state' is the final and definitive answer.[5]

Neo-liberalism was built on the ideas of the Austrian School (e.g. Hayek: 1944; 1960; 1988), the Chicago School (e.g. Friedman with Friedman, 1962; Friedman and Friedman, 1980) and the Public Choice School (e.g. Buchanan and Tullock, 1962). Economists working within this broad field of neo-liberalism drew philosophical sustenance from three mid-twentieth-century reinterpretations of classical liberalism: Popper (1945), Berlin (1958) and Nozick (1974). According to the credo of neo-liberalism, politics and the economy should be seen as entirely different realms. It championed – and continues to champion – the small state, but the implication of its 'small state' ideology is to bring wholly new areas of human activity under the domain of transactional exchange and to make them subject to market relations. The idea of the *small* state was, in other words, premised on the reality of an increasingly *strong* state. The embedded liberalism of the Keynesian post–World War II settlement, in which free markets were embedded in a web of social and political constraints, was swept away. In its wake came an ideology not only of the free and unregulated market but of social control through the mechanism of market relations. Economic austerity is an instrument of that ideology.[6]

If, as Skidelsky claims, the Washington Consensus represented a radical break at the level of underlying philosophy, it also allowed for significant institutional continuities.

---

[4] See Amin (2014), Brass (2011), Ness (2016) for analyses of the global impact of market liberalization, and Holborow (2015) for an analysis of neo-liberalism as an ideology that permeates everyday language use and helps shape organizational cultures.

[5] See Madrick (2010) for the counterargument.

[6] On the one hand, the reintroduction of protectionism (the practice of shielding domestic industries from foreign competition by taxing imports) by the Trump administration, and the consequent retreat from trade liberalism, may suggest that we are entering a period of post–neo-liberalism. On the other hand, the emphasis on financial deregulation by the Trump administration is a clear indication that some of the core elements of neo-liberalism are still alive and well in the United States.

Chief among these were the IMF and the World Bank. With the breakup of the Bretton Woods system the IMF was in theory rendered redundant. In reality, however, it came to have a key role in the new regime. With the aid of the World Bank it exerted considerable control over the structural adjustments required to achieve economic stability across currencies. Moreover, it established a framework for structural adjustment that placed an overriding emphasis on the need to minimize fiscal deficits, inflation and tariffs; maximize privatization and the liberalization of finance; and break up trade unions. 'The result', writes Mark Blyth (2015: 162–3), 'was a series of one-size-fits-all policies that were applied from Azerbaijan to Zambia'. These 'one-size-fits-all policies' were in effect the precursor of 'expansionary fiscal contraction', and the IMF – in systematically applying those policies – was a vital means of institutionalizing and normalizing what were to become the defining assumptions of economic austerity.[7]

Maastricht and beyond

Germany, with its history of low inflation and price stability, maintained the role of monetary anchor from the late 1970s to the end of the century. During that period, as Heiner Flassbeck and Costas Lapavitsas (2015: 9) put it, 'the political will to adhere to economic policies and a monetary model similar to that pursued by Germany shaped the European debate on monetary policy and exchange rates to a very large extent.' This political resolve was stiffened with the fall of Communism in 1989 and the ensuing collapse of the USSR. This defining moment opened up the possibility of an extended or developed Europe – a 'Greater Europe' – and was seen in some neo-liberal quarters not only as the end of the Cold War but as 'the end of history'. It was, argued Francis Fukuyama (1992), the vindication of Western liberal democracy as the final form of human government and of economic liberalism as the apotheosis of global capitalism.[8] The IMF, with its emphasis on the minimization of fiscal deficits, inflation and tariffs and the maximization of privatization and the liberalization of finance, sat very comfortably within the new neo-liberal orthodoxy. Throughout the 1980s it became increasingly difficult for policymakers to think outside that frame. 'There is no alternative' became the guiding assumption.[9]

Following the Maastricht Treaty and the establishment of the European Union (EU) on 1 November 1993, the construction of a more expansive and sustainable Economic Monetary Union (EMU) became a major policy objective.[10] The inclusion

---

[7] The 'expansionary fiscal contraction hypothesis' can be traced back to Alesina and Ardagna (1998; 2010) and Alesina and Perotti (1995; 1997). Perotti (2011) later seriously questioned the validity of the hypothesis.

[8] History, of course, immediately spoke back to 'the end of history' thesis with a forceful reminder – in the form of the decade-long wars and the accompanying atrocities and war crimes perpetrated in the former Yugoslavia – that it was still very much alive and kicking.

[9] The statement 'there is no alternative' is ascribed to Margaret Thatcher. The initial letters of the four words comprising the statement went on to form an acronym – TINA – which became one of Thatcher's nicknames.

[10] The EU should not be confused with the forty-seven–nation Council of Europe founded in 1949. Its greatest achievement is the European Convention on Human Rights (ECHR), which was adopted in 1950. The ECHR enshrines in European law fundamental human rights and has been evoked in support of, for example, gay and lesbian rights, the right of privacy and employment rights.

of a larger group of countries – some of a similar size and economic power to that of the now reunited Germany – suggested the need for a common bank that was independent of any single currency. That need was eventually met when on 1 June 1998 the European Central Bank (ECB) was established. In creating the ECB – and significantly extending the powers of the European Commission (EC) in respect of the formulation and clarification of policy – the Maastricht Treaty paved the way for the introduction of the euro and the creation of what is now termed the 'eurozone'. The snake having been recast as the ecu now gave way to the euro. Paul Wallace highlights the significance of this event:

> On 1 January [1999], the founder states, which included the four big economies of Germany, France, Italy and Spain, locked their exchange-rates irrevocably against one another. Even though it would take three years until euro notes and coins replaced national money in circulation, at the start of 2002, the ECB based in Frankfurt now set interest rates for the whole of the euro area, affecting over 290 million people living in eleven countries sharing a common currency. (2016: 30)

The establishment of the ECB put in place the final element of what is commonly referred to as 'the Troika': the newly established ECB, the newly empowered EC and the long-established powerbase of the IMF. These are the three institutional pillars of European governance that shape – and to a large extent determine – economic policy across the EU. Operating according to the principles already established within the existing EMU, the Troika has shaped the economic policies not only of those countries comprising the Eurozone but also those member states that retain their own currencies. Indeed, some of the latter – notably the United Kingdom – have been among the most persistent and uncompromising advocates of the monetary policies and principles established by the Troika. Austerity – having been institutionalized and normalized – had become the new economic orthodoxy. So, when the financial crisis of 2007/08 occurred, the institutional conditions necessary for economic austerity were already firmly established.

Those conditions require any European state seeking to restructure its national debt to adopt austerity measures in order to meet the conditions laid down by the Troika. Any country not doing so faces exclusion from the EU and the economic and social consequences that would necessarily follow from that exclusion. The economic orthodoxy is reinforced by an institutionalized policy framework that can – particularly in the case of heavily indebted states – ride roughshod over the political will of democratically elected governments by imposing upon them a standard set of disciplinary and liberalizing policy prescriptions: the removal of capital controls and tariffs, privatization, deregulation and the reining in of public debt (see, for example, Iglesias, 2015, and Varoufakis, 2011 and 2016). George Soros, who has been an outspoken critic of Europe's response to the financial crisis and of Germany's role in shaping that response, characterizes the situation as follows:

> The European Union was meant to be a voluntary association of equals but the euro crisis turned it into a relationship between debtors and creditors where the debtors

have difficulties in meeting their obligations and the creditors set the conditions
that the debtors have to meet. That relationship is neither voluntary nor equal ...
[T]he very survival of the EU is at risk. (Soros and Schmitz, 2016: 36)[11]

Critiques of austerity

Moving from the institutional history of austerity Europe to its present conditions,
two points are glaringly obvious: the economic arguments against austerity carry considerable weight and yet they have been largely ignored or sidelined by national governments and the European bureaucracy. These arguments focus on the fairness and
fitness for purpose of austerity policies but also on the assumptions underlying them.
They are advanced by major authorities within the field of economics but also have
implications for those working in the related field of political philosophy. These critics
of austerity disagree on many points of detail, but are undivided in their view that austerity is a political choice not an economic necessity and that any judgement regarding
its efficacy should be based on that assumption.

Is it fair? Does it work?

First, there are those who argue that the austerity measures implemented post-2007/
08 have resulted in escalating economic inequalities which have in turn led to increasing social exclusion. Such measures are, it is claimed, unjust since the inequalities
they produce cannot be justified with reference to innate capacity or just desert. They
are simply unfair. Different economists focus on different aspects of inequality. For
example, Joseph Stiglitz, a Nobel laureate who served as chairman of the Council of
Economic Advisers in the Clinton administration and as chief economist at the World
Bank during the Asian financial crisis of the late 1990s, has focused throughout his
career on the extremes of income and wealth *at the top* particularly but not exclusively within the US context. His most recent publications continue to focus on these
extremes and their social and political consequences. But they also point to alternative
ways forward: through, for example, high marginal tax rates on the rich and increased
investment in public infrastructure, education and technology (Stiglitz, 2012; 2015a;
2015b; Stiglitz and Greenwald, 2014)

Focusing more specifically on the UK and Europeans contexts, Anthony Atkinson
has, in the course of a long and distinguished career working in the field of public
economics, concentrated on the increase of poverty *at the bottom* (see, for example,
Atkinson, 1969; 1972; 1975; 1999). More recently he too has proposed, in his 2015
Inequality: What Can Be Done?, a set of fully costed and evidence-based policies that
avoid what he sees as the deleterious consequences of the current UK government's

---

[11] Heisbourg (2013), Offe (2016), Sinn (2014) and Stiglitz (2016) also point to what they see as the
design flaws in the eurozone, in particular its shackling together of quite diverse economies in a
common currency without a common treasury.

economic agenda.[12] Writing from within continental Europe but addressing a much wider constituency, Thomas Piketty in his groundbreaking 2014 *Capital in the Twenty-First Century* focuses – as the title of his widely read and widely reviewed book suggests – on the accumulation of capital and in particular its reproduction through lineage and family dynasties (see also Piketty, 2016).[13] The originality of Piketty's approach as yet lies less in his alternative policy formulations than in his and his colleagues' innovative use of hitherto untapped sources of tax data. Nevertheless, his argument, like those of Stiglitz and Atkinson, highlights the impact of inequality on individuals and groups and points to alternative policy orientations by way of a close examination of the direct and indirect causal links between austerity and inequality.[14]

Second, there are those who highlight the failure of the current system to activate growth and productivity and thereby stimulate human flourishing at both the individual level and the level of the local community. Austerity measures are, it is claimed, at best ineffective and at worst counterproductive. The argument, as the former leader of the British Labour Party puts it, is 'that inequality isn't just unfair but that it actually inhibits economic growth' (Miliband, 2015: 19). In support of this line of argument Mark Blyth (2015) provides an analysis of historic cases in which austerity has in his view undoubtedly failed on its own terms and more positive cases where it has arguably succeeded. He concludes that the conditions that made the latter cases possible are absent in Europe at the moment: while one state may be able to cut its way to growth, it cannot work when all states try it simultaneously. Applied universally, thrift is counterproductive since it drives down demand. That is why, from Blyth's perspective, the only way in which Europe can deal with its debts is through taxes and not through austerity: 'Not because austerity is unfair, which it is, not because there are more debtors than creditors, which there are, and not because democracy has an inflationary bias, which it doesn't, but because austerity simply doesn't work' (244).[15]

Larry Liu (2015), too, bases his argument on a detailed analysis of specific cases. Having studied the social and economic consequences of austerity policies in seven European countries (Cyprus, Ireland, Italy, Latvia, Spain, Portugal and the United Kingdom), he argues that the austerity policies pursued have not only increased social suffering for significant groups within these national regions but have also impeded economic growth and increased national debt. Austerity has, he concludes, failed to deliver on its twin promises of deficit reduction and economic expansion. Paul Krugman (2012) – another Nobel Prize winning economist and one of today's leading interpreters of Keynes – argues along similar lines that fiscal cuts and austerity measures simply serve to deprive the economy of funds that could be circulating and

---

[12] These proposals are succinctly summarized in Atkinson (2016).

[13] Piketty is in fact concerned with both wealth and capital, a distinction which Atkinson (2015: 104) argues is crucial given that those who own wealth are not necessarily those who utilize it as capital: 'The power of capital is exercised by the fund managers not by the beneficial owners.'

[14] For an account of the educational and social impact of increased economic inequality among young people, see Putnam, 2015; for a study of the impact of inequality on student lives, see Antonucci, 2016; and for analyses of the impact of inequality on health and physical well-being, see Marmot, 2015, McKee et al., 2012 and Stuckler and Basu, 2013.

[15] Although more guarded in its wording, the 2015 Organization for Economic Cooperation and Development (OECD) report *In it Together: Why Less Inequality Benefits All* makes a similar case.

adding to economic growth (see also Krugman, 2008). He dismisses as 'the confidence fairy' the idea put forward by what he terms the 'Austerians' that such measures raise market expectations and attract private investment – the idea, that is, of 'expansionary fiscal contraction'. The idea, he argues, is based on the highly questionable assumption that the economy remains stable or continues to grow while the austerity policies are implemented. It thereby fails to take into account the economic ripple effects – or back-wash – of austerity whereby the economy is subject to contraction.

Nor does he accept the idea that public investment depresses the economy by 'crowding out' private spending and investment, since government spending not only compensates for lack of private spending but pays for itself in projects such as schools, houses, transport infrastructure and green energy that create value for the economy. While acknowledging that it is necessary to cut debt, Blyth, Liu and Krugman all insist that the worst moment to do so is when an economy has suffered severe finan-cial shocks.[16] If people are unable to spend, markets cannot thrive. The discrepancy between supply and demand that thereby results may partially – and in the short term – be resolved through wage restraint and an increased reliance on overseas mar-kets. But if competing economies within the same monetary union are chasing the same export markets, then there will inevitably be a widening gap between the more advanced economies that are able to meet the market demands and those economies that for historic reasons are less well placed to do so.

This widening gap between the winners and losers calls into question not only the efficacy and viability of the monetary union but also its long-term sustainability – and if the union itself becomes unsustainable, then the economies of its member states, particularly those comprising the inner core of the eurozone, are in jeopardy. This is precisely the situation created by the terms set for membership of the EU. Those terms constitute for any state that for whatever reason chooses not to conform to the precepts and principles of austerity what Heiner Flassbeck and Costas Lapavitsas (2015: 76) call an 'impossible triad'. It is, they argue, impossible for Eurozone members in particular and EU states in general to accomplish all three of the following: 'first, achieving effec-tive restructuring of the debt; second, abandoning austerity; and third, continuing to operate within the institutional framework of the EU and particularly the EMU'.

The 'disembedded' economy

A third critical perspective focuses not so much on the policies themselves – and their consequences – but on the conception of economics that underlies them: the notion of a 'disembedded' economy that is self-sustaining and self-adjusting and that can be managed through the application of specialist technical knowledge. This line of argu-ment was advanced consistently and powerfully by the Hungarian political economist Karl Polanyi, whose life's vocation, as his biographer Gareth Dale (2016: 28) puts it, 'was to subject the commercial ethic to moral critique and the market economy to

---

[16] On this point, as on many others, they follow Keynes who famously declared in an article pub-lished in *The Times* in January 1937: 'The boom, not the slump, is the right time for austerity at the Treasury' (2015: 402).

scientific critique'. His 1944 magnum opus, *The Great Transformation*, provided both a history of market society and an analysis of how – by reducing citizens to egotistical incentive seekers – such a society becomes increasingly atomised (see also Dale, 2010: 188–207).

With the market economy, he argued, came a new type of society and, crucially, a new conception of the economic:

> an 'economic sphere' came into existence that was sharply delimited from other institutions in society. Since no human aggregation can survive without functioning productive apparatus, this had the effect of making the 'rest' of society a mere appendage to that sphere. This autonomous sphere, again, was regulated by a mechanism that controlled its functioning. As a result, that controlling mechanism became determinative of the life of the whole body social ... 'Economic motives' now reigned supreme in a world of their own. (Polanyi, 2014: 35)[17]

Polanyi challenges the idea that markets and governments are separate and autonomous entities. Similarly, the playwright and public intellectual David Hare (2016: 27) makes the point that 'we do not live in a free market. No such thing as a free market exists. Nor can it. The world is far too complex, far too interconnected. All markets are rigged. The only question that need concern us is: in whose interest?' An ungoverned market, Polanyi argues, is a market that ignores that question. It is a market cut loose from its political and social moorings. While acknowledging that markets are necessary for any functioning economy, he insists that any attempt to create a 'market society' – a society based entirely on market principles and dependent on material goods alone – threatens the relational fabric of human life. It denies the very nonmaterial goods – mutuality, reciprocity, recognition – that open up the possibility of a just society and a vibrant polity. Polanyi's critique, in other words, is not just an economic critique of the policies themselves but a moral and political critique of the assumptions underlying those policies.

Polanyi's more general critique is implicit, if not always explicit, in the argument put forward by Atkinson, Piketty and Stiglitz (among others) that austerity is unjust and in the complementary argument advanced by Blyth, Krugman and Liu (among others) that it is at best ineffective and at worst counterproductive. Polanyi's claim that its underlying principles are morally and politically void underpins both lines of argument. Edmund Phelps (2013) – another Nobel laureate – reinforces these various lines of argument from a neo-Aristotelian ethical standpoint. Justice, he argues, is not everything people need from an economy. They also need the wherewithal to fulfil their potential and, in so doing, to prosper. He sees European economies in particular as having failed in respect of what he terms 'mass flourishing' and calls for a reorientation of education towards a greater emphasis on creativity and imagination: a reorientation that, he argues, requires a rebalancing of the curriculum in favour of the arts and

---

[17] This quotation is from an undated conference paper entitled 'Economics and the freedom to shape our social destiny'. Given that some portions of this paper appeared in an article published in 1947, it is reasonable to assume therefore that the conference paper was delivered in the late 1940s.

humanities.[18] He argues that the economy should provide gains in experience rather than just in material reward, although he acknowledges that material gains may be a means to nonmaterial ends. To view the economy as morally and politically 'disembedded' means seeing it as ethically disconnected in terms of self-realization and the fulfilment of individual potential.

It also means that economic security comes to be defined wholly in terms of government bookkeeping. To function well, markets depend on rules, norms and regulations, so questions then arise as to who determines what those rules, norms and regulations will be and in whose interests they operate. Since, as Danielle Allen (2016: 27) argues, such questions are addressed within the political sphere, it is that sphere that 'sets the terms according to which the economic game is played'. So discussions relating to the economy cannot be contained within the economic sphere alone, but need to come back round to the political sphere. Indeed, the idea that the economy is an isolated and impermeable sphere was one of the factors contributing to the financial crisis of 2007/ 08, which had much less to do with public expenditure and public deficits than with the way in which global banks were allowed to extend vast amounts of credit on the basis of very little core capital. The global economy has become increasingly subject to what the author and *Time* economic columnist Rana Foroohar (2016) terms 'financialisation', the trend whereby debt-fuelled speculation takes precedence over productive lending with the result that most of the money in the system is used for lending against existing assets (see Turner, 2015). The banks took immense risks, were bailed out by the public when the risks failed to pay off, and paid huge bonuses to those responsible for the ensuing crisis, thereby squandering the trust and good will of the public. 'In an incredibly short space of time', as James Meek (2016: 7) puts it, 'the banks swelled to grotesque size, then popped.'

Moreover, far from restoring confidence and encouraging investment, the constant emphasis on economic vulnerability and the dire consequences of failing to balance the books has had the effect of chasing away long-term investment that might have provided a more resilient base. 'Austerity, justified by fear', as Phillip Inman (2016) puts it, 'is the reason businesses have been so reluctant to invest.' That reluctance to invest in turn stalls social mobility for key groups within society. Mike Savage et al. (2015) have shown how, within the UK context, this stalling of social mobility is particularly pronounced within the bottom and top layers of society. Within the middle layers there is some evidence of social mobility, but in the bottom and top layers there remains closure and stasis. This, they argue, is because of the complex interaction between cultural, economic and social capital. To inherit all three forms of capital greatly reduces the risk of social de-escalation, while to lack all three greatly reduces the possibility of social escalation. Some emergent groups in between the top and bottom layers may have the opportunity to combine elements of cultural, economic and social capital in such a way as to allow some room for manoeuvrability. The relation between economic capital, on the one hand, and social and cultural capital, on the other, is crucial to understanding how privilege and inequality accumulate over time.

---

[18] Arguing for a broad-based and liberal education, Nussbaum (2010) makes out a similar case for the central importance of the humanities in the school and college curriculum. (see also Nussbaum, 1997).

The only beneficiaries of the 'disembodied' economy, argues the political economist Robert B. Reich (2015: 12), are the rich and powerful: 'as economic and political power have once again moved into the hands of a relatively few large corporations and wealthy individuals, "freedom" is again being used to justify the multitude of ways they entrench and enlarge that power by influencing the rules of the game' (see also Reich, 2012.) Economies that bestow such gains on small groups at the top are inherently unstable. They generate dissatisfaction and social unrest among those at the bottom that can – as is increasingly apparent across Europe – all too easily be channelled into forms of authoritarian populism and directed against vulnerable minorities including immigrants and those dependent on social welfare. In this way the social consequences flowing from the 'disembedded' economy impact on the quality – and, ultimately, the very survival – of democratic politics. The economy not only shapes but is also shaped by the cultural and social conditions within which it is located.

Austerity's legacy

The three critical perspectives outlined above are closely related and, in the main, mutually supportive. Moreover, they have been – and continue to be – advanced by some of the most respected and authoritative economists whose opinions are informed by years of original research and theoretical enquiry. (In addition to the authors previously cited, see, for example: Arestis and Pelagidis, 2010; Flassbeck and Lapavitsas, 2015; Islam and Chowdhury, 2010; Moyo, 2011.) It is remarkable, therefore, that their arguments have not only had so little purchase on policy but have been so summarily dismissed. Of course, economists will always disagree, but the dismissal of the case against austerity is not a case of honest disagreements honestly pursued. The carefully reasoned arguments of economists who oppose austerity are ignored, sidelined or simply vilified. Deployed against them is the full panoply of what Arthur O. Hirschman (1991) termed 'the rhetoric of reaction': the age-old rhetorical ploys used to discredit critics of the status quo on the grounds that their arguments are perverse, futile or present a threat.

To ignore admissible arguments against austerity is to deny austerity's troubled legacy. The critics of austerity highlight its unfairness, its unfitness for purpose and its reification of the economy as an autonomous or 'disembedded' sphere. These critiques point to a legacy in which active citizenship becomes increasingly marginalized within an ever more bureaucratic democracy and in which the impact of austerity is concentrated on a particular generation whose offspring will also bear the full consequences of the austerity measures currently being employed and enforced. So, the question as to why the arguments of the 'Austerians' hold sway while the counterarguments are barely considered necessarily raises the further question, 'What are they hiding?'

The democratic deficit

The Oxford economist Simon Wren-Lewis (2015: 11) suggests that part of the answer lies in the self-interest of corporate business and its alliance with large sections of the press. He highlights the particular problem, as he sees it, of the influence of working in the City (London's financial hub): 'There are some wise and experienced City economists, but there are also many with limited expertise and sometimes fanciful views. Their main job is to keep their firm's clients happy.' Part of the job of these economists, he points out, is ensuring that they are readily available when the media needs a swift response. Those sections of the print media with a clear political agenda might be expected to rely on such spokespersons, but other sections of the media may also find it convenient to draw on them given their accessibility and availability. 'There is', suggests Wren-Lewis, 'obvious self-interest here: the more market reaction is thought to be important, the more the media will want to talk to City economists.'

Writing with specific reference to the United Kingdom, Krugman (2015: 32) suggests that the answer lies not only in the collusion between corporate business and the press but also in the combination of an ill-informed and misinformed citizenry ('a public that doesn't understand the rationale for government spending, that tends to think of the government budget via analogies with family finances') and a government that is willing to take advantage of – and actively encourage – this lack of public awareness: 'scare talk about debt and deficits is often used as a cover for a very different agenda, namely an attempt to reduce the overall size of government and especially spending on social insurance' (33). Since large sections of the press have played – and continue to play – a major part in maintaining and promoting this cover story, Krugman's analysis highlights the urgent need for a greater emphasis on economic and political awareness at all levels of the education system – a need that is unlikely to be fully met in the immediate future given the UK government's increasing control of the education system and what Krugman sees as its hidden agenda.[19]

Implicit in Wren-Lewis's and Krugman's argument is the notion of an increasingly acquiescent citizenry at the mercy of 'big business', a predominantly right-wing press and government 'spin'. There is more than a grain of truth to this characterization of the citizen as acquiescent and uncritical subject: this citizen-as-subject for whom austerity is reassuring in both its recourse to homespun analogies with family finances and its insistence that the economy is best left to the technocrats. Austerity is presented as at once so simple that we can all intuitively grasp its underlying logic and so complex that we require experts to operationalize it. The ideal citizen-as-subject is both an assiduous and thrifty saver and an inveterate and creditworthy spender; both ruthlessly competitive and socially philanthropic; both dedicated to home building and wedded to work.

Caught in this web of contradictions, the acquiescent citizen is perfectly adapted to what Sheldon S. Wolin (2010) has termed 'the managed democracy': a democracy outsourced – as Wolin sees it – to an oligarchy comprising the super-rich, the political elite

---

[19] Skidelsky's (2009: 188–90) call for a reform of the way in which economics is studied at universities at both undergraduate and postgraduate levels is relevant at this point. Arguing for a shift of emphasis from microeconomics to macroeconomics, he proposes that undergraduate degrees should be more broadly based and that postgraduate study should combine the study of macroeconomics with relevant non-economic components such as history, philosophy, sociology, politics, international relations, biology and anthropology. 'Such a reconstruction', he argues, 'would loosen the discipline's Newtonian anchor and give it a less regressive research agenda' (190). See also Earle, Moran and Ward-Perkins (2016), who as undergraduates studying economics at the University of Manchester at the time of the 2007/08 crisis helped set up the student-led Post-Crash Economics Society, which gave rise to the more broadly based Rethinking Economics network.

and corporate business. This 'managed democracy' relies not only on an acquiescent citizenry but also on institutions that are 'thin' in terms of engagement and participation and increasingly centralized with regard to both their internal management and audit structures and their external control and accountability systems. The civic spaces between the individual and the state – the institutional spaces of civic association that straddle the public and private – are thereby hollowed out through a combination of disengagement and bureaucratic managerialism and squeezed out by increased centralized control coupled with creeping privatization (see Elliott and Atkinson, 2016; Meek, 2014).

What emerges from these various responses is a democratic deficit at the heart of democratic Europe. Power has become increasingly concentrated in a small and largely unaccountable elite: in effect, as David Harvey points out, a new 'ruling class' for which the political class acts as proxy:

> Only now, as the state steps in to bail out the financiers, has it become clear to all that state and capital are more tightly intertwined than ever, both institutionally and personally. The ruling class, rather than the political class that acts as its surrogate, is now actually seen to rule. (2011, 219)

Generational stratification

This ruling class does not go unchallenged. Across Europe there are significant instances of renewed democratic participation and political engagement: Greece's Syriza coalition, Spain's Podemos party and the United Kingdom's Momentum are, for example, working through parliamentary channels or as social movements with close links to political parties; similarly, community groups are operating at a local level in an attempt to meet the immediate economic, political and social needs of particular communities; there are also protest groups that are mobilizing not only across Europe but worldwide (see Fominaya and Cox, 2013; Katsambekis, 2015; Kioupkiolis and Katsambekis, 2014; Ness, 2016; Roberts et. al., 2016; Wainwright, 2009). The rise of these various forms of 'citizen politics' can be attributed to diverse sources. 'The common thread that runs through nearly all of them, though', argues Jack Shenker (2016, 4–5), 'is a relationship between the expansion of financial markets and a diminution of the autonomy afforded to citizens as individuals and as collectives – be they living under dictatorships or long-established democracies'.

Although cross-generational in their support base and membership, 'citizen politics' gains much of its impetus from the millennial generation (the 'Gen Y') of those born between 1980 and 1999. This cohort of young adults, with ages ranging from mid-teens to mid-thirties, is growing up in what Erik Brynjolfsson and Andrew McAfee (2014) have termed 'the second machine age', during which automation becomes an increasingly disruptive factor within the labour market. Used as a means of reducing labour costs and thereby increasing profit, technological innovation inevitably leads to rising unemployment. Of course, new employment opportunities open up in those industries dedicated to technological research and development. But these job opportunities are in the main only open to those who are highly educated and with a particular skill set.

So, the millennial generation is increasingly split between what Savage et al. (2015, 165–81) have identified as an emergent 'technical middle class' and an increasingly disenfranchised 'precariat'. The former are under increasing pressure within a highly competitive and volatile labour market beset by graduate unemployment, while the latter are lucky to find any secure employment and are bearing the brunt of cutbacks in public expenditure (see also Savage, 2010, and Prieur and Savage, 2009.) Both groups are – albeit in different ways and to a different extent – vulnerable to the pressures and tensions of late capitalism's 'second machine age'. The millennial generation is not only set apart from earlier generations who were the beneficiaries of a more benign 'welfar-ism' but also increasingly fractured within itself.

Nick Srnicek and Alex Williamson (2015) argue for a policy response that acknow-ledges the need for a transition to what they see as a future post-work world. Such a response would, they argue, involve embracing full automation coupled with higher wages and reduced working hours together with a universal basic income which would enable everyone to reorder her or his life work balance towards more socially useful ends. Their proposed policy response is an attempt to maximize the economic ben-efits of automation while minimizing its social fallout: to locate automation within a broader socio-economic strategy aimed at prioritizing social inclusion in 'a world without work'.

Atkinson addresses the same problem of the social exclusion and fragmen-tation resulting from austerity, but outlines a very different policy response. He argues for stronger steerage by the state of the course of technological progress. As a major investor in technological progress, the state could encourage innovation in a form that, as he puts it, 'increases the employability of workers and emphasises the human dimension of service provision' (Atkinson, 2015: 118–19). He argues that its failure to do so renders the plight of the 'precariat' ever more precarious and highlights the irrationality of an economic system that encourages technological innovation at the expense of social well-being: 'Governments should take an active interest in the direction of technological change; after all, their grants and labs are responsible for much of the underlying research. When allocating public research funds, governments should consider employment and other social needs.' He cites as an example the possibility of 'shift[ing] priorities from driverless cars, which will likely reduce jobs, to technology that helps the elderly stay in their homes, which would increase the demand for caregivers' (2016: 30). His central point is the need to rethink technical innovation in terms of what makes for a good and fair society – both for the generation most directly affected by the economic crisis and its fallout and for subsequent generations.

A divided Europe

The responsibility for implementing austerity policies is frequently shifted down the line from centre to periphery. This shift – from regional to national, national to local, and local to institutional – sits conveniently within the political rhetoric of decen-tralization. In reality, however, it is very often the imposition of centralized control by proxy. The EU requires member states to adopt austerity measures; nation states require localities and/or sectors to implement those measures; and the local and/or sector-wide authorities then require particular institutions to fulfil those requirements. Within the United Kingdom, for example, local authorities are prohibited from deficit budgeting. Should a local authority choose to defy austerity budgeting in isolation, central government has the means and the will to impose rule by technocrats. Moreover, each shift in the level of implementation represents an increase in the level of complexity since the devil lies in the detail. A strategic decision taken at the centre becomes at the local and institutional level a highly intricate and multifaceted exercise in the management of change.

It is at the local and institutional level that the impact of austerity is felt most keenly by both the professional practitioners involved and members of the general public who rely on their services. Initially, therefore, the erosion of public trust that follows from cuts in public services and amenities is likely to be experienced at this level. This partly explains why, as Harvey (2011: 217) puts it, 'legitimation crises typically unfold at a different pace and rhythm to stock market crises'. It takes time for whatever policies are put in place to impact on a critical mass of the population, but it takes even longer for responsibility to be traced back from the periphery where that impact is experienced to its central source. Moreover, in the current situation, the central source is adept at presenting its own imposition of austerity policies as a benign exercise in democratic devolution. The result is erosion of public trust in the institutions and professional groups upon which they have traditionally relied – a trust which once lost is extremely difficult to regain.

But it would be a mistake to think of institutional erosion solely in terms of cuts to public services. 'Austerity', as Aditya Chakrabortty (2016: 29) puts it, 'is far bigger than that: it is a project irreversibly to transfer wealth from the poorest to the richest'. Privatization is the centrepiece of this project. 'At best', writes Chakrabortty, 'privatisation is a short-term gain for a long-term loss ... Sure, we pocket a couple of billion now – but we lose far more in the long run'. Public investment in the institutional infrastructure – built up sometimes over generations – is thus sold off to small groups of private investors with a view to balancing the books and thereby justifying the pursuit of austerity measures. Over time the private investors then reap the rewards.

It is important to bear in mind what exactly is being eroded. Institutions form the associative mesh that binds society. They constitute the civic space between the individual and the state. As such they have the potential for becoming what Axel Honneth (2014: 49) has termed 'institutions of recognition': spaces of realization for 'intersubjective freedom' and 'mutual recognition' (see also Honneth, 1995). When public trust in the institutional fabric of society is eroded communities become fractured and individuals atomized, public professionals become demoralized, and institutions themselves become marginalized and threatened. Institutional erosion deeply affects social cohesion. It cuts in at precisely the point where human beings are most vulnerable and where their moral and political affiliations are formed. It thereby endangers the polity by providing a space for anti-democratic forces to exploit marginalized and vulnerable groups on the basis of populist manifestos.

The journalist and columnist Jonathan Freedland (2016a: 28) points to the spread of these anti-democratic forces as a global phenomenon: 'While every case is different, it is undeniable that populists and demagogues are making extraordinary strides, the examples almost too numerous to list.' He cites the rise of Hindu nationalism in India, the Justice and Development Party (AKP) in Turkey, the nativist Front National in France, the far-right Alternative für Deutschland in Germany, the Danish People's Party, the Swedish Democrats (which has roots in neo-Nazism), the Finns Party (formerly known as the True Finns), the People's Party of Switzerland and the populist UK Independence Party (UKIP). One could add to this list Poland's Law and Justice Party, Greece's neo-Nazi Golden Dawn and Hungary's third-strongest party, Jobbik, which has pushed the ruling national conservative Fidesz party towards increasingly hard-line policies.

The individual contexts are different, but as Freedland argues, this disparate collection of parties feeds on the same discontent: 'You might have imagined that the crash would have channelled the fury in a different direction, that the backlash would have been against capitalism rather than democracy. Yet perhaps too many voters believe the system cannot be changed, that there is no alternative to capitalism.' It is, he concludes, 'no wonder voters turn their ire on democracy instead' (2016a: 29). The political historian Jan-Werner Müller (2016: 6) points out that while the anger may be turned on democracy itself, right-wing parties are not averse to co-opting the language of democracy for their own political ends and purposes: 'They have all successfully usurped the language of democracy and, in the case of Marine Le Pen, French Republicanism. They claim faithfully to represent the people's will and to uphold the ideal of national sovereignty.'

The rise of such parties across Europe and more widely is a clear indication that democracy faces a looming crisis of legitimacy. It is that looming crisis that the economic sociologist Wolfgang Streeck alludes to in his gloomy prognosis of the future of Europe: 'What seems most likely, unfortunately, is a big and long-lasting mess … There will be a decade of bad blood, muttering incrimination, temporary fixes and ever-declining respect for centrist parties, national governments and international institutions' (Streeck, 2016: 10). The 'big and long-lasting mess' to which Streeck refers involves an increasing uneasiness regarding the viability and sustainability of Europe as an idea and as an ideal.

Streeck's piece was published just weeks before the June 2016 UK referendum on membership of the EU. The referendum campaigns as conducted by both the 'Brexit' and 'Remain' camps were degrading affairs that descended into mutual recrimination supported by the wilful misrepresentation of statistics clearly designed to mislead the public on all the major issues. UKIP (part of 'Brexit') focused almost exclusively on immigration and towards the end of the campaign resorted to blatantly racist tactics designed to draw the support of those social groups that had been hardest hit by austerity. The final result with its narrow majority for exit (51.9 per cent for 'out' and 48.1 per cent for 'remain') exposed deep fault lines in British society between the large metropolitan areas that have benefitted from globalization and the broad swathes of post-industrial England that have borne the brunt of cuts in public expenditure and the erosion of the welfare state.

In the wake of the 'Brexit' victory, racist incidents rose significantly within the UK, and right-wing political groupings across Europe voiced their approval for what they saw as a victory for the far right. Anne Corbett (2016) commented at the time that the 'Brexit vote has, in its first days, brought political chaos, economic meltdown and racist attacks', while the writer and journalist John Lanchester (2016: 6) stated that 'there is a real darkness in this country, a xenophobic, racist sickness of heart that is closer to the surface today than it has been for decades. That is a direct result of the referendum campaign.' Freedland (2016b: 8) added his own 'howl of rage' when, commenting on Brexit and its aftermath, he wrote that 'the consequences have been disastrous. A whirlwind has torn through Britain, exposing rifts that have to be healed and destroying much that was precious. And no one seems to have any idea when, how, or if it can ever be made whole again' (See also Barber, 2016, for an immediate but considered response to the UK referendum result.)

Zygmunt Bauman's (2004: 89) idea of Europe as 'an unfinished adventure' – its 'composite totality, bringing many languages and cultural strands into daily contact and conversation with each other … a natural soil for hermeneutics, the art of interpretation and understanding … a homeland of perpetual translation' – is foundering on the fundamentalist principles of economic austerity. When trust between communities, nations and peoples breaks down, shared understanding becomes increasingly difficult; and, when understanding becomes increasingly difficult, we need as never before those institutions – Honneth's (2014, 49) 'institutions of recognition' – that value understanding and exist to ensure its transition from generation to generation. The stakes are high, which is the point Hans-Georg Gadamer was making in 1985: 'we have to learn together what our European task means to us and we have to do this for the future of humanity as a whole' (1992: 234).

Higher education and the time of austerity

While the economy may or may not recover – and while the policy regime of economic austerity may or may not give way to alternative regimes – the impact of the austerity measures imposed across Europe will have a trickle-down effect at least into the next generation, and in all probability well beyond. Austerity was not some kind of mild influenza which we will be able to shake off and forget about. It is now in the DNA of our organizational structures, institutional systems, professional practices and ways of thinking. To understand its enduring impact on institutions and on civil society generally is therefore a matter of considerable importance.

Higher education faces a hard choice: either it continues to acquiesce in the reproduction of inequality or it challenges its own role in that reproductive cycle. The choice is between two sharply contrasting visions of society and the place of higher education within it. The first is of a society that lacks cohesion and is economically sluggish and politically disengaged. It relies on subjects who know their place in society and are punctilious in the protection of their own private interests. It focuses on the past and views inequality as inevitable. At the bottom of this society are, as Stiglitz (2012: 289) shows, 'millions of young people alienated and without hope'. Within this vision of society, higher education contributes to the private gain of those individuals who are in the fortunate position of being able to afford it.

The second vision is of a society that embraces difference and is economically resilient and democratically purposeful. It requires citizens who demand their place within the polity and consider their own interests to be inextricably entwined with the public interest. It focuses on alternative futures and challenges the legacy of inequality. It is a society where, as Stiglitz again puts it, 'the gap between the haves and the have-nots has been narrowed, where there is a sense of shared destiny, [and] a common commitment to opportunity and fairness' (289). Within this vision, higher education contributes to the public good of society as a whole and is accessible to anyone able to benefit from it regardless of whether they can pay for it.

This second vision was partially endorsed both by the Conference of European Ministers Responsible for Higher Education convened in April 2009 under the auspices of the Bologna Process and by the United Nations Educational, Scientific and Cultural Organization (UNESCO) in its communiqué of July 2009. The Bologna communiqué acknowledged that 'our societies currently face the consequences of a global and economic crisis', while stating that 'we consider investment in higher education of utmost priority' (Bologna Process, 2009). Similarly, the UNESCO communiqué acknowledged that 'the current economic downturn may widen the gap in access and quality between developed and developing countries as well as within countries' and stated that, 'as a public good and a strategic imperative for all levels of education and as the basis for research, innovation and creativity, higher education must be a matter of responsibility and economic support of all governments'. It went on to assert that 'Higher Education as a public good is the responsibility of all stakeholders, especially governments' (UNESCO, 2009).

Subsequent Bologna communiqués have become increasingly enmeshed in an ill-defined distinction between higher education as a public good and higher education as a public responsibility. The distinction may be a fine one, but it is crucial in terms of government policy. It had in fact been implicit in the 2009 Bologna communiqué which, while asserting that 'within the framework of public responsibility we confirm that public funding remains the main priority to guarantee equitable access and further sustainable development of autonomous higher education institutions', insisted that 'greater attention should be paid to seeking new and diversified sources and methods': public responsibility for higher education could, in other words, include private investment and/or a combination of private and public sources of funding.

The following chapters offer various perspectives from across Europe on how education is faring in austerity Europe. As editor, I have been anxious to include contributors from Eastern and Southern Europe, since the debate on higher education so often focuses on Western Europe, where the major European institutions of culture and governance are based. The book does not intend to offer either a unified voice or a programme for reform. Its aim is to begin to document the impact of economic austerity on higher education within Europe and highlight some of the key issues that will need to be addressed in the coming years. The book has a tripartite structure, with Part 1 addressing some trans-European concerns and perspectives, Part 2 focusing on some of the 'hard cases' from within specific national systems and Part 3 suggesting some post-austerity perspectives. The concluding chapter comprising responses from authors outside Europe highlights the global implications of austerity Europe.

Trans-European perspectives

The chapters comprising Part 1 challenge the notion of 'the disembedded economy' through counternarratives that reveal the complex interplay between the economic, institutional, social and political factors operating within the history of post–World War II Europe. Marek Kwiek (Chapter 1) provides a sociopolitical analysis of 'welfarism' as developed across Europe in response to the needs, priorities and histories of different national systems. He shows how 'welfarism' – as an idea and as a political reality – led to a significant widening of student access to higher education and an increase in the opportunities for lifelong learning. Have the economic policies associated with austerity Europe, asks Kwiek, put at permanent risk the educational and social benefits of the welfare state? While far from sanguine in his response to that question, Kwiek insists that the only way of countering the long-term effects of austerity is to rebuild public trust in – and support for – higher education as a common good.

Åse Gornitzka (Chapter 2) provides an alternative counternarrative informed by institutional theory and policy analysis. The prime focus of her account is the continuing struggle to achieve a workable balance between national, sectoral and regional interests in the development of a Europe-wide 'governance site' for educational policy. She shows how that balance is highly vulnerable to unforeseeable shocks and ongoing turbulence – including those occasioned by fluctuations in the economy. But, she argues, the institutional frameworks of governance as they have evolved – and are still evolving – have been instrumental in safeguarding higher education from some of the more damaging effects of economic austerity. They have, she claims, on occasion provided a significant site for asserting the interests and values of the higher education sector as a whole in the face of national policies that place those values and interests at risk.

In the final chapter of Part 1, Paolo Landri, Rosaria Lumino and Roberto Serpieri (Chapter 3) show how austerity has operated through a regime of accountability aimed at controlling its institutional performances. Through detailed policy analysis they demonstrate how standardization operates as a complex game – based on the principle of *Calculemus* or 'Let's calculate!' – the rules of which remain largely implicit and subliminal but exert immense influence on funding outcomes and the overall landscape of higher education. Addressing a theme that emerges throughout subsequent chapters, Landri, Lumino and Serpieri highlight the way in which austerity may operate covertly – or, at least, under the guise of principles that would seem to underlie its true intent. *Calculemus*, they suggest, is one of the underlying codes of austerity as it impacts upon higher education. But they also imply that we need to learn how to play that game and, in so doing, play both within and against austerity Europe.

Europe from the inside

In shifting from trans-European perspectives to specific cases, the chapters included in Part 2 show how austerity is mediated by the histories, politics, traditions and systems of different nation states. Dorota Dakowska (Chapter 4) invites us to reconsider the temporal and political aspects of the reconfiguration of higher education with regard to austerity measures. Dakowska argues that, for two main reasons, the financial crisis of 2007/08 cannot be viewed as the main trigger of Poland's redesign of the higher education sector: first, the Polish economy has not been hit by this economic turmoil as hard as some West European countries; secondly, the structural austerity measures which have affected the country's public sector followed the 1989 fall of the Communist regime and the 'shock therapy' implemented by the first democratic governments. These neo-liberal policy measures set up in the beginning of the 1990s have led to a far-reaching privatization of higher education. The period 2007/08 is more appropriately seen as a caesura in the post-1989 history of Polish higher education, providing an opportunity for the new liberal government to undertake several important measures to reform the sector in the name of competitiveness, diversification and excellence.

In focusing on Croatia, Danijela Dolenc (Chapter 5) also locates the financial crisis of 2007/08 within a broader time frame. Since the 1990s the Western Balkans have, like many other regions of the world, been characterized by the massification of higher education. But unlike some other regions, argues Dolenc, this trend was coupled with poor economic performance. This has meant that Western Balkan countries have failed to secure adequate public funding for higher education, jeopardizing the success of ambitious reforms envisaged by the Bologna and Lisbon processes. At the same time, the Bologna Process and the Lisbon Agenda have contributed to an increasingly instrumental concept of higher education as a vehicle of competitiveness and economic development. Given this context, the intensification of neo-liberal policies in higher education that have occurred since the 2007/08 economic crisis have further amplified the impact of low public investment combined with the increasing emphasis on cost effectiveness. Framing her argument within a broader discussion of the political economy of higher education in Croatia – and relying on two rounds of Eurostudent survey data, implemented in 2010 and 2014 respectively – Dolenc explores the impact of these neo-liberal policies on the socioeconomic profile of students.

Marnie Holborow and John O'Sullivan (Chapter 6) also adopt a political economy perspective in focusing on the impact of austerity measures on higher education within the Republic of Ireland. These measures, they argue, have given momentum to a shift from what was mainly public to what is now increasingly private funding (including funding from industry, corporate capital, grants for specific research activities and individual students). While this push towards privatization follows an international trend, its full impact in Ireland has been felt only recently as a result of the government's response to the terms of the EU bailout as agreed in 2010. Holborow and O'Sullivan argue that corporate elites, employers and other private interests have been the main beneficiaries from the restructuring of higher education, since the shift in ideology and ethos that it denotes suits their 'human capital' needs. They also explore – with reference to the social composition of universities, the option of emigration and political legacies – the reasons for the relatively muted resistance to the policies that have driven the restructuring of higher education and the push towards privatization.

Greece, having been in deep recession for the past six years, is one of the countries within Europe that has been most affected by the economic crisis of 2007/08. As Daphne Kyriaki-Manessi (Chapter 7) shows, the crisis led to the worsening of employment conditions and an increase in the 'brain drain' with respect to Greece's young highly qualified graduates. This 'brain drain', apart from its huge social implications, is having a long-term deleterious impact on the economy, since the better educated members of the labour force are dispersing: a trend which is particularly apparent among the younger graduate population. Since education in Greece is regarded as the state's responsibility – tuition being free at all levels of the system including higher education – austerity measures have brought about budget cuts, staff reductions and salary cuts. This, in turn, has affected the quality of higher education provision nationally, thereby compounding both the economic and social problems facing the country.

Definitions of 'the small state' differ, but with a population dipping just below the three-million mark Lithuania falls well within that category (as do Croatia and the Republic of Ireland according to some definitions).[20] As such it shares with other small states a particular set of problems and challenges particularly as these relate to economies of scale. Almantas Samalavičius (Chapter 8) provides an account of how Lithuania has responded to this situation through an increased reliance on student self-funding, together with the rebranding, amalgamation and in some cases closure of institutions, and a greater emphasis on competition and marketization in the overall management of institutions. Samalavičius challenges the current policy orientation on the grounds that it is driven by what he sees as a market mentality: a set of assumptions regarding the nature of the university that denies – or at the very least obfuscates – its central role as a free space of intellectual debate and development.

Beyond austerity Europe

Part 3 looks to some possible ways forward. None of the chapters is prescriptive in the sense of proposing a detailed programme. Nor do the authors adopt a universalist perspective but rather ground their arguments in the specificity of the conditions within which they think and work. They provide conceptual reorientations: ways of thinking about the relation between theory and practice. Drawing on the work of Hannah Arendt and Michel Foucault, Ari-Elmeri Hyvönen and Esko Harni (Chapter 9) provide some theoretical resources for critically assessing what they see as a long-term political strategy of creating a neo-liberal 'entrepreneurial university'. Focusing specifically on the humanities – and locating their discussion within the context of Finnish higher education in particular – they argue that the increasing emphasis on entrepreneurship education is jeopardizing the role of the university in sustaining critical thinking and political dialogue. The urgent task for the university, they insist, is to provide a space within which these capacities can be nurtured and developed: a space, that is, in which to think beyond austerity.

Nicole Rege Colet (Chapter 10) also grounds her analysis within a particular national and institutional locality. She describes the choices made and the projects implemented to build up the research, teaching and learning capacities in the regional

---

[20] The World Bank (2009) defines 'the small state' as any state with a population of less than 1.5 million, while the Commonwealth Secretariat (2009) employs a cut-off point of 5 million. Martin and Bray (2012) in their discussion of higher education in small states set the cut-off point at 3 million.

context of Alsace, the strip of French land bordering Germany and Switzerland. This, as she puts it, has meant 'stepping out of the field of austerity'. It has meant designing innovative programmes and taking tough decisions, working within and against authority in order to move beyond it. The challenge, she argues, has been to let go of traditional constraints and explore beyond disciplinary and national boundaries to develop new ways of working together as fellow academics and look anew at what academic development might mean. Her approach is to draw in theoretical insights, but to do so within the context of a collaboratively driven and practice-oriented programme of change at the level of institutional and cross-institutional practice.

In the final chapter of Part 3 Ourania Filippakou (Chapter 11) argues that the economic and political context within which higher education is now located requires a reimagining of the focus and study of higher education: a conceptual frame within which to address anew the question of what higher education is for. The world as mirrored in the existing disciplines has changed and poses problems that require new theories and methodologies, new concepts and analytical frameworks, new ideas. There is, Filippakou maintains, a shift in the cultural form of European higher education systems. In order to grasp the significance of this shift, higher education research and scholarship will need to rethink its relation to policy and practice. What is needed is a critical engagement with the underlying codes of higher education policy and practice: their implicit ends and purposes, their moral grammar. This, she argues, is an ethical task of the utmost importance – a task which looks beyond 'austerity Europe'

By way of conclusion Tanya Fitzgerald, Manja Klemenčič and Jae Park (Chapter 12) offer some comparative points of reference from Australia, the United States and Asia respectively. They highlight commonalties and differences. They remind us that 'austerity Europe' is a phenomenon that arises from a global crisis that had – and continues to have – global repercussions. They remind us, in short, that ours is a common if divided world.

Conclusion

'Any great failure', wrote Skidelsky (2009: 168–9), 'should force us to rethink fundamental ideas. The present economic crisis is a great failure of the market system.' But, as Skidelsky went on to argue, 'the crisis also represents a moral failure: that of a system built on money values. At the heart of the moral failure is the worship of money for its own sake, rather than as a way to achieve the good life.' As I have argued throughout this chapter, most of the European nation states – together with the major international institutions with responsibility for the economic well-being of Europe – have not only failed to acknowledge that failure but have deliberately and systematically ignored, sidelined and debunked those who have attempted to do so.

The contributors to this volume differ significantly in their methods of analysis and ideological orientations, their cultural and intellectual affiliations and their mother-tongue backgrounds. But they all share a common concern with the impact of austerity on the academic practices, organizational structures and sector-wide systems of higher education. Each in her or his own way confronts the 'failure of the market system'. By evidencing, analysing and looking beyond that failure, contributors not only highlight some of the major issues that need to be addressed in developing the capacity of higher education across the nation states of Europe but also identify key areas for future research and development within the broad field of higher education policy and practice. They provide a timely reminder of the need to think not only within and against austerity – but beyond it. 'We need', as Judt (2010: 161) put it, 'to re-learn how to criticize those who govern us.'

One final point: three major events – the decision by the United Kingdom to exit the EU, the election of Donald Trump to the US presidency and the electoral success of far right parties across Europe – occurred after most of the contributions to this volume had been finalized. The impact of these events on the global economy, the geopolitical world order and the social stability of nation states is as yet unclear. (I am writing during the first few weeks of the Trump administration and in the immediate aftermath of the UK government resolving to trigger Article 50 of the December 2007 Lisbon Treaty.) What is clear is that Europe is now a much more uncertain place in respect of its economic, political and social future; that new and emergent forms of populism and demagogy now dominate the political scene; and that nationalism has re-emerged as a powerful and mobilizing rhetoric across the Continent. (Those who draw parallels with 1930s Europe are not being fanciful.) These developments are a stark reminder that – as Wolin (2016) reminded us – democracy is inherently 'fugitive': forever vulnerable to the destabilization of the separation of powers that is one of its defining features. I briefly discuss the implications of these developments for higher education in the Coda.

References

Alesina, A., and S. Ardagna. (1998). Tales of fiscal adjustments, *Economic Policy* 13(27): 489–545.

Alesina, A., and S. Ardagna. (2010). Large changes in fiscal policy: Taxes versus spending, in J. R. Brown (ed.), *Tax, Policy and the Economy*, vol. 24. National Bureau of Economic Research Tax Policy and the Economy. Chicago: University of Chicago Press. 35–68.

Alesina, A., and R. Perotti. (1995). Fiscal Expansions and fiscal adjustments in OECD countries, National Bureau of Economic Research (NBER) Working Paper No. 5214, Cambridge, MA: NBER

Alesina, A., and R. Perotti. (1997). Fiscal adjustments in OECD countries: Composition and macroeconomic effects, *Staff Papers. International Monetary Fund* 44(2): 210–48.

Allen, D. (2016). Equality and American democracy: why politics trumps economics, *Foreign Affairs* 95, 1 (January/February): 23–8.

Amin, S. (2014). *The Implosion of Capitalism*. London: Pluto Press

Antonucci, L. (2016). *Student Lives in Crisis: Deepening Inequality in Times of Austerity*. Bristol: Policy Press.

Arestis, P., and T. Pelagidis. (2010). Absurd austerity policies in Europe, *Challenge* 53(6): 54–61.

Atkinson, A. B. (1969). *Poverty in Britain and the Reform of Social Security*. Cambridge: Cambridge University Press.

Atkinson, A. B. (1972). *Unequal Shares: Wealth in Britain*. London: Allen Lane Press and Penguin.

Atkinson, A. B. (1975). *Economics and Inequality*. Oxford: Oxford University Press.

Atkinson, A. B. (1999). *The Economic Consequences of Rolling Back the Welfare State* (Munich Lectures in Economics). Cambridge, MA, and London (in cooperation with the Center for Economic Studies at the University of Munich).

Atkinson, A. B. (2015). *Inequality: What Can Be Done?* Cambridge, MA, and London: Harvard University Press.

Atkinson, A. B. (2016). How to spread wealth: Practical policies for reducing inequality, *Foreign Affairs* 95(1): 29–33.

Barber, T. (2016). Haunted Europe, *Financial Times*, 27 June, 11.

Bauman, Z. (2004). *Europe: An Unfinished Adventure*. Cambridge and Malden, MA: Polity.

Berlin, I. (1969). 'Two concepts of liberty' (Inaugural Lecture), in *Four Essays on Liberty*. Oxford: Oxford University Press. 118–172.

Blyth, M. (2015). *Austerity: The History of a Dangerous Idea*. Oxford: Oxford University Press.

Bologna Process (2009). *The Bologna Process 2020 – The European Higher Education Area in the New Decade: Communiqué of the Conference of European Ministers Responsible for Higher Education*, Leuven and Louvain-la-Neuve, 28–29 April 2009.

Brass, T. (2011). *Labour Regime Change in the Twenty-First Century: Unfreedom, Capitalism and Primitive Accumulation*. Leiden: Brill.

Brynjolfsson, E., and A. McAfee. (2014). *The Second Machine Age: Work, Progress and Prosperity in a Time of Brilliant Technologies*. New York: Norton.

Buchanan, J. M., and G. Tullock. (1962). *The Calculus of Consent*. Ann Arbor: University of Michigan Press.

Callinicos, A. (2010). *Bonfire of Illusions: The Two Crises of the Liberal World*. Cambridge and Malden, MA: Polity Press.

Chakrabortty, A. (2016). Austerity is far more than just cuts :It's about privatising everything we own, *The Guardian*, 24 May, 29.

Commonwealth Secretariat (2009) *Small States: Economic Review and Basic Statistics, vol. 13*. London: The Commonwealth Secretariat.

Corbett, A. (2016). United Kingdom universities in a post-Brexit world, *University World News Global Edition*, issue 421, 5 June, http://www.universityworldnews.com/article.php?story=20160705101034144.

Dale, G. (2010). *Karl Polanyi: The Limits of the Market*. Cambridge, UK, and Malden, MA: Polity Press.

Elliott, L., and D. Atkinson. (2016). *Europe Isn't Working*. New Haven, CT: Yale University Press.

Earle, J., C. Moran and Z. Ward-Perkins. (2016). *The Econocracy: The Perils of Leaving Economics to the Experts*. Manchester: Manchester University Press.

Flassbeck, H., and C. Lapavitsas. (2015). *Against the Troika: Crisis and Austerity in the Eurozone*. London and New York: Verso.

Fominaya, C. F., and L. Cox (eds) (2013). *Understanding European Movements: New Social Movements, Global Justice Struggles, Anti-Austerity Protest*. Abingdon, Oxon and New York: Routledge.

Foroohar, R. (2016). *The Rise of Finance and the Fall of American Business*. New York: Crown Business (Penguin Random House, LLC).

Freedland, J. (2016a). Welcome to the age of Trump, *The Guardian*, 19 May, 27–9.

Freedland, J. (2016b). A howl of rage, *New York Review of Books*, August 18–September 28, 4–8.

Friedman, M., with R. D. Friedman. (1962). *Capitalism and Freedom*. Chicago: University of Chicago Press.

Friedman, M., and R. D. Friedman. (1980). *Free to Choose*. New York: Harcourt Brace Jovanovich.

Fukuyama, F. (1992). *The End of History and the Lost Man*. London: Penguin.

Gadamer, H.-G. (1992). *Hans-Georg Gadamer on Education, Poetry, and History*. Edited by D. Misgeld and G. Nicholson; Translated by L. Schmidt and M. Reuss. Albany, NY: State University of New York Press.

Gardner, R. N. (1956). *Sterling-Dollar Diplomacy: Anglo-American Collaboration in the Reconstruction of Multilateral Trade*. Oxford: Clarendon Press.

Hare, D. (2016). Why the Tory project is bust, *The Guardian*, 8 March, 25–7 (Edited version of 'Putting the clock back: A playwright's view of dismal conservatism', 2016 Richard Hillary Lecture, 3 March, Oxford University).

Harvey, D. (2011). *The Enigma of Capital and the Crises of Capitalism*. London: Profile Books.

Hayek, F. A. (1944). *The Road to Serfdom*. London: Routledge.

Hayek, F. A. (1960). *The Constitution of Liberty*. London: Routledge.

Hayek, F. A. (1988). *The Fatal Conceit* (3 volumes). Chicago: University of Chicago Press.

Heisbourg, F. (2013). *La Fin du Rêve Européen*. Paris: Stock.

Hirschman, A. O. (1991). *The Rhetoric of Reaction: Perversity, Futility, Jeopardy*. Cambridge, MA, and London: The Belknap Press of Harvard University Press.

Holborow, M. (2015). *Language and Neoliberalism*. London and New York: Routledge.

Honneth, A. (1995). *The Struggle for Recognition: The Moral Grammar of Social Conflicts*. Translated by J. Anderson. Cambridge: Polity Press.

Honneth, A. (2014). *Freedom's Right: The Social Foundations of Democratic Life*. Translated by J. Ganahl. Cambridge: Polity Press.

Iglesias, P. (2015). *Politics in a Time of Crisis: Podemos and the Future of a Democratic Europe*. Translated by L. S. Fox. London: Verso.

Inman, P. (2016). Wages of fear stifle cry of 'Hail, Caesar!' *The Guardian*, 7 March, 21.

Islam, I., and A. Chowdhury. (2010). The fallacy of austerity-based fiscal consolidation, *G-24*, Policy Brief No. 58 (August 15).

Judt, T. (2005). *Postwar: A History of Europe Since 1945*. London: Vintage.

Judt, T. (2010). *Ill Fares the Land: A Treatise on Our Present Discontents*. London and New York: Allen Lane/Penguin Press.

Katsambekis, G. (2015). The rise of the Greek radical left to power: Notes on Syriza's discourse and strategy, *Linea Sur* 3(9): 152–61.

Keynes, J. M. (1919). *The Economic Consequences of the Peace*. London: Macmillan.

Keynes, J. M. (1935). *General Theory of Employment, Interest, and Money*. London: Palgrave Macmillan.

Keynes, J. M. (2015). *The Essential Keynes*. Edited by R. Skidelsky. London: Penguin Classics.

King, M. (2016). *The End of Alchemy: Money, Banking and the Future of the Global Economy*. London: Little, Brown.

Kioupkiolis, A., and G. Katsambekis (eds) (2014). *Radical Democracy and Collective Movements Today: The Biopolitics of the Multitude versus the Hegemony of the People*, Farnham, UK, and Burlington, VT: Ashgate.

Krugman, P. (2008). *The Return of Depression Economics and the Crisis of 2008*. London: Penguin Books.

Krugman, P. (2012). *End This Depression Now*. New York: Norton.

Krugman, P. (2015). The austerity delusion, *The Guardian*, 29 April, 31–3.

Lanchester, J. (2016). Brexit blues, *London Review of Books*, 28 July, 3–6.

Liu, L. L. (2015). *The Austerity Trap: Economic and Social Consequences of Fiscal Consolidation in Europe*. CreateSpace Independent Publishing Platform.

McKee, M., M. Karanikolos, P. Belcher and D. Stuckler. (2012). Austerity: A failed experiment on the people of Europe, *Clinical Medicine* 12(4): 346–50.

Madrick, J. (2010). *The Case for Big Government*. Princeton and Oxford: Princeton University Press.

Marmot, M. (2015). *The Health Gap: The Challenge of an Unequal World*. London and New York: Bloomsbury.

Martin, M., and M. Bray. (2012). Higher education in small states, in B. Adamson, J. Nixon and F. Su (eds), *The Reorientation of Higher Education: Challenging the East West Dichotomy*. CERC Studies in Comparative Education 31. Hong Kong: Springer in association with CERC, University of Hong Kong.

Meek, J. (2014). *Private Island: Why Britain Belongs to Someone Else*. London: Verso.

Meek, J. (2016). Robin Hood in a time of austerity, *London Review of Books*, 18 February, 3–8.

Miliband, E. (2015). The inequality problem, *London Review of Books*, 4 February, 19–20.

Moyo, D. (2011). *How the West Was Lost: Fifty Years of Economic Folly – And the Stark Choices Ahead*. London: Allen Lane.

Müller, J-W. (2016). Europe's sullen child, *London Review of Books*, 2 June, 3–6.

Ness, I. (2016). *Southern Insurgency: The Coming of the Global Working Class*. London: Pluto.

Nozick, R. (1974). *Anarchy, State, and Utopia*. New York: Basic Books.

Nussbaum, M. C. (1997). *Cultivating Humanity: A Classical Defence of Reform in Liberal Education*. Cambridge, MA, and London, UK: Harvard University Press.

Nussbaum, M.C. (2010). *Not for Profit: Why Democracy Needs the Humanities*. Princeton and Oxford: Princeton University Press.

OECD (2015). *In It Together: Why Less Inequality Benefits All*. Paris: OECD Publishing. doi:http://dx.doi.org/10.1787/9789264235120-en.

Offe, C. (2016). *Europe Entrapped*. Cambridge: Polity.

Perotti, R. (2011). The 'austerity myth': Gain without pain? Bank for International Settlements (BIS) Working Papers No 362, Basel: BIS.

Phelps, E. (2013). *Mass Flourishing: How Grassroots Innovation Created Jobs, Challenge and Change*. Princeton and Oxford: Princeton University Press.

Piketty, T. (2014). *Capital in the Twenty-First Century*. Translated by A. Goldhammer. Cambridge, MA: Belknap Press/Harvard University.

Piketty, T. (2016). *Chronicles: On Our Troubled Times*. Translated by S. Ackerman. New York: Viking.

Polanyi, K. (1944). *The Great Transformation: The Political and Economic Origins of Our Time*. New York: Farrar and Rinehart.

Polanyi, K. (2014). *For a New West: Essays, 1919–1958*. Edited by G. Resta and M. Catanzariti. Cambridge, UK, and Malden, MA: Polity.

Popper, K. (1945). *The Open Society and its Enemies*. London: Routledge.

Prieur, A., and M. Savage. (2013). Emerging forms of cultural capital, *European Societies* 15(2): 246–67.

Putnam, R. D. (2015). *Our Kids: The American Dream in Crisis*. New York: Simon and Schuster.

Reich, R. B. (2012). *Beyond Outrage: What Has Gone Wrong with Our Economy and Our Democracy, and How to Fix It*, expanded ed. New York: Vintage Books.

Reich, R. B. (2015). *Saving Capitalism: For the Many Not the Few*. New York: Alfred A. Knopf.

Roberts, A., M. J. Willis, R. McCarthy and T. G. Ash (eds) (2016). *Civil Resistance in the Arab Spring: Triumphs and Disasters*. Oxford: Oxford University Press.

Savage, M. (2010). *Identities and Social Change since 1940: The Politics of Method*. Oxford: Oxford University Press.

Savage, M., N. Cunningham, F. Devine, S. Friedman, D. Laurison, L. McKennzie, A. Miles, H. Snee and P. Wakeling. (2015). *Social Class in the 21st Century*. London: Penguin.

Shenker, J. (2016). *The Egyptians: A Radical Story*. London: Allen Lane.

Sinn, H-W. (2014). *The Euro Trap: On Bursting Bubbles, Budgets, and Beliefs*. Oxford: Oxford University Press.

Skidelsky, R. (2004). *John Maynard Keynes 1883–1946: Economist, Philosopher, Statesman*, compiled and abridged one-volume ed. London, Basingstoke and Oxford: Pan Books.

Skidelsky, R. (2009). *Keynes: The Return of the Master*. London: Allen Lane.

Soros, G., and G. P. Schmitz. (2016). The EU is on the verge of collapse – an interview, *New York Review of Books*, 11–24 February, 35–7.

Srnicek, N., and A. Williams. (2015). *Inventing the Future: Postcolonialism and a World without Work*. London and New York: Verso.

Stallings, A. E. (2016). Austerity measures, in K. van Dyck (ed.) *Austerity Measures: The New Greek Poetry*. London: Penguin.

Steil, B. (2013). *The Battle of Bretton Woods: John Maynard Keynes, Harry Dexter White, and the Making of a New World Order*. Princeton: Council on Foreign Relations/ Princeton University Press.

Stiglitz, J. E. (2012). *The Price of Inequality: How Today's Divided Society Endangers Our Future*. New York: Norton.

Stiglitz, J. E. (2015a). *The Great Divide: Unequal Societies and What We Can Do about Them*. New York: Norton.

Stiglitz, J. E. (2015b). *Rewriting the Rules of the American Economy: An Agenda for Growth and Shared Prosperity*. New York: The Roosevelt Institute. Available at www. rewritingtherules.org.

Stiglitz, J. E. (2016). *The Euro: How a Common Currency Threatens the Future of Europe*. New York: W. W. Norton.

Stiglitz, J., and B. C. Greenwald. (2014). *Creating a Learning Society: A New Approach to Growth, Development, and Social Progress*. New York: Columbia University Press.

Streeck, W. (2016). Scenario for a wonderful tomorrow, *London Review of Books*, 31 March, 7–10.

Stuckler, D., and S. Basu. (2013). *The Body Economic: Why Austerity Kills*. New York: Basic Books.

Turner, A. (2015). *Between Debt and the Devil: Money, Credit, and Fixing Global Finance*. Princeton: Princeton University Press.

United Nations Educational, Scientific and Cultural Organization (UNESCO) (2009). *Communiqué 8 July 2009* (2009 World Conference on Higher Education: The New Dynamics of Higher Education and Research for Social Change and Development). Paris: UNESCO.

van Dormael, A. (1978). *Bretton Woods: The Birth of a Monetary System*. New York: Holmes and Meier.

Varoufakis, Y. (2011). *The Global Minotaur: America, the True Origins of the Financial Crisis and the Future of the World Economy*. London and New York: Zed Books.

Varoufakis, Y. (2016). *And The Weak Suffer What They Must?* London: Bodley Head

Wainwright, H. (2009). *Reclaim the State: Experiments in Popular Democracy*, rev. ed. Calcutta: Seagull Books.

Wallace, P. (2016). *The Euro Experiment*. Cambridge: Cambridge University Press.

Wolin, S. S. (2010). *Democracy Incorporated: Managing Democracy and the Specter of Inverted Totalitarianism*. Princeton and Oxford: Princeton University Press.

Wolin, S. S. (2016). *Fugitive Democracy and Other Essays*. Edited by N. Xenos. Princeton and Oxford: Princeton University Press.

World Bank (2009). Small states, www.worldbank.org/smallstates.

Wren-Lewis, S. (2015). The austerity con, *London Review of Books*, 19 February, 9–11.

Part One

Pan-European Perspectives

Europe – as well as being a geopolitical reality – is also an idea: the idea, that is, of achieving unity across nation states, while resisting uniformity; of recognizing cultural, national, social and constitutional differences, while avoiding division; of building unity on the basis of diversity and respecting the rights and interests of minorities. With regard to higher education – its practices, organizational structures and sector-wide systems – three crucial areas of policy development have a direct bearing on the realization of this idea: the viability of a vibrant public sector, the legitimacy of sector-wide governance and the maintenance of fair and accountable systems of standardization. The following chapters show how these policy areas have developed over time – but also how, since the 2007/08 crisis, they have been shaped by the politics of economic austerity.

Part One

Pan-European Perspectives

1

Higher Education, Welfare States and Austerity: Pressures on Competing Public Institutions

Marek Kwiek

Both welfare states and universities are currently changing under adverse financial conditions caused by an array of interrelated and mutually reinforcing forces, and their long-term financial sustainability is at stake across Europe. However, the problems of sustainability did not start with the financial crisis of 2008 – they had been growing since the 1970s (Bonoli and Natali, 2012; Hay and Wincott, 2012; Schäfer and Streeck, 2013). Nor should financial austerity be seen as an exclusively post-crisis phenomenon. As a concept, it was used in welfare state research at least a decade earlier, although it does not seem to have been used in higher education studies until recently. As Paul Pierson emphasized at the turn of the century,

> Signs of strain are everywhere. The struggle to balance budgets is unending, even as many governments cope with levels of debt unprecedented in peace-time.... . Despite their striking resilience over a quarter-century of 'crisis', welfare states are widely held to be under siege. (2001a: 80)
> The welfare state now faces a context of essentially permanent austerity. Changes in the global economy, the sharp slowdown in economic growth, the maturation of governmental commitments, and population aging all generate considerable fiscal stress. There is little reason to expect these pressures to diminish over the next few decades. If anything, they are likely to intensify. (2001b: 411)

Indeed, thinking specifically about universities, 'signs of strain' are everywhere, and 'permanent austerity' determines their daily operations and institutional strategies for the future.

The welfare state is a 'particular trademark of the European social model' (Svallfors, 2012: 1), 'the jewel in the crown' and a 'fundamental part of what Europe stands for' (Giddens, 2006: 14), as are tuition-free universities, the cornerstone of intergenerational social mobility in Continental Europe (Kwiek, 2015c). The past trajectories of major types of welfare states and of universities in Europe tend to go hand in hand: first, vast expansion following World War II, and especially in the 1960s and 1970s, and then a state of permanent, resource-driven and legitimacy-based 'crisis' in the last two decades. Welfare states and universities, two critically important public institutions, seem to be under heavy attack from the public, the media and politicians. Their long-term sustainability is being questioned, and solutions to their (real and perceived) problems are being sought at global, European and national levels. Despite vastly different national circumstances – welfare state regimes and universities being born in different national contexts (see Kwiek, 2005, on Central Europe; Christensen et al., 2014, on the Nordic countries) – both of these public institutions have been operating under increasingly adverse financial conditions and exposed to large-scale systemic reforms across both Western and Eastern Europe (Stensaker et al., 2012; Zgaga et al., 2015).

This chapter is not about reforms and their current and future directions in the public sector, though. It is about increasing internal competition between major components of the widely understood welfare state architecture as it has emerged in the last half century: in particular, between old-age pensions, health-care systems and higher education and academic research as major claimants to the public purse. The competition is not only for public funding, although the financial dimension of ongoing transformations is of paramount importance (Kwiek, 2015b), but also for the place these three public institutions hold in the global, European and national social imagination. The assumption of this chapter is that public institutions cannot thrive without powerful supportive discourses concerning their social roles. When these discourses – which provide social legitimation combined with public funding – weaken, institutions weaken together with them. I focus on an ongoing and still largely latent struggle between major public institutions, with some predictions about its outcome.

Historically, the welfare state after the 'Golden Age' of the 1960s and the early 1970s entered an era of austerity that forced it 'off the path of ever-increasing social spending and ever-expanding state responsibilities' (Leibfried and Mau, 2008: xiii). Similarly, public higher education and research in Europe stopped being a permanent 'growth industry', and the 'expansive regime' in science of the post–World War II period, with the rate of accumulation steadily accelerating over time, was replaced with a new regime that John Ziman termed 'science in a "steady state"' (1994: 67 and 90). Europe has been struggling with the long-term consequences of both processes in both sectors for several decades now, with a varying pace, nature and depth of change in different countries. The ever-expanding 'endless frontier' in science promoted by Vannevar Bush (1945) is no longer with us, and in the last two decades universities have been exposed to large-scale reform attempts, as widely analysed in higher education research (see especially recent collective volumes on reform dynamics in Europe: Enders et al., 2011; Kwiek, 2015a; Schuetze et al., 2012; Stensaker et al., 2012; Zgaga et al., 2015).

From 'national glue' to 'national wealth'

I assume, following John S. Dryzek's theory of institutional design (1996; see also Goodin, 1996), that 'no institution can operate without an associated and supportive discourse (or discourses). Discourses may best be treated as institutional software';

furthermore, 'society's discourses are intertwined with its institutions' (Dryzek, 1996: 104 and 103). Institutional design – or reform-related changes in public institutions – results from 'reshaping the constellation of discourses in society' (Dryzek, 1996: 104). Both welfare state and universities are highly dependent on their supportive discourses, as they are highly reliant on public funding and highly sensitive to changing relationships with their environments – and as their discourses are under constant global construction and global renegotiation.

Historically, the power of the modern university over the last 200 years resulted from the power of the accompanying (supportive) discourse of modernity in which the university held a central, highlighted, specific (and carefully secured) place in European societies (Kwiek, 2006: 139–270; Kwiek, 2013: 107–90; Rothblatt and Wittrock, 1993; Wittrock, 1993). Modern universities as knowledge-producing institutions were born together with the nation state (and its nineteenth-century industrialism). Björn Wittrock, in his historical essay about the modern university, wrote that 'universities form part and parcel of the very same process which manifests itself in the emergence of an industrial economic order and the nation-state as the most typical and most important form of political organization' (1993: 305). The modern university was producing national glue and national consciousness, holding together emergent European nation states. The idea of a research-oriented university was born in the minds of German Idealist philosophers (Kwiek, 2006: 81–138) and still captures the imagination of European societies, recently reinforced by the idea of nationally located world-class universities. Keeping the institution's high position in the future social, cultural and economic architecture of European nations requires a strong supporting discourse to sustain – if not increase – public confidence, without which it is hard to maintain a high level of public trust (and public funding).

The struggles over the future forms of such public institutions as the university are also, perhaps above all, the struggles over discourses legitimizing their social, cultural and economic standing. In the last decade, those struggles have intensified and for the first time become global, with ever stronger engagement of international and transnational organizations and institutions (see 'international incentives for national policymaking', in Martens and Jakobi, 2010, and 'internationalized education policy', in Jakobi, 2009). To a large extent, the future of European universities and the level of their public subsidization will depend on the social and political acceptance of new legitimizing discourses currently being produced about them. These discourses are being produced especially at supranational levels and increasingly accepted in national policymaking communities across Europe, albeit with stronger or lighter 'national filters' or with an interplay between 'global reform scripts' for universities and their regional 'epistemic and normative "counterscripts"' (as explored in the Nordic context by Christensen et al., 2014: 45).

Widely accepted supportive discourses for public universities seem to be still in the making, amidst transformations of their environments (Välimaa and Hoffman, 2008). From a longer historical perspective, despite strong academic reluctance across the globe, it might be the case that 'science must be expected to keep up with the times' and that the only arguments to carry any weight for the expansion of science may be those that emphasize its 'promise of future wealth or other tangible benefits'

(Ziman, 1994: 84 and 85), hence, in more current parlance, the increasing popularity in European policy circles of the knowledge economy discourse (for research) and the private goods logics (for teaching).

Major questions about the future of the university are parallel to those about the future of the welfare state. As Pierre Pestieau expressed it elegantly in the context of the latter: 'the key issue is to figure out what we really want. Do we want the welfare state as it is, a market economy with no social protection, or a market economy with protection provided by the private sector?' (2006: 67). 'What we really want' in his formulation means, in various national circumstances, powerful supportive discourses resulting from various interrelated factors. Regarding the university of the future we need to know what we want and need to promote in society and the ideas that explain why we want it. We also need to make sure this voice is strong – as there is direct competition with other voices in favour of other social needs (Kwiek, 2015b), and as there are competing supportive discourses in favour of something else – something much less in favour of universities or in favour of universities being conceived of (and, especially, governed and funded) differently than we academics conceive them. The core of this strong voice conveying an academic message should be, in my view, increased institutional autonomy combined with at least maintained, and hopefully increased, levels of public funding. Public universities in Continental Europe need substantial public funding to continue their missions – and this message needs continued justification. To refer to John Ziman again, 'Any activity requiring a total layout of several percent of the national GNP is in serious competition with other desirable items of public or private expenditure, and has to be justified in that context' (1994: 83).

In any competition there are always winners and losers, and the outcome of the cross-generational and intranational competition to be at the top of publicly funded social priorities is unpredictable. Financial, ideological and electoral pressures on the reconfiguration of spending priorities are bound to intensify across Europe. In Central Europe, they emerged in the 1990s due to financial austerity experienced following the collapse of communism in 1989 (Kwiek, 2007), and the institution of the university was among the losers. Its supporting discourse was far too weak – and its access to public funds was not viewed as a social priority (Kwiek, 2012), with long-term negative implications.

From 'expansion' to 'steady state' to 'permanent austerity'

In the post-war period, there was no explicit internal competition between different social needs and the various components of the welfare state. Booming higher education and academic research were not in direct competition with expanding pension and health-care systems at that time. (In the expansion period, universities were also in much less competition internally, while in the current period, 'project is weighted against project, programme against programme, and field against field, according to criteria that are heavily influenced by political or commercial priorities', as Ziman (1994: 84) suggested two decades ago.) Public funding for the three sectors was substantial, and the pillars of favourable social attitudes to them were solid. National piles of tax-derived public funds available were expanding. However, 'growth industries' can always slow down or stop for financial, ideological and electoral reasons. And in times of financial austerity – lasting for at least two decades now, and intensified since 2008 in Europe – social configurations in which various public institutions function can be radically redefined, with unpredictable implications for the future.

The stagnation which started in the mid-seventies in Europe was perhaps the first sign that the welfare system in the form designed for one period (i.e., the post–World War II reconstruction of Europe) might be not be working in a different period. As Gøsta Esping-Andersen, a pioneering figure in European welfare studies, put it, 'most European social protection systems were constructed in an era with a very different distribution and intensity of risks and needs than exist today.... As a consequence, the welfare state is burdened with responsibilities for which it was not designed' (2001: 138). The post–World War II social contract was related to an industrial economy in a period of considerable growth; the male breadwinner model of work; and closed, national economies with largely national competition for investment, goods, products and services (see Kwiek, 2005). Since the seventies, the marriage of the nation state and the welfare state has been under powerful internal and external pressures. As Alex Dumas and Bryan S. Turner (2009: 49) point out, from a longer historical perspective, 'old age and retirement are products of the demographic transition (from high to low fertility and increased life expectancy) and industrialization'. Consequently, the social agenda of the eighties and nineties changed radically: after the policies of the 'Golden Age' of expansion, European welfare states have been shaped by Pierson's concept of 'permanent austerity' (2001b).

The post–World War II period of growth in higher education in Europe coincided with the development of post-war welfare states across the Continent. Massification processes in European higher education were closely linked to the growth and consolidation of European welfare states. Currently, while massification processes in higher education are in full swing across Europe, welfare states are under the most far-reaching restructuring in their post–World War II history (Bonoli and Natali, 2012; Connelly and Hayward, 2012; Häusermann, 2010; Hemerijck, 2013; Palier, 2010). Furthermore, European welfare states may be at risk of becoming a 'crisis casualty in the cascade of violent economic, social, and political aftershocks, unleashed by the global financial crisis' (Hemerijck, 2013: 1). In more general terms, the aftermath of the global financial crisis may mark a 'stress test' for the whole construction of the welfare state in Europe (Hemerijck, 2013: 68).

Or, as Peter Starke and colleagues argue in their study of policy responses to economic crisis across Europe, 'a huge pile of public debt restricts the room for manoeuvre, and makes even some conventional state functions appear like luxuries. Austerity is bound to remain the guiding force in years to come and painful cuts are the only thing left to be distributed' (2013: 2). The current restructuring of the foundations of the welfare state may change the way both policymakers and European societies view higher education. The financial dimension of ongoing changes in both the welfare state and higher education seems crucial, especially as the total costs generated by welfare state components, as well as each of them separately, cannot be easily reduced.

'University attitudes' and 'welfare attitudes': social legitimacy and public funding

Universities (and all public sector services) are not only heavily dependent on the public purse, or on the national financial context in which they are embedded, but also – of interest to me here – heavily dependent on the social fabric in which they are embedded. They are closely linked in individual countries (traditional nation states) to their usually shrinking tax base, or at least the tax base increasingly insufficient to mounting social and infrastructural needs. They are also closely linked to weak or strong social 'attitudes', expressed in larger weak or strong social supportive discourses.

Historically, the tax base for the components of the welfare state was in place. Moreover, social attitudes were highly favourable and supportive discourses were powerful. From the beginning of the modern European university in the early nineteenth century, the high social and economic standing of the university has remained unchallenged. The power of the modern university rested in the power of the modern nation state: the social contract between the two was as strong in the nineteenth century as it was in the period of its massive expansion in the post–World War II period (see Kwiek, 2006). Not surprisingly, the period of the most impressive growth of higher education Europe coincided with the period of the most impressive growth of European welfare states, and especially with its 'Golden Age' of the third quarter of the twentieth century. In the European social imagination (both in the capitalist West and in the socialist East), optimism regarding the future prevailed: growth seemed unimpeded and financial limits seemed distant. Welfare state entitlements grew in every generation, and universities and academic research grew exponentially. In short, citizens were ever better entitled and secured against social ills, and there were ever more ever better scientifically equipped researchers, as if the sky were the limit. Researchers were working 'under conditions of continuous expansion' and on the tacit assumption that expansion 'will never cease' (Ziman, 1994: 13). Until, that is, there appeared 'limits to growth'. The emergent limits were financial. Higher education in its traditional European forms has been largely publicly funded. As Gareth Williams points out, 'by the mid-1970s the idea of higher education as a publicly provided service was overwhelmingly the dominant model' (1992: 135).

In a similar vein, European citizens were being ever more protected against all sorts of social ills troubling them in the pre–World War II period, with affordable and effective public healthcare and reasonable, if not lavish, old-age pension systems termed at the time as 'welfare state maturation' (Pierson, 2001a: 88–92). The current increased fiscal demands on the welfare state come predominantly from these two major components – healthcare and pensions (neither linked to globalization and economic integration) – in the context of rapid population ageing.

Public institutions change over time, and social attitudes to public institutions also change. What I term here 'university attitudes' in European societies today may be studied in parallel to recently investigated 'welfare attitudes'. Stefan Svallfors's large-scale comparative research project on 'welfare attitudes' examined the legitimacy of current welfare state arrangements across European countries and the United States: 'Attitudes toward the welfare state and other public institutions should be seen as central components of social order, governance, and legitimacy of modern societies. They tell us something about whether or not existing social arrangements are legitimate' (2012: 2). Thus, in general, changing attitudes towards the welfare state and other public institutions (including universities) may lead to change in the founding ideas of public institutions, and reforms of public institutions may be – although do not have to be – a reflection of changing attitudes. However, if changing fiscal environments (towards less friendly) coincide with changing attitudes (towards less supportive), higher education reforms may be deeper and policy changes more abrupt. This may be the case in some European countries, potentially especially in Central Europe, which saw large cuts in public funding after 2008 (see Kwiek, 2016).

The modernization of European universities – as promoted, for instance, by the European Commission – can be viewed in parallel to what Silja Häuserman (2010: 1) has termed 'modernization in hard times' with reference to the transformations of the Continental welfare state: '*modernization* refers to the adaptation of existing institutional arrangements to the economic and social structures of post-industrialism ... The *hard times* result from the gap between declining resources and the growing (financial) needs that these modernization processes entail' (original emphasis). Most Organization for Economic Cooperation and Development (OECD) countries are currently experiencing a shrinking tax base. As Pierre Pestieau put it a decade ago, 'the share of regular, steady salaried labor is declining in a large number of countries, and thus the share of payroll tax base in the GDP is shrinking' (2006: 35). The constraints on public revenues are combined with growing social needs due to the ageing of European societies, increasingly costly past entitlements in the pension sector, an increasingly effective but also an expensive healthcare sector and changing family structures as well as the pressures of economic globalization. As Pierson explained in 2001, long before the recent financial crisis occurred, 'a context of essentially permanent austerity' was linked to a long list of factors inherent to the development of welfare states (2001b: 411).

The age structure of our societies increasingly matters. In ageing societies, the priorities of older generations (such as healthcare and pensions) may be stronger than ever before, leaving higher education (rather than general education) lower on the list of social priorities. Resources can be steered 'toward pensions and health care and away from educational investments for younger generations. As age conflict increases, the possibilities for age integration decline' (Dumas and Turner, 2009: 51). Reforms to both sectors may occur in parallel, according to similar 'global scripts' produced at a supranational level, but their outcomes may depend on wider social intergenerational conflicts. In the overall context of welfare state expenditures, healthcare, in comparison with pensions and unemployment benefits, has not shown signs of retrenchment, at least until the recent crisis (Pavolini and Guillén, 2013: 276; Rothgang et al., 2010: 247). But healthcare is 'in a state of permanent transformation' caused by the following tension:

> As demographic change and advancements in medical technology increase the demand for healthcare, globalization limits the amount of public funds that can go into it. As a result, the need for reforms that assure cost containment and at the same time guarantee high quality healthcare services for the population has increased. (Rothgang et al., 2010: 3)

Financial, ideological and electoral pressures
on public institutions

There are three separate types of pressures on public services which need to be kept in mind in discussing the future of the institution of the university: financial, ideological and electoral. They are all closely related to and influence one another, with electoral pressures possibly being most important.

First, financial pressures are relatively easily defined: the public costs of teaching and academic research are escalating, as are those of maintaining advanced health-care systems (Rothgang et al., 2010) and pension systems for ageing European populations. As Alex Dumas and Bryan S. Turner (2009: 50) argue, 'it is well recognized that the welfare states of Europe have rested on an explicit social contract between generations'. Any changes in the contract are bound to produce both winners and losers among different welfare state components. Some state responsibilities in some policy areas may have to be scaled down. One of the possible areas for social renegotiation is clearly the mass public subsidization of higher education. Even though its outcome is still undetermined, in several European countries the pressure to pump ever more private funding into higher education (through fees and business contracts) has been mounting, with the United Kingdom as a prime example.

Second, ideological pressures come mainly from global financial institutions and international organizations involved in the data collection and analysis of broader public sector services, especially the World Bank. They tend to disseminate the view – in different countries to different degrees – that, in general, the public sector is less efficient than the private sector; that its maintenance costs may exceed social benefits brought by it; and that it deserves less unconditional social trust combined with less unconditional public funding. While detailed arguments in favour of reforms vary over time and across European countries, overall they seem to be increasingly convergent, especially at transnational levels (OECD, World Bank and, following the 2008 economic crisis, the European Commission). The former two organizations have been the major providers of analytical frameworks, definitions, large-scale comparative datasets and extended analyses of pensions, healthcare, and higher education in the last decade. Global interests lead to global agendas along with global diffusion on the one hand and global data collection and analysis on the other (Jakobi, 2009). The role of global ideas in national policymaking increases (Martens and Jakobi, 2010). The OECD is a global health, pensions and education actor. It singles out important issues and sets agendas, presents visions and values, develops scenarios and defines guiding principles and concepts. Finally, 'it identifies present tendencies and future problems that are later discussed at national level' (Martens and Jakobi, 2010: 9). Not surprisingly, education policy statements 'sound increasingly and astonishingly similar all over the world' (Jakobi, 2009: 2). Soft mechanisms involved in 'OECD governance' include 'idea production', 'policy evaluation' and 'data production' (Martens and Jakobi, 2010: 266–8).

Finally, there are changeable electoral or public pressures, linked to both financial and ideological ones through public discussions, media coverage and personal experiences. Electoral perceptions of the public sector in general (like public attitudes towards welfare services) may gradually influence electoral perceptions of universities and the ways they should be financed in the future. Newly emergent 'university attitudes' across Europe – focusing on private goods and individual benefits rather than public goods and collective benefits produced through them – may be gradually changing the social circumstances in which universities are embedded. These attitudes may be more hostile to traditional Continental European mechanisms of full public subsidization, and more open to high fees/high loans mechanisms prevalent in the Anglo-Saxon world, with powerful implications for the nature of the institution.

So, as well as dealing with financial and ideological pressures, universities must also deal with the long-term effects of changes in the beliefs of European electorates as being of key importance for changes in the positions of leading national political parties across the Continent. Within economic constraints, 'the overall size of the welfare state and the extent of redistribution remain a matter of political choice' (Scharpf and Schmidt, 2000: 336). In democracies, voters play a crucial role – and in Europe they are currently attached to both the two major components of the welfare state (publicly funded pensions and tax-based healthcare) and to tuition-free public higher education (Altbach et al., 2010), Europe still being 'one of the last hold-outs of free higher education' (Marcucci, 2013: 19). However, under pressure from increasing competition for public resources between various claimants, the steering of resources away from educational investments should not be excluded. Otherwise generational interests would be on a collision course (Dumas and Turner, 2009: 51–2).

Although we cannot define the long-term impact of the economic crisis on higher education, we can provisionally assume that 'welfare attitudes' in general will not differ substantially from 'university attitudes' in particular, and that globally supported funding solutions for mass higher education systems will be more popular in Europe than nationally promoted ones, except perhaps for selected small and ultrarich European countries such as Norway or Switzerland.

Final thoughts

There are four reasons why universities (and academic research) in these times of permanent financial austerity need more social trust and stronger public support to maintain or increase their public subsidization.

First, growing intergenerational conflicts in ageing European societies do increase the power of arguments in support of higher public funding for the other two high spenders: pensions and healthcare, which are in direct competition with universities (with 'age wars' possibly replacing 'class wars' in the future; Dumas and Turner, 2009: 51). Universities have to confront increasing public support for the other two high spenders.

Second, current entitlements in both pensions and health-care systems (even redefined and recalibrated: either 'rationalized' or 'updated'; Pierson, 2001a: 425–7) have been growing exponentially due to decisions during the expansion period, with the accompanying large-scale social acceptance for both systems across Europe. Universities have to confront the accumulation of past entitlements in the other two high spenders, which makes competition more difficult than in the past.

Third, while the two high spenders clearly follow the logic of public goods in their functioning, universities are being increasingly reconceptualized, especially at a supra-national level, as following the logic of private goods in both teaching (students reconceptualized as consumers) and research (research results reconceptualized as sellable, commercialized commodities). The logic of public goods used by the other two high spenders is intrinsically linked to high public subsidization, while that of private goods is not. Universities have to confront the different normative basis of the other two high spenders in the competition for legitimacy and public funding.

And fourth, the rules of a zero-sum game apply more in tight fiscal times than in relaxed ones: as European societies in the post-2008 period entered a period of permanent financial austerity, higher public expenditures in one sector occur at the expense of expenditures in other sectors. Universities have to confront the task of showing their greater social usefulness compared with all other high spenders (as societies may increasingly value what universities produce 'relative to how those resources could be used elsewhere' (Salerno, 2007: 121).

The current condition of permanent financial austerity may redefine the nature of the European university as a public institution. Its future depends, to a considerable extent, on favourable social attitudes and strong supporting public discourses, both changeable under economic, ideological and electoral pressures. Therefore, no public institution should take for granted its survival in an untouched form without powerful social support. No rights seem to have been given forever, and public trust does not seem to have been guaranteed: both need to be thoughtfully and continuously fought for. Their combination indirectly determines the level of public subsidization, which, after a long period of post–World War II growth when the cross-sectoral competition between the different public sector claimants for public funding was not present, is being redefined. Although relatively friendly towards each other prior to the age of financial austerity, different public services in Europe are now beginning to operate in the context of increasing, albeit still latent, competition: for social trust, public support and public funding.

To thrive in the age of permanent financial austerity, the academic profession needs to know what their preferred image of the university is, how they want to function within it and why they want it – in order to be able to promote a strong supporting discourse about the key social and economic relevance of their institutions and themselves. In tough times, under adverse economic conditions, the preferred image needs to be clear and widely promoted. Confronting the two competing high spenders, pensions and health-care systems, does not seem to be easy in the context of growing cross-generational conflicts over public resources. However, optimistically, European governments most often follow public attitudes, and electoral pressures still do matter. All we need to do as academics is to promote universities in our societies as (still) highly legitimate, socially useful and publicly fundable institutions, and count on public trust and public support in the future. If we do not do this, why should anyone else?

Acknowledgements

The author gratefully acknowledges the support of the National Research Council (NCN) through its MAESTRO grant DEC-2011/02/A/HS6/00183 (2012–2017).

References

Altbach, P. G., L. Reisberg and L. E. Rumbley. (2010). *Trends in Global Higher Education. Tracking an Academic Revolution.* Rotterdam: Sense.

Bonoli, G., and D. Natali. (2012). *The Politics of the New Welfare State.* Oxford: Oxford University Press.

Bush, V. (1945). *Science: The Endless Frontier.* A Report to the President on a Program for Postwar Scientific Research. Reprinted July 1960, Washington DC: National Science Foundation.

Christensen, T., A. Gornitzka and P. Maassen. (2014). Global pressures and national cultures: A Nordic university template?, in P. Mattei (ed.), *University Adaptation in Difficult Economic Times.* Oxford: Oxford University Press. 30–51.

Connelly, J., and J. Hayward (eds) (2012). *The Withering of the Welfare State: Regression.* Basingstoke: Palgrave Macmillan.

Dryzek, J. S. (1996). The informal logic of institutional design, in R. E. Goodin (ed.), *The Theory of Institutional Design.* Cambridge: Cambridge University Press. 103–25.

Dumas, A., and B. S. Turner. (2009). Aging in post-industrial societies: Intergenerational conflict and solidarity, in J. Powell and J. Hendrick (eds), *The Welfare State and Postindustrial Society: A Global Analysis.* New York: Springer. 41–56.

Enders, J., H. F. de Boer and D. F. Westerheijden (eds) (2011). *Reform of Higher Education in Europe.* Rotterdam: Sense Publishers.

Giddens, A. (2006). A social model for Europe?, in A. Giddens, P. Diamond and R. Liddle (eds), *Global Europe, Social Europe.* Cambridge: Polity. 14–36.

Goodin, R. E. (1996). Institutions and their design, in R. E. Goodin (ed.), *The Theory of Institutional Design.* Cambridge: Cambridge University Press. 1–53.

Gøsta, E.-A. (ed.) (2001). *Incomplete Revolution: Adapting Welfare States to Women's NewRoles.* Cambridge: Polity Press.

Häusermann, S. (2010). *The Politics of Welfare State Reform in Continental Europe: Modernization in Hard Times.* Cambridge: Cambridge University Press.

Hay, C., and D. Wincott. (2012). *The Political Economy of European Welfare States.* New York: Palgrave.

Hemerijck, A. (2013). *Changing Welfare States.* Oxford: Oxford University Press.

Hurrelmann, A., S. Leibfried, K. Martens and P. Mayer. (2007). The golden-age nation state and its transformation: A framework for analysis, in A. Hurrelmann, S. Leibfried, K. Martens and P. Mayer (eds), *Transforming the Golden-Age Nation State.* Basingstoke: Palgrave Macmillan. 1–23.

Jakobi, A. P. (2009). *International Organizations and Lifelong Learning: From Global Agendas to Policy Diffusion.* Basingstoke: Palgrave Macmillan.

Kwiek, M. (2005). The university and the state in a global age: Renegotiating the traditional social contract?, *European Educational Research Journal* 4(4): 324–41.

Kwiek, M. (2006). *The University and the State: A Study into Global Transformations.* Frankfurt a/Main and New York: Peter Lang.

Kwiek, M. (2007). The university and the welfare state in transition: Changing public services in a wider context, in D. Epstein, R. Boden, R. Deem, F. Rizvi and S. Wright (eds), *Geographies of Knowledge, Geometries of Power: Framing the Future of Higher Education*. New York: Routledge. 32–50.

Kwiek, M. (2009). Globalisation: Re-reading its impact on the nation-state, the university, and educational policies in Europe, in M. Simons, M. Olssen and M. E. Peters (eds), *Re-Reading Education Policies: A Handbook Studying the Policy Agenda of the 21st Century*. Rotterdam: Sense Publishers. 195–215.

Kwiek, M. (2012). Changing higher education policies: From the deinstitutionalization to the reinstitutionalization of the research mission in Polish universities, *Science and Public Policy* 39(5): 641–54.

Kwiek, M. (2013). *Knowledge Production in European Universities: States, Markets, and Academic Entrepreneurialism*. Frankfurt a/Main and New York: Peter Lang.

Kwiek, M. (2015a). Reforming European universities: The welfare state as a missing context, in P. Zgaga, U. Teichler, H. G. Schuetze and A. Wolter (eds), *Higher Education Reform: Looking Back – Looking Forward*. Frankfurt a/Main and New York: Peter Lang. 93–118.

Kwiek, M. (2015b). Competing for public resources: Higher education and academic research in Europe; a cross-sectoral perspective, in J. C. Brada, W. Bienkowski and M. Kuboniwa (eds), *International Perspectives on Financing Higher Education*. London: Palgrave Macmillan. 6–24.

Kwiek, M. (2015c). European universities and educational and occupational intergenerational social mobility, in H.-O. Otto (ed.), *Facing Trajectories from School to Work. Towards a Capability-Friendly Youth Policy in Europe*. Dordrecht: Springer. 87–114.

Kwiek, M. (2016). From privatization (of the Expansion Era) to de-privatization (of the contraction era): A national counter-trend in a global context, in S. Slaughter and B. J. Taylor (eds), *Higher Education, Stratification, and Workforce Development: Competitive Advantage in Europe, the US and Canada*. Dordrecht: Springer. 311–30.

Leibfried, S., and S. Mau (eds) (2008). *Welfare States: Construction, Deconstruction, Reconstruction. Volume I: Analytical Approaches*. Cheltenham: Edward Elgar.

Marcucci, P. (2013). The politics of student funding policies from a comparative perspective, in D. E. Heller and C. Callender (eds), *Student Financing of Higher Education. A Comparative Perspective*. New York: Routledge. 9–31.

Martens, K., and A. P. Jakobi (eds) (2010). *Mechanisms of OECD Governance: International Incentives for National Policy-Making?* Oxford: Oxford University Press.

Palier, B. (ed.) (2010). *A Long Goodbye to Bismarck? The Politics of Welfare Reform in Continental Europe*. Amsterdam: Amsterdam University Press.

Pavolini, E., and A. M. Guillén (eds) (2013). *Health Care Systems in Europe under Austerity. Institutional Reforms and Performance*. New York: Palgrave.

Pestieau, P. (2006). *The Welfare State in the European Union: Economic and Social Perspectives*. Oxford, UK: Oxford University Press.

Pierson, P. (2001a). Post-industrial pressures on the mature welfare states, in P. Pierson (ed.), *The New Politics of the Welfare State*. Oxford: Oxford University Press. 80–106.

Pierson, P. (2001b). Coping with permanent austerity: Welfare state restructuring in affluent democracies, in P. Pierson (ed.), *The New Politics of the Welfare State*. Oxford: Oxford University Press. 410–56.

Rothblatt, S., and B. Wittrock (eds) (1993). *The European and American University since 1800: Historical and Sociological Essays*. Cambridge: Cambridge University Press.

Rothgang, H., M. Cacace, L. Frisina, S. Grimmeisen, A. Schmid and C. Wendt. (2010). *The State and Healthcare: Comparing OECD Countries*. Basingstoke: Palgrave Macmillan.

Salerno, C. (2007). A service enterprise: The market vision, in P. Maassen and J. P. Olsen (eds), *University Dynamics and European Integration*. Dordrecht: Springer. 119–32.

Schäfer, A., and W. Streeck. (2013). Introduction: Politics in the age of austerity, in A. Schäfer and W. Streeck (eds), *Politics in the Age of Austerity*. Cambridge: Polity Press. 1–25.

Scharpf, F. W., and V. A. Schmidt (eds) (2000). *Welfare and Work in the Open Economy. Vol. 1: From Vulnerability to Competitiveness*. Oxford: Oxford University Press.

Starke, P., A. Kaasch and F. van Hooren. (2013). *The Welfare State as Crisis Manager: Explaining the Diversity of Policy Responses to Economic Crisis*. New York: Palgrave.

Stensaker, B., J. Välimaa and C. S. Sarrico (eds) (2012). *Managing Reform in Universities. The Dynamics of Culture, Identity and Organizational Change*. New York: Palgrave.

Svallfors, S. (2012). Welfare states and welfare attitudes, in S. Svallfors (ed.), *Contested Welfare States: Welfare Attitudes in Europe and Beyond*. Stanford: Stanford University Press. 1–24.

Tanzi, V. (2011). *Government versus Market: The Changing Economic Role of the State*. Cambridge: Cambridge University Press.

Välimaa, J., and D. Hoffman. (2008). *Knowledge society discourse and higher education, Higher Education* (56): 265–85.

Williams, Gareth. (1992). *Changing Patterns of Finance in Higher Education*. Buckingham: Open University Press.

Wittrock, B. (1993). The modern university: The three transformations, in S. Rothblatt and B. Wittrock (eds), *The European and American University since 1800: Historical and Sociological Essays*. Cambridge: Cambridge University Press. 303–62.

Zgaga, P., U. Teichler, H. G. Schütze and A. Wolter (eds) (2015). *Higher Education Reform: Looking Back – Looking Forward*. Frankfurt a/Main and New York: Peter Lang.

Ziman, John. (1994). *Prometheus Bound: Science in a Dynamic Steady-State*. Cambridge: Cambridge University Press.

2

The European Governance of Education Policy: Crises, Collisions and Sectoral Defence

Åse Gornitzka

Few, if any, governance sites operate in splendid isolation but rather are part of larger political orders, that is, the set of political institutions that make and implement collective decisions. Some are centrally placed and tightly connected to other elements of such an order, whereas others are on the periphery and loosely connected to other governance sites. In the context of the emerging *European* political order, the governance of education and training has been far from the centre. This stands in contrast to the central position of the governance of education in national politics, that is, the ability of individual states to make and enforce rules regulating teaching and learning and to deliver services in education. Public education systems have traditionally played a key role in the state and nation building. Historically, education governance has been contested and has often been a battleground for the clash between the state and the church, between centre and periphery and/or between levels of government. The timing and dynamics related to the institutionalizing of mass education systems have also varied considerably (Rokkan, 1966; Soysal and Strang, 1989).

The emerging European political order entails serious challenges to the state-centred order. Shifts in authority and development of governance capacity lead to fuzzy demarcations between the responsibilities of territorial levels in formulating, deciding on and implementing rules and policies (Egeberg, 2005). This challenge, however, has not formally been present in education governance, which has remained an area where the European Union (EU) treaties only assign a supporting role for the EU. In some respect we could argue that compulsory education stays within the realm of 'core state powers', although this term has not been used in this way (Rittberger et al., 2013). What we can observe, nonetheless, is a soft challenge to the nation-state prerogative in education, higher education and vocational training when national political orders in Europe have been Europeanized.

At the turn of the century the Lisbon Summit and later the EU's strategy for growth and jobs had important repercussions for cooperation in the field of education. They represented in several respects a critical juncture. A new *governance site* in education was established with the concept of the open method of coordination (OMC) as its main framework (Gornitzka, 2007). It created a platform for profiling the sector in the wider context of the EU and for legitimating its place in European integration. The new cooperation within education policy came to be known as 'Education and Training 2010' and later as 'Education and Training 2020'. By insiders it was referred to simply as 'ET'.

The introduction of the OMC can also be seen as an instance of innovation that brought a new template for organizing governance within this sector in the EU. In this respect the OMC is an appropriate case for examining how new governance sites emerge and evolve – this being the main concern of this chapter. Building on previous studies of the emergence of these governance sites (Gornitzka, 2006, 2007), the current chapter examines how crisis and exogenous events shape how governance sites develop. Consequently, I trace the trajectory that this site has followed over a fifteen-year period through different stages: from its prehistory before the launch of the EU's Lisbon Strategy; to its initial inception stage in which the education sector picked up the OMC concept and started building the new governance site; to the consolidation phase; to, finally, the stage in which we can expect such a governance site to be challenged by the general systemic crisis, that is, the context and wake of the Eurozone crisis.[1]

The processes involved in developing new governance sites are multidynamic and cannot be fully understood with reference to any single theoretical account. Two main arguments drawn from institutional scholarship are explored in this chapter: one concerns a performance crisis and exogenous shocks as catalysts for institutional change, and the other concerns the horizontal dynamics of change where different sectors of society collide and challenge each other. On the basis of these two arguments I explore three possible scenarios for how governance sites develop:

- First scenario: we can expect a weak and marginal governance site to be crushed by ruptures in its surroundings, leading to institutional decay and even 'death'.
- Second scenario: if the governance site is loosely coupled to the overall political-administrative order (Cohen et al., 2012), then it is relatively invariant to crises (be it a performance or legitimacy crisis) in other parts of the system and can continue to operate relatively independently. The impact of crises is cushioned.
- Third scenario: actors can in times of crisis and turbulence use the established governance site as a platform to defend their interests, values and ideas and in doing so confirm its effectiveness and legitimacy: what might be referred to as a dynamic of sectoral defence (whereby crisis leads to stronger governance capacity).

These theoretical arguments are spelled out below. The chapter then proceeds to follow the case of ET 2010/2020 through different stages, before I conclude by identifying what this case can tell us about the dynamics of education governance in a Europeanized political order.

---

[1] See Gornitzka (2007) for a broader account and comparative analysis of the first phases of 'knowledge governance' sites in the EU's Lisbon Strategy.

Institutional change and resilience:
theoretical expectations

From the perspective of institutional theory, institutional arrangements are path dependent and cannot be readily changed by shifts in political will and power constellation, deliberate design and reorganization or environmental 'necessities' (March and Olsen, 1989). As institutional structures mature and grow in density over time, they gain operational autonomy and become infused with value 'beyond the technical requirement of the task at hand' (Selznick, 1966: 17). They thereby become 'embedded in structures of meaning and resources that are *relatively invariant* in the face of turnover of individuals and *relatively resilient* to the idiosyncratic preferences and expectations of individuals and changing external circumstances' (March and Olsen, 2006: 3; my emphasis).

Institutional and sectoral spheres acquire their own operational logic and principles that legitimize them, and institutional spheres of society become disassociated from one another (Eisenstadt, 1964). Public governance arrangements are specialized according to what societal sectors they address. With each sector having its own organized governance capacity, there is a potential problem of coordination across sectoral divides. A robust finding in the study of public bureaucracies is that coordinating within organizational boundaries is significantly easier than coordinating across them (Simon, 1976 [1945]). To the extent that such sectoral decision-making segments share basic ideas and understandings about appropriate policy objectives and legitimate concerns within a particular policy domain, sectorally differentiated institutions carry and perpetuate distinct policy paradigms and legacies. These are relatively predictable frames for action within a policy domain defining what are appropriate problems and solutions and who are the relevant actors.

Such insights underline how institutional spheres are relatively closed and 'sticky', not easily changed by people who come and go or by changing circumstances. Yet this does not mean that they are static. There are dynamics of change even within an institutionalized system, three of which provide the focus of this chapter.

First, there is the question of how institutions exist within a larger institutional setting (or 'order') that is rarely in a state of equilibrium. Change can occur in the interface and interaction between institutions (Holm, 1995) and can be understood in terms of 'interaction and collisions among competing institutional structures, norms, rules, identities and practices' (March and Olsen, 2006: 14–15). It can result in radical change if goals, interests, understandings and actors from one sphere *invade* another. Paradigmatic change would be observed if the fundamental understanding of the purposes of societal institutions embodied in public policy were replaced by another. Less dramatic cases of the effects of intersectoral interaction involve the gradual change in understanding of the constitutive principles of societal spheres – as when, for example, market-like solutions are imported to adjust the governance mechanisms in the social policy sphere without changing the overall policy paradigm or threatening the constitutive principles of a policy or the societal institutions it addresses (Hall, 1993). When the logic and governing arrangements of one sector are perceived to be challenged by another, it may trigger contestation and sectoral defence mechanisms (Gornitzka and Olsen, 2006;Olsen, 1997; Olsen 2007). This notion of institutional change suggests that the development of government sites is likely to be affected by developments in neighbouring sectors.

Secondly, organized governance capacity, once having been established, tends to gain relative independence. This is especially the case when the capacity for coordination between governance sites is weak as a result of a piecemeal and departmental 'silo approach' to governance having been adopted. In loosely coupled systems (Orton and Weick, 1990) governance sites can live semi-parallel lives. The downside is a lack of coordination and contradictory policies (e.g., where competition policies directly contradict environmental regulations or where agricultural policy contradicts health policy). The upside can be that a crisis in one part of the system may not necessarily cause disruption within other parts of the system. Under such conditions a breakdown, for instance, in EU economic governance, would have weak, indirect and belated consequences for the governance of other parts of the EU. Loose couplings insulate against the immediate onset of a domino effect of crisis in a system.

Thirdly, we would expect to see radical change at 'critical moments' of performance failure and crisis. Such moments call into question existing normative and causal beliefs regarding, for example, the effectiveness and legitimacy of existing governance arrangements, what constitutes appropriate problems and solutions, how resources should be distributed and who the legitimate actors are within a specific policy domain. Performance crisis is thus a key determinant of deinstitutionalization (Oliver, 1992): interventions and changes that at other times are unacceptable become possible in times of performance and legitimacy crises (Olsen, 2009). This was the case, for instance, when the EU governance of food safety was changed in the wake of the Bovine spongiform encephalopathy (BSE) crisis (Ugland and Veggeland, 2006) and when the wave of emigrants brought about by the collapse of the Soviet Union led to the entry of migration and policing policy into the EU agenda and the Maastricht Treaty (Turnbull and Sandholtz, 2001). This does not imply, however, that exogenous shocks and performance failure *automatically* trigger institutional change. For change to occur, crises and dramatic external events have to be translated into action.

If we are attempting to account for how governance sites develop with reference to these three arguments about institutional change, then this has implications for how we study them. First, it requires a diachronic approach where the establishment and fate of a governance site can be followed and traced in a sequence of events. Second, given that the focus here is on the role of contingent events and environments that surround new governance sites, the process of creation and institutionalization has to be placed in time and context. This chapter is structured according to such an approach, identifying the main stages. The analysis is based on eighteen semi-structured interviews conducted during 2005–7 with people (Commission officers, participants from national ministries and independent experts – all of whom have been involved in these processes at the European level) as well as on document analysis. The latter includes analyses of reports/publications that have been produced by working groups and expert groups, and official documentary records from the EU Consilium (minutes from the European Council and the Council of the EU's education meetings).

Stage I: European governance level in education before the turn of the century

Much of the history of the European Commission (EC)/EU's involvement in education as a policy area has been described as the national defence of the systemic borders and the sovereignty of nation-state systemic control (Corbett, 2006; De Wit and Verhoeven, 2001; Murphy, 2003). Education has been perceived as an area of legitimate national diversity. In Europe considerable national systemic diversity – both in terms of structure and content – reflects national traditions and links between education and the nation state. In their democratic role, schools and higher education institutions provide youth with civic education, which is a necessary component of a well-functioning democracy and a critical public sphere. At the level of tertiary education, one of the basic functions of the university has traditionally been to educate national elites and prepare them for entry into core national institutions, in particular the civil service and the national legal system. In the development of the welfare state, access to education at all levels has been seen as a key index of social equity.

Efforts to establish a European dimension to education and a common policy approach to education have encountered fundamental challenges. The integration of education systems has been off limits in terms of legal harmonization and regarded as of marginal interest for the European integration labelled as 'other matters' (Corbett, 2005: 133–41). The boundaries of education systems and the public responsibility for education by and large coincided with the boundaries of the nation state, especially as regards compulsory education. Also, with respect to higher education and vocational training, the idea of 'national systems' has been strong. European-level responsibility has been focused on mobility, that is, on dealing with the implications of and encouraging the crossing of systemic boundaries. The decisions to establish the EU's education programmes were core events. Education was also seen as least nationally sensitive in its economic rationale and more sensitive when perceived as a carrier of cultural and social values. The EC/EU's stronger legal foundation in the area of vocational training compared to other areas of education illustrates how this policy area and the issue of the free flow of skilled manpower, with its link to European integration as a market-building project, have historically been seen as an appropriate part of European integration (Shaw, 1999).

A gradual institutionalization of the policy area took place prior to the 2000s (Beukel, 2001). The supranational level institutionalized education as a policy area through the establishment of the EC's Director-General (DG) for education. With it education became subject to sustained attention and policy-making capacity at the European level. Even though, in terms of European budgets, the EU still was according 'more importance to a cow than a hundred students',[2] the education programmes expanded in scope and size. They became the basis for establishing many of the networks the Commission forged with national administrations, transnational and

---

[2] Comment made by the Commissioner Manuel Marín in connection with the Erasmus decision in 1986–87, quoted in Corbett, 2005: 140.

subnational actors (Gornitzka, 2009). At the European level the Commission's DG for education has been far from the only actor in education policy. The DG for education has been in interplay with other European institutions, with the Education Council and the Education Committee and the parallel committee in the European Parliament. Also, the European Court has played a very important role in defining the role of the European level (Beerkens, 2008; Shaw, 1999).

In sum, the European governance level showed signs of sectoral differentiation and capacity building. The EU's capacity for action in education did not rival that of most other policy areas of the EU and was, of course, completely dwarfed by the legal and financial means of governance that nation states had at their disposal.

Stage II: The inception of a new governance site in European education policy: 2000–4

As we have seen, the EU's involvement in European education was not an invention of the Lisbon European Council. Nonetheless, the Lisbon Process is a landmark for European education policy: in the context of the Lisbon Process the education sector was linked to and influenced by developments in other policy areas. It placed education on the interface between the EU's economic policy and social policy. Education received attention in Lisbon as part of a much larger agenda and political project. The whole knowledge and skills area was defined in Lisbon as a necessary component of an economic and social reform strategy. In particular, the Commission pitched the education sector's contribution to the Lisbon Strategy in an urgent tone of voice. Already in the early stage of the Lisbon Strategy it was clear that this process implied a strengthening of the visibility of the education sector as higher education and training were defined as part of a set of policy areas open to 'competitiveness'. The Lisbon Strategy expressed at an ideational level greater expectations of coordination not only between territorial levels but across sectors, an opportunity for horizontal integration that could trigger the kind of collisions and interaction between policy sectors that had operated largely independent of each other. The reference that the Lisbon Spring Council (heads of state in the EU Member States) in 2000 made to the OMC also opened up a procedural way forward for how education sector actors could organize in a different way, that is, a new governance template to match the new ideas about the EU's transition to the knowledge economy.

In 2001 three strategic objectives were adopted that concerned the improved quality and effectiveness of education, access to education and the opening up of national education and training systems to society and 'the wider world'[3]. This was turned into a ten-year work programme comprising thirteen specified objectives.[4] The Commission

---

[3] Adopted by the European Council, Stockholm 2001 (Presidency Conclusions 23–24 March 2001), The Archive of European Integration.

[4] See 'Detailed work programme on the follow-up of the objectives of education and training systems in Europe', adopted by the Education Council and the Commission 14.02.02. OJ C 142. Brussels 14 June 2002). Work programme approved by the European Council 2002 (Presidency Conclusions 15–16 March, 2002), The Archive of European Integration.

prepared the documents, and the Education Council quickly agreed on these strategic goals. The goals that the education ministers agreed on were very general and hardly touched any overtly controversial or sensitive issues. Nonetheless, the establishment of OMC education indicates a change of attitude towards European coordinating efforts among European ministers of education: a change described by one informant as going from education ministers 'meeting to celebrate national diversity to acknowledging common challenges'.[5]

The Commission started setting up an institutional model for the OMC. From early 2004 two other parallel processes, the intergovernmental process towards establishing the European Higher Education Area (the Bologna Process), and the EU's 'Copenhagen Process' for vocational education and training, were added in order to include the whole range and all the forms of education. From then on the OMC process in education was referred to as 'Education and Training 2010'. The political agreement, anchored in the Education Council and legitimized by the European Council, on the content of the new cooperation formed the basis for future development.

Two types of exogenous shocks inside the sector but outside the EU added to this dynamic. In 1999, the same ministers who had agreed to revise their ways of cooperating within the EU had put their signatures on the Bologna declaration. These signatures led them to embark on the process towards establishing a European higher education area, notably as an outside EU process where the actors within the sector were in the driver's seat, and supranational institutions (read the Commission) were initially not invited to sit at the decision-making table (Ravinet, 2008). Still, this was an unprecedented initiative in the history of European integration and (higher) education and a surprising procedural innovation in European governance of higher education.

The second (and more painful) shock came from the Organization for Economic Cooperation and Development (OECD) and the community of education experts: in December 2001 the results of the Programme for International Student Assessment (PISA) 2000 comparative study of schoolchildren's basic skills were made public. Notably, several of the national Ministries of Education were in a state of shock due to the scores of their students.[6] Moreover, the role of the Education Council/Education Committee notwithstanding, the inception of the OMC into EU education policy was from the very start marked by active role of the Commission's DG. The Directorate-General Education, Youth, Sport and Culture (DG EAC) acted as a procedural and ideational entrepreneur for creating a new governance site and maintaining it. The DG EAC in its follow-up to the Lisbon Strategy emphasized the need for common action to modernize European education.

Stage III: Consolidating a sector-specific governance site

The DG EAC prepared, organized and orchestrated the practical implementation of the OMC governance site.[7] The DG EAC also provided organizational capacities to

---

[5] Informant interview December 2005.
[6] Informant interview December 2005.
[7] Informant interview August 2006.

the process and found a budget line in the SOCRATES programme to finance OMC activities at the European level. The DG's officials were crucial in determining the content and working procedures of the OMC groups. Not all working groups under the OMC procedure were strongly energized – especially those groups that were characterized by unclear cognitive structures and little common understanding of the agenda were killed softly by waning energy from the participants and the DG's informal assessment of their operations. Other groups could operate on the basis of strong cognitive and normative structures and were able to perform stocktaking, provide information and 'deliver'.

The national experts who served on these working groups were predominantly drawn from national Ministries of Education, and few came from national agencies or expert/academic communities. The way in which the OMC was practised in this sector brought the Commission close to national political-administrative leadership in some of the subpolicy areas. In addition over thirty different social partners and stakeholder organizations[8] were represented, and in some cases, the secretariats of international organizations, most notably the OECD and the Council of Europe. These actors were brought together in the new governance site in iterative interaction at the European level in most areas of education policy: access, approaches to teaching and learning basic skills, funding and organizational issues, counselling, ICT and so on. The new governance site was filled with the core actors in the field and enhanced and expanded the European networks of national administrations and stakeholders.

In 2005 the OMC structure was partly reorganized[9] and new areas of attention were included. Two new organizational elements were added that further institutionalized the OMC: a High-Level Group (only national administrations represented) charged with maintaining stronger links to national administrations and producing input to the reporting processes, and a large ET 2010 coordination group, which also included the social partners. A new governance site was undoubtedly being institutionalized, but not all elements were equally 'taken for granted'.

In this period – halfway into the Lisbon Strategy – the OMC approach to European integration came under fire (see Tholoniat, 2010, for a summary of this period). The list of grievances directed at the governance approach was long: Member States' refusal to report, non-committal to agreed objectives, wishful thinking, the gap between ambition and performance and so on. The High-Level Group, led by Win Kok, spoke of cheap talk that came with heavy administrative reporting burdens and processes dominated by technocrats. The aura that had surrounded the OMC as a new method seemingly lost some of its glow. Some of the smaller OMCs did not survive this 'public

---

[8] Most notably, European-level associations such as Union of Industrial and Employers' Confederations of Europe (UNICE), European Trade Union Committee for Education (ETUCE), Education International, European School Heads Association, European Parent's Association, European University Association, National Union of Students in Europe.

[9] Cluster on Modernisation of higher education, on Teachers and Trainers in VET, on making best use of resources, on Maths, Science and Technology, on Access and Social Inclusion in LLL, on Key Competencies and ICT, on Recognition of learning outcomes, Adult learning, and lifelong guide policy network. Most of these were a continuation of the working groups that had been established in the infancy of the OMC.

attack'. The OMC governance site in education did. Yet, it felt the impact of the revised Lisbon Strategy. The reorganization that was instituted in this period was in line with the overall revision and relaunch of the Lisbon Strategy. Furthermore, in substantive terms the process towards the modernized European education system that was heralded in the beginning of the Lisbon Process was, with one major exception (increasing graduates in maths, sciences and engineering), very far from being attained, and there was no major evidence to suggest that the workings of this governance site had produced substantive outcomes in national education policy. Nonetheless, several of the elements of the new governance site increasingly showed signs of institutionalization in this consolidation phase.

The quantified aspects of the OMC process were most deeply institutionalized. The quantification of European cooperation in education policy was persistently pushed in order to provide 'strong policy relevant messages'.[10] After its establishment the Standing Group on Indicators and Benchmarks gained acceptance from the Member States and also within the DG EAC, and to date it continues to have a strong position within the OMC structure with high attendance rates and a legitimated and visible role in the ET 2010 programme. The significance attached to indicators was confirmed by the establishment of a centre that formed part of the Commission Joint Research Centre in Italy in 2005 with a view to supporting the EU's indicator development in the area of lifelong learning. Furthermore, in 2005 the Council decided on new indicators, and the following year the legal basis for the Statistical Office of the European Communities (EUROSTAT's) education statistics was strengthened. (The centre continues to monitor the EU 2020 headline targets in education and training and conducts analysis to feed policy decisions at the EU level.) Reporting from the implementation of ET 2010 became fairly well established as a routine.[11]

However, the organization and practices for policy learning and peer reviewing lived in a tensile balance between institutionalization, experimentation and disintegration. There were no obviously established and accepted criteria for certifying the experiences of other countries as good examples to guide national policy reform or adjustment. When the DG EAC reorganized the OMC infrastructure in 2005/06, it focused on the need to provide a clearer working methodology for learning. The DG EAC set up eight 'clusters' that corresponded to key priorities identified in the ET 2010 work programme. Ten to twenty-five Member States could participate in each cluster according to their own priorities. Each cluster was coordinated by an official from the DG EAC. The format for the 'clusters' implied organizing learning through the so-called peer learning activities (PLAs) (Lange and Alexiadou, 2010).[12]

Stage IV: Navigating the crisis?

Towards the end of the first decade of the twenty-first century this governance site had settled into becoming a fairly regularized activity at the EU level, extending its

---

[10] SGIB minutes from 3 July 2002, first meeting: p. 5.
[11] Council Conclusions of 12.05.09 on ET 2020, 2009/C 119/02.
[12] PLAs are organized by clusters and include site visits and in situ peer reviewing.

activities to the national level with the PLAs and national reporting. Signs of output legitimacy in terms of the domestic impact of the eight- to ten-year-old governance site were scant (Alexiadou et al., 2010; Lange and Alexiadou, 2010). Yet the governance site had expanded its territory. In addition to the annual reports on the progress towards the common European objectives in education and training, it produced the backup and input to a string of Commission communications and recommendations that made it into the regular decision-making procedures of the EU institutions in this area – for example, its issuing of educational standards through the European Qualifications Framework (EQF) adopted in 2008 (Elken, 2015) and of guidelines for quality in vocational education and training (EQAVET), together with work on the modernization agenda of the European universities (Gornitzka, 2010).

In June 2010, EU leaders adopted the 'Europe 2020' strategy, to replace the Lisbon Strategy with the aim of creating jobs and promoting 'smart, sustainable and inclusive growth'. This also implied a major overhaul of the governance architecture. This reform should be seen against the backdrop of the acute financial and sovereign debt crisis in the EU, a crisis that rocked the foundations of the EU's political, economic and social order. What the implications were for the governance architecture of the EU is still under debate. Still, one major change in the governance architecture is particularly relevant here: the introduction of the European Semester in 2011, which combines governance instruments in economic and social governance of the EU within one single annual policy coordination cycle (Zeitlin and Vanhercke, 2014). The aim of the European Semester was to improve economic policy coordination in the Union and push towards implementation of the EU's economic rules.[13] The European Semester setup gave the Commission a clearer and stronger role in policy coordination – not only would the Commission in autumn of each year set out the EU priorities for the coming year (Annual Growth Survey) but it should also publish its opinions on each country's draft budgetary plan. Moreover, the Commission took on a new role in issuing country-specific recommendations (CSRs) for budgetary and economic policies, after each country had presented its Stability/Convergence Programme and its National Reform Programme (later, in the spring). The latter sets out the Member States' budgetary and economic policies. The Council discusses these recommendations, amends them if deemed appropriate and adopts them (Darvas and Leandro, 2015: 4).

What were the implications of this and connected arrangements for EU education governance?

The education sectors still hung on to the overall political project of the EU. One of the seven 'flagship initiatives' for growth and employment of the Europe2020 agenda was 'Youth on the Move', aimed at 'improv[ing] the performance and international attractiveness of our higher education institutions and raise the quality of all levels of education and training in the EU, combining both excellence and equity'.[14] Moreover, the 2020 strategy proposed five headline targets, amongst them one centred on two heartland education policy issues: cutting the school dropout rate from 15 per cent to

---

[13] The Stability and Growth Pact (SGP) and the macroeconomic imbalance procedure (MIP).
[14] Commission 2010: COM (2010) 2020 final, EUROPE 2020 – A strategy for smart, sustainable and inclusive growth. Brussels, 03.03.2010.

below 10 per cent and increasing the number of young people with a university degree or diploma from less than a third to at least 40 per cent. In May 2010 the EU's education ministers agreed to recommend the numerical average targets that the Commission had proposed as part of the Europe 2020 strategy. These had met with considerable resistance from Germany, especially from the federal states.[15]

The Commission's attempts to issue country-specific recommendations to Member States met with a mixed reception from national ministries. For instance, the United Kingdom responded with overt defiance,[16] whereas Hungary dismissed the target for dropout rates as 'unrealistic'.[17] After years of operating within an OMC-style governance site at the European level, these initiatives were perceived as attempts to step outside the formal remit of the Commission in the area of education. This rekindled lines of traditional territorial conflict between the supranational and the national/federal/state levels. Yet within the framework of the European Semester, the Commission did issue country-specific recommendations which frequently encompassed recommendations with respect to education policy. In fact all country recommendations that the Commission issued in 2013 contained recommendations on education, with the exception of the recommendation for the Netherlands, urging in many cases the Member States to exempt education from budget cuts in order to pursue 'growth friendly consolidation paths' (Bekker, 2014: 8 and13).

The numerical target connected to education also implied continued or increasing investments in education. Since education was an area of heavy public spending, such an emphasis was problematic given the financial difficulties that most of the Member States were facing in the wake of the financial and economic crisis at the time. However, the Commission's approach to this situation was not to abandon continued and renewed support for the education and skills sector. Moreover, the crisis did not prompt a withdrawal of support on the part of the Commission for common EU education governance. Rather, in its subsequent reporting on ET 2020, the opposite was the case. The DG EAC's response was to use the economic crisis and recession to further underline the need for concerted action and a common strategy on the part of the EU, as it had done at the inception of the ET 2010. The sector's input on the Europe 2020 strategy actively referred to both skills and education as the main solution for Europe's economic predicament and to the need for investment in the education sector. The assertiveness of the sector so far seems to have been enhanced in the context of the new overall strategy, pushing even further its message of what education can do for the economy and the labour market. The sector-specific governance site is still in operative mode. Actors inside the education domain – and those outside it – did not use the general crisis as an opportunity to question and deinstitutionalize this governance site.

---

[15] Euractiv 18/08/2010.

[16] The United Kingdom conveyed that it did agree with the European Commission's interpretation of how the 'Europe 2020' strategy should be implemented in the field of education. The United Kingdom insisted that the headline targets agreed by the European Council in June 2010 were not formally binding on Member States. The UK representative argued that individual countries should 'set their own level of ambition' when it comes to translating these targets into national policies, in order for the specific characteristics of different education systems to be taken into account. (Euractiv 15–16/02/2011).

[17] Euractiv 21/07/2010.

Since 2011 the Commission's DG EAC has published an annual Education and Training Monitor with in-depth country reports accompanying it.[18] Ideationally, education has over the past fifteen years become more strongly embedded as an instrument for other social and economic goals and for horizontal coordination. Overall the governance site established on the basis of the OMC survived the economic crisis and has been further strengthened as part of the Europe 2020 strategy. Also the EU's Education, Youth, Culture and Sport (EYCS) Council continues to pursue a sectoral-defence approach. For example, European education ministers stated with respect to the 2014 European Semester,

> With a view to increasing the visibility of education and training in the 2014 European Semester, the Council agreed to focus on: facilitating long-term investment in the modernisation of education and training and the development of skills, equipping people in all age groups with better and more relevant skills, smoothing the transition from school to work, notably by promoting work-based schemes, continuing to modernise and improve educational methods and making full use of the digital learning opportunities. (Press Release, 3296th Council meeting, Education, Youth, Culture and Sport, Brussels, 24 February 2014)

The extent to which European talk results in national action, however, is another matter – from 2000 to 2013 the spending on education dropped in terms of the EU average and in the majority of the Member States. This fact has been bemoaned both in the overall country recommendation included in the European Semester and in the comments and communications from the DG EAC specifically. Clearly, this is a case of sectoral defence that takes place at the European level. The transversal problem-solver approach has been no less relevant in the wake of the crisis: for example, the Council adopted in 2016 a resolution on promoting socio-economic development and inclusiveness in the EU through education (5685/1/16 REV 1), again calling for targeted reforms and prioritized investment in education systems and for education to work more closely with the employment sector.

The 2016 New Skills Agenda for Europe also illustrates the continued interplay between labour market policy and the education policy sphere. Here the new organizational setup of the Commission with stronger coordination of policy approaches at the political level (new super-commissioners initiated by the Juncker Commission) is an interesting development. The commissioners' perspectives – 'sector goggles' – demonstrate how the framing of education/labour market policy items remains a constant feature of the discussions.

The horizontalization of education is increasingly visible at the EU level – and in ways other than through the framework of ET, the European Semester and economic and social policy coordination. It is visible, for example, in areas such as EU–US trade negotiations and the disputed role of education as tradable service, and in the collision between national higher education policy and implementation of the EU's service directive.

---

[18] European Commission, *The Education and Training Monitor*, httm://ec.europa.eu/education/tools/et-monitor_en.htm.

The security and migration crisis illustrates a similar cross-sectoral dynamic: the emphasis on 'skills for life', and not just for work, becomes an instrument in the policy for integration and the fight against extremism and for the deradicalization of youth (Council meeting 24.02.16). The traditional role of education as a socializing institution which installs fundamental European values and democracy is rekindled at this governance site. Once again the Commission and the Council in the education sector responded to the crisis situation by offering the use of education and training strategies for integrating recently arrived immigrants (Council 23-11-15). As argued by the French minister of education during a Council meeting in 2015, 'Education and training must be a bulwark against fanaticism' (Vallaud-Belkacem 23.11.15).

Conclusion

The larger context of the Lisbon Process and later on the EU's strategy for growth and jobs (Europe 2020) had important repercussions for cooperation in the field of education and represented in several respects a critical juncture. A new site of voluntary policy coordination in education was established that created a platform for profiling the sector in the wider context of the EU, and for legitimating its place in European integration. The story of education policy and the Lisbon Process and the EU 2020 strategy also demonstrate how at the European level a nationally sensitive policy domain was (re)framed in substantive terms within an economic competitiveness agenda and as an instrument for facing the challenges of the globalized knowledge economy. The demand that education policy should have a more prominent place on the political agenda was reinforced by the demand that it should be integrated within the overall political and economic objectives of the EU. Hence the new governance site was placed in an area of tension between different policy sectors and ideas about the role of education (economic, cultural, democratic and social roles) in a changing political and economic order.

How this purportedly fragile site for voluntary policy coordination developed cannot be accounted for unless we factor in the larger context of the European political order. Faced with exogenous shocks and key events, actors within the EU education policy domain actively used these external conditions to defend the educational domain (especially against the 'intrusion' of employment policy) and to couple the governance of education and training to the wide ambitions of the EU. Neither the overt crisis in EU governance, policy failures within the education policy domain and even more so outside this domain, nor resistance from Member States guarding their education policy prerogative have (so far) led to a decay of this governance site.

References

Alexiadou, N., D. Fink-Hafner and B. Lange. (2010). Education policy convergence through the Open Method of Coordination: Theoretical reflections and implementation in 'old' and 'new' national contexts, *European Educational Research Journal* 9(3): 345–58.

Bartolini, S. (2005). *Restructuring Europe: Centre Formation, System Building and Political Structuring between the Nation-State and the European Union*. Oxford: Oxford University Press.

Beerkens, E. (2008). The emergence and institutionalisation of the European higher education and research area, *European Journal of Education* 43(4): 407–24.

Bekker, S. (2014). EU economic governance in action: Coordinating employment and social policies in the third European Semester, *Tilburg Law School Research Paper Series* 14.

Beukel, E. (2001). Educational policy: Institutionalization and multi-level governance, in S. S. Andersen and K. A. Eliassen (eds), *Making Policy in Europe*. London: Sage. 124–45.

Cohen, M. D., J. G. March and J. P. Olsen. (2012). 'A garbage can model' at forty: A solution that still attracts problems, in A. Lomi and J. R. Harrison (eds), *The Garbage Can Model of Organizational Choice: Looking Forward at Forty*. Bingley, UK: Emerald Group Publishing Limited. 19–30.

Corbett, A. (2005). *Universities and the Europe of knowledge: Ideas, institutions and policy entrepreneurship in European Union higher education policy, 1955–2005*. Basingstoke: Palgrave Macmillan.

Corbett, A. (2006). Higher education as a form of European integration: How novel is the Bologna Process?, *Arena Working Paper* 15.

Curtin, D., and M. Egeberg. (2008). Tradition and innovation: Europe's accumulated executive order, *West European Politics* 31(4): 639–61.

Darvas, Z., and Á. Leandro. (2015). The limitations of policy coordination in the euro area under the European semester, *Bruegel Policy Contribution* 18.

De Wit, K., and J. C. Verhoeven. (2001). Higher education policy of the European Union: With or against the Member States?, in J. Huisman, P. Maassen and G. Neave (eds), *Higher Education and the Nation State*. Amsterdam: Pergamon Press. 175–231.

Egeberg, M. (2005). EU institutions and the transformation of European-level politics: How to understand profound change (if it occurs), *Comparative European Politics* 3(1): 102–17.

Eisenstadt, S. N. (1964). Social change, differentiation and evolution, *American Sociological Review* 29(3): 375–86.

Elken, M. (2015). New EU instruments for education: Vertical, horizontal and internal tensions in the European Qualifications Framework, *Journal of Contemporary European Research* 11(1): 69–83.

Fukuyama, F. (2013). What is governance?, *Governance* 26(3): 347–68.

Gornitzka, Å. (2006). The open method of coordination as practice: A watershed in European education policy?, Arena Working Papers 16/06, Arena Centre for European Studies, Oslo.

Gornitzka, Å. (2007). The Lisbon Process: A supranational policy perspective, in P. Maassen and J. P. Olsen (eds), *University Dynamics and European Integration*. Dordrecht: Springer. 155–78.

Gornitzka, Å. (2009). Networking administration in areas of national sensitivity: The Commission and European higher education, in A. Amaral, P. Maassen, C. Musselin and G. Neave (eds), *European Integration and the Governance of Higher Education and Research*. Dordrecht: Springer. 109–31.

Gornitzka, Å. (2010). Bologna in context: A horizontal perspective on the dynamics of governance sites for a Europe of knowledge, *European Journal of Education* 45(4): 535–48.

Gornitzka, Å., and J. P. Olsen. (2006). Europeiske endringsprosesser og høyere utdanningsinstitusjoner, *Tidsskrift for Samfunnsforskning* 47(2): 259–74.

Hall, P. A. (1993). Policy paradigms, social learning, and the state: The case of economic policy-making in Britain, *Comparative Politics* 25(3): 275–96.

Holm, P. (1995). The dynamics of institutionalization: Transformation processes in Norwegian fisheries, *Administrative Science Quarterly* 40(3): 398–422.

Jones, E., R. D. Kelemen and S. Meunier. (2016). Failing forward? The euro crisis and the incomplete nature of European integration, *Comparative Political Studies* 49(7): 1010–34.

Lange, B., and N. Alexiadou. (2010). Policy learning and governance of education policy in the EU, *Journal of Education Policy* 25(4): 443–63.

March, J. G., and J. P. Olsen. (1989). *Rediscovering Institutions: The Organizational Basis of Politics*. New York: Free Press.

March, J. G., and J. P. Olsen. (2006). Elaborating the 'new institutionalism', in R. A. W. Rhodes, S. Binder and B. Rockman (eds), *The Oxford Handbook of Political Institutions*. Oxford: Oxford University Press. 3–20.

Murphy, M. (2003). Covert action? Education, social policy and law in the European Union, *Journal of Education Policy* 18(5): 551–62.

Oliver, C. (1992). The antecedents of deinstitutionalization, *Organization Studies* 13(4): 563–88.

Olsen, J. P. (1997). Institutional design in democratic contexts, *Journal of Political Philosophy* 5(3): 203–29.

Olsen, J. P. (2007). *Europe in Search of Political Order: An Institutional Perspective on Unity/Diversity, Citizens/Their Helpers, Democratic Design/Historical Drift, and the Co-Existence of Orders*. Oxford: Oxford University Press.

Olsen, J. P. (2009). Democratic government, institutional autonomy and the dynamics of change, *West European Politics* 32(3): 439–65.

Orren, K., and S. Skowronek. (2004). *The Search for American Political Development*. Cambridge: Cambridge University Press.

Orton, J. D., and K. E. Weick. (1990). Loosely coupled systems: A reconceptualization, *Academy of Management Review* 15(2): 203–23.

Pochet, P. (2005). The OMC and the construction of social Europe, in J. Zeitlin and P. Pochet (eds), *The Open Method of Coordination in Action*. Brussels: P. I. E. Peter Lang, 37–82.

Ravinet, P. (2008). From voluntary participation to monitored coordination: Why European countries feel increasingly bound by their commitment to the Bologna process, *European Journal of Education* 43(3): 353–67.

Rittberger, B., D. Leuffen, F. Schimmelfennig, P. Genschel and M. Jachtenfuchs (2013). Differentiated integration of core state powers, in Philipp Genschel and Markus Jachtenfuchs (eds), *Beyond the Regulatory Polity? The European Integration of Core State Powers*. Oxford: Oxford University Press. 183–210.

Rokkan, S. (1966). Norway: Numerical democracy and corporate pluralism, in R. A. Dahl (ed.), *Political Oppositions in Western Democracies*. New Haven: Yale University Press. 70–115.

Selznick, P. (1966). *Leadership in Administration: A Sociological Interpretation*. New York: Harper & Row.

Shaw, J. (1999). From margins to centre: Education and training law and policy, in P. Craig and G. de Búrca (eds), *The Evolution of EU Law*. Oxford: Oxford University Press. 555–95.

Simon, H. A. (1976 [1945]). *Administrative Behavior: A Study of Decision-Making Processes in Administrative Organization*, 3rd ed. New York: Free Press.

Soysal, Y. N., and D. Strang. (1989). Construction of the first mass education systems in nineteenth-century Europe, *Sociology of Education* 62(4): 277–88.

Tholoniat, L. (2010). The career of the Open Method of Coordination: Lessons from a 'soft' EU instrument, *West European Politics* 33(1): 93–117.

Turnbull, P., and W. Sandholtz. (2001). Policing and immigration: The creation of new policy spaces, in A. S. Sweet, W. Sandholtz and N. Fligstein (eds), *The Institutionalization of Europe*. Oxford: Oxford University Press. 194–220.

Ugland, T., and F. Veggeland. (2006). The European Commission and the integration of food safety policies across levels, in M. Egeberg (ed.), *Multilevel Union Administration: The Transformation of Executive Politics in Europe*. Houndmills: Palgrave Macmillan. 143–62.

Zeitlin, J., and B. Vanhercke. (2014). Socializing the European Semester? Economic governance and social policy coordination in Europe 2020. 1 October. Watson Institute for International Studies Research Paper No. 2014-17. Watson Institute of International Studies, Brown University. Available at SSRN: https://ssrn.com/abstract=2511031 or http://dx.doi.org/10.2139/ssrn.2511031.

3

Complex Games of Standardization in Higher Education: *Calculemus*

Paolo Landri, Rosaria Lumino and Roberto Serpieri[1]

Higher education in Europe is under pressure from a new regime of accountability aimed at putting its institutional performance under control. This new regime was well established before the global economic crisis of 2007/08 and relies on a long-standing project of standardization that has been underway since the initial steps of the Bologna Process and the inauguration of the European Higher Education Area (EHEA). In this chapter we argue that standardization does not in practice necessarily lead to the end of the heterogeneities within the EHEA. While education standards are 'normative specifications for the steering of educational systems' (Waldow, 2014: 50), standardization is a dynamic process based on the stability but also on the malleability of standards. Recently, the history of standardization has been interwoven with the adoption of austerity measures and with the need for fostering competitiveness in higher education. However, as we seek to show, 'trade-offs' between, on the one hand, the expectations of meeting high standards of outcomes and, on the other hand, the obligation of placing public spending under control are being worked through in some European countries.

So we focus on the complex games of standardization of higher education within Europe, by considering education standards as epistemic objects (Knorr-Cetina, 2001; Mulcahy, 2011). This perspective considers standards as incomplete, question generating and unfolding (Knorr-Cetina, 2001; Miettinen, 2005) and invites us to look at how standards are enacted in practice. Standardization does not lead necessarily to increasing uniformity nor to the rejection of the diversity of practices which it is intended to regulate (Busch, 2011). Here, it means looking at the history of standardization within higher education in Europe, in order to highlight: (a) how it is fabricating spaces of commensuration and (b) how it draws on education standards that are flexible, fluid objects, always incomplete over time.

---

[1] This chapter is a work of shared authorship. For the purpose of identifying individual contributions, the introductory section was written by Roberto Serpieri; the section on the standardization of higher education in Europe by Paolo Landri; and the section on the drive to performance-based funding in European universities by Rosaria Lumino; the conclusions were jointly drafted by Paolo Landri, Rosaria Lumino and Roberto Serpieri.

Empirically, the chapter relies on (a) a historiography of higher education policy in the European Union (EU) (Gale, 2001) and (b) comparative reviews of the scorecard indicator frames included in reporting on the progress of the Bologna Process and of the range of such indicators related to funding universities through a set of performance values in European countries. In particular, we we seek to show how, through the Bologna Process, higher education can achieve greater consistency in the application of those performance values. In the second section we draw attention to how austerity is witnessing the fragmentation of performance-based funding (PBF) in the higher education systems of Europe. PBF is a widespread standard relating higher education outcomes to the share of financing. We highlight how (a) the alignment to this standard testifies to the increasing calculability of higher education and (b) the implementation of performance-based funding (PBF) is far from being univocal and, during austerity times, carries the risk of amplifying inequalities across and within the EHEA via a standardized differentiation.

Standardization of higher education in Europe

There are many ways of retracing the history of the standardization of higher education in Europe as different interpretations bring to the forefront various aspects of the dynamics under investigation (Brøgger, 2016; Corbett, 2011; Gornitzka, 2010; Pépin, 2007; Ravinet, 2008). However, the turning point is recognized as the inception of the Bologna Process and notably the 'shock' of the Sorbonne Declaration in May 1998. Here, four ministers of education (from Germany, France, Italy and the United Kingdom), on the occasion of the 800th anniversary of the Sorbonne, invited other European member states of the EU and other countries to constitute the EHEA.

In June 1999, almost one year later, ministers of twenty-nine European countries signed the Bologna Declaration and agreed to coordinate national policies on six objectives: the development of a system of comparable degrees; the adoption of a two main cycle system; a credit system (such as the European Credit Transfer and Accumulation System (ECTS)), cooperation in quality assurance, promotion of mobility and promotion of the European dimension. This was the point of departure for the Bologna Process, which aimed at building an EHEA by 2010.

Since then, ministers of education who signed the declaration have met every two years to monitor progress and to take decisions about further actions to adjust the overall process. The meetings took place in Prague (2001), Berlin (2003), Bergen (2005), London (2007), Leuven (2009), Budapest-Vienna (2010), Bucharest (2012) and, lastly, in 2015 in Yerevan. In the Budapest-Vienna Communiquè, the final declaration stated that the objective of making an EHEA was accomplished and that the Bologna Process was entering a new period devoted to consolidation and the realization of the common objectives of harmonization. At this time, forty-seven countries have signed the declaration, and there is broad consensus on considering this process to be the most powerful force for change in the European higher education policy arena. The Bologna Process is not limited to EU boundaries and extends to

European countries, not EU members. It is not a legally binding process, since no texts are signed, and there is no risk of sanctions for those countries that signed the declaration in the event that the commonly agreed objectives are not fulfilled. It is a voluntary intergovernmental coordination, consolidated within a 'monitored coordination' (Ravinet, 2008).

The historical reconstruction of the process underlines how a fragile initial process became more and more formalized and paved the way to a sociomaterial assemblage between two overlapping, and initially colliding, projects of reform: on the one hand, the intergovernmental cooperation of the Bologna Process in higher education and, on the other hand, the horizontal dynamics of the Lisbon Strategy and the education and training (E&T) platform that describes a landscape of inclusive higher education in the discourse of a knowledge society – and in the overall agenda of lifelong learning (Corbett, 2011; Gornitzka, 2010). It was only in 2004 that higher education participated in the Lisbon Agenda when the Council of EU accepted the Commission's proposal to include the Bologna targets in the E&T work programme (Gornitzka, 2010). In 2005, the decision was institutionalized, and an expert group was created by the Commission to follow E&T 2010 into the EHEA. When this occurred, it was considered that progress on the targets of the Bologna process was the contribution of the higher education sector to the realization of the Lisbon Agenda.

There are open discussions about the reciprocal interplay between the Bologna Process and the Lisbon Agenda, and how this overlap contributes to shaping policymaking with regard to higher education and, more generally, the Europeanization of education. Nonetheless, the two projects of reform shared a similar 'policy ontology', that is, a common orientation towards the standardization of higher education (Brøgger, 2016). Notably, the intense commitment to standardization translates EHEA into a space of commensuration. Policy instrumentation and tools are fabricated to make comparable and compatible higher education systems and to monitor progress in the accomplishment of the agreed-upon targets of coordination. To some extent, it is a double standardization: it is related to the higher education systems of the countries and to the toolbox that supports the follow-up mechanism. The combination of the two levels of standardization constitutes a space of commensuration that allows for a cross-cutting analysis of the Bologna Process and the gathering of information regarding the overall degree of coordination of the EHEA. The status of commensuration is made visible, in particular, through the national reports, the stocktaking, and the scorecard.

The national reports were objects of standardization in the period between 1999 and 2005. It was then possible to have a clearer idea of the implementation of the Bologna Process in the individual countries by following a template that made them comparable. Moreover, from 2003 to 2005 additional instrumentation permitted complex visualizations of the EHEA as a space of commensuration. In preparation for the Bergen Conference 2005, the Bologna follow-up group set up a stocktaking exercise, defined as an appraisal and progress report on the accomplishment of the Bologna targets. The stocktaking focused on three priorities: (a) quality assurance, (b) the 2-cycle system and (c) the recognition of degrees and period of study. The working group in charge of the definition of the methodology proposed changing from text to scorecards in order to have a visual display of the process.

The source of inspiration was the *Balanced Scorecard*, taken from the business literature and the *Lisbon Scorecard*, created by a London think tank to monitor year by year the realization of the Lisbon Strategy. The working group decided on criteria for measuring the progress in the three priorities and on benchmarks in each area of priority. The performance of each country was coloured from dark green (excellent performance) to red (poor progress in the accomplishment of the target), with the idea that the colours provided a soft ranking approach. The exercise of stocktaking drew on existing data sources (national reports, Eurydice, additional sources from the European Commission) and produced synthetic summaries for each scorecard indicator where it was possible to visualize the progress made in the Bologna Process and the situation of each country in the form of a coloured display.

This was the first time that a synthetic and widely distributed report on the Bologna Process had been made. At this stage, the method for realizing the visualization resembled the Open Method of Coordination of the Lisbon Strategy (Ravinet, 2008). The stocktaking exercise was repeated three times in preparation for the meeting of the Ministries of Education before the launch of the EHEA (see Table 3.1).

Table 3.1 Scorecard indicators until the launch of the EHEA (* New scorecard indicators; ** Newly refined scorecard indicators)

Report/Policies	2005	2007	2009
Degree and Qualification			
• Implementation of 2-cycle system	*	*	**
• Student enrolment in 2-cycle system	*	--	--
• Access to the next cycle	*	**	*
• Implementation of national qualifications framework	--	*	**
Quality Assurance			
• Development of quality assurance system	*	--	--
• Key elements of evaluation systems	*	--	--
• Implementation of ENQA guidelines	--	*	--
• Development of External QA system	--	*	**
• Level of participation of students	*	*	**
• Level of international collaboration	*	**	**
Recognition of Degrees and Study Periods			
• Implementation of the Diploma Supplement	*	**	**
• Ratification of the Lisbon Recognition Convention	*	--	--
• Implementation of the Lisbon Recognition Convention	--	*	*
• Implementation of ECTS	*	**	**
• Recognition of prior learning	--	*	*
• Establishment and recognition of joint degrees	--	*	--

Source: Our elaboration from Bologna Stocktaking Reports (2005, 2007, 2009)

Initially, the stocktaking focused on the scorecard indicators; however, further information about the dynamics of higher education systems was collected and additional comparisons were made. After the launch of the EHEA, the scorecard indicators were included in a wider publication reporting on the implementation of the Bologna Process at this stage and as conceived within the overall framework of Horizon 2020. Here, the stocktaking exercise was diluted in the implementation report, while the benchmarks still played a core information role in the progress of the implementation (see Table 3.2).

However, a cross-cut analysis of these education standards reveals their ontology as epistemic objects, that is, their incompleteness and fluidity. By comparing the lists of scorecard indicators from the first to the third exercise of stocktaking on the three policy priorities (*Degree, Quality Assurance* and *Recognition*), a dynamic of change in the education standards for the Bologna Process is apparent (see Table 3.1). This dynamic implies the following operations: (a) the introduction of the new scorecards (b) the abandonment of some indicators or the merging of past ones and (c) the refinement of benchmarks. Moreover, while each stocktaking drew on the previous stocktaking exercise, each new release introduced new demanding and challenging criteria. In some cases, scorecard indicators maintain the same name, but the scorecard categories are restructured.

The comparison between these present and past scorecard indicators is based on the assumption of different scales. In particular, 'dark green' (excellence) is increasingly difficult to reach, and the implementation dynamics is oriented towards moving, hard-to-reach and ever more specific targets. The stocktaking exercises are only apparently comparable. The list of scorecards becomes more stable after the launch of the EHEA (see Table 3.2). The Bologna Process here is confronted with Horizon 2020, and the implementation reports include a restructuring of the scorecards and the policy priorities. The key areas of the Bologna Process were confirmed in 2012. In particular, the Bologna tools – Two Cycles, the ECTS, the Diploma Supplement and the National Framework of Qualification – were grouped together in the area of Degree and Qualifications. The Quality Assurance scorecards were articulated with more precise and stricter criteria and the introduction of a new scorecard (Level of openness to cross-border quality assurance activity of the European Equality Assurance Register (EQAR)). New policy priorities were added: the social dimension and the internationalization of higher education, each with new scorecards. The description of these changes reveals a fluidity across the scorecards and the incompleteness of the standardization. The comparison between the Standards and Guidelines for Quality Assurance in the European Higher Education Area documents published in 2005 and 2015 (ENQA, 2005; ENQA, 2015) confirms the malleability of standards.

The tendency is to change quality assurance standards by considering the new conditions of teaching and learning in higher education institutions (student-centred learning, digital learning and so on) and to refine the education standards and guidelines to make them clearer and to some extent sharper than before. The documents clarify as well the 'philosophy of standards': (a) the refusal of a 'monolithic' perspective and (b) a high level of generality to make standards of quality assurance applicable to the plurality of higher education provision.

Table 3.2 Scorecard indicators after the launch of the EHEA (* New scorecard indicators; ** Newly refined scorecard indicators)

Report/Policies	2012	2015
Degree and Qualification		
• Implementation of 2-cycle system	*	*
• Access to the next cycle	**	*
• Implementation of national qualifications framework	**	*
• Implementation of ECTS	*	*
• Implementation of the Diploma Supplement	*	*
Quality Assurance		
• Development of External QA system	**	*
• Level of student participation in external QA system	**	*
• Level of international collaboration in external QA system	**	*
• Level of openness to cross border QA activity of EQAR registered agencies	--	*
Social Dimension		
• Recognition of prior learning	*	*
• Measures to support the participation of disadvantaged students	--	*
Internationalization and Mobility		
• Portability of public grants and publicly subsidized loans	--	*
• Financial mobility support to disadvantaged students	--	*

Source: Our elaboration from Bologna Process Implementation Reports (2012, 2015)

The history of the standardization of higher education and a close look at the transformation of the scorecards from the first exercise of stocktaking to the implementation report of the Bologna Process after the launch of the EHEA highlight an open and dynamic process. Thus the standard setting looks less like the implementation of an a priori model of agreed and concerted practice and more an emergent discovery in the process of implementation. In the next section, we consider, in particular, the alignment of standard setting to the standard of PBF. Even in that case, the alignment does not occur in a straightforward way, and the standard appears to be designed more to allow differentiation than uniformity.

Towards performance-based regimes: a matter of standardized differentiation

A full understanding of the contemporary history of standardization in European higher education systems requires a parallel appreciation of the recent efforts at performance-oriented reforms of higher education institutions. These manifest themselves largely through the demand for increased information, reporting requirements and budgetary reforms, all of which are seen as essential assets for ensuring the sustainability of institutions of higher education.

In the complex scenario following the financial crisis of 2007/08 there was a decisive impulse towards performance standards in the funding formulas, with a view to controlling at a distance the costs of higher education and to strategically orienting the sector towards the benchmarks of the Bologna Process and of the overall Horizon 2020 agenda. To some extent, the crisis accelerated the objectification of teaching and learning and brought to the forefront the measurable aspects of the activity of research.

References to 'performance' in relation to the Lisbon objectives appear in the communication of the European Commission on 'Supporting Growth and Jobs – and Agenda for the Modernization of Europe's Higher Education Systems' (EC, 2011/567): member states and higher education institutions are encouraged to implement funding mechanisms 'linked to performance including an element of competition'. The Council of the European Union (2011) confirms this approach and invokes an explicit link between performance and funding systems. The subsequent 2012 communication on 'A Reinforced European Research Area Partnership for Excellence and Growth' (EC, 2012/392) identifies performance-based PBF as a standard mechanism promoting competition in research and increasing the effectiveness of national expenditures. In the same vein, the Bucharest Communiqué (2012) and the Europe 2020 strategy and its Innovation Union policy flagship (EC, 2014/339) stress the importance of developing more efficient governance and managerial structures within higher education institutions.

Traditional modes of funding based on historical allocation or funding schemes drawing on input indicators (e.g., student numbers) have been at least partially replaced by the standard of PBF. PBF introduces an explicit link between performance and financial allocation schemes (Burke, 2002) relying either on ex-post assessment of (research) outputs (Hicks, 2012) or on the achievement of specific policy goals via ex-ante evaluation of future performances (i.e., performance agreements/contracts).

The size and relevance of performance-funding instruments differ substantially across EU member states, because they are mixed up in block grants relying on different allocation mechanisms: a funding formula grounded in input or output criteria, performance contracts or historically determined distribution, project-based funding and/or excellence award mechanisms (Pruvot et al., 2015).

The complexity of financing mechanisms across Europe makes the comparison a challenging exercise as sometimes different allocation mechanisms are combined. While the size and timeline of performance-funding policies can differ substantially from state to state, the competitive policy premise behind these policies is largely the same. The policy ontology turns on the notion of accountability, by appealing to material and symbolic incentives: the former represented by financial resources, the latter concerning reputation and the 'goals' developed through a competitiveness frame. These, in turn, have a long-term influence on the access of higher education institutions to resources (attractiveness to students, staff, collaborators, the attainment of project funding and so on). As Herbst (2007: 90) stresses, 'the rationale of performance funding is that funds should flow to institutions where performance is manifest: "performing" institutions should receive more income than lesser performing institutions, which would provide performers with a competitive edge and would stimulate less performing institutions to perform'.

However, the rationales provided by governments for their PBFs orbit different independent issues: reducing resources, encouraging international publication, stimulating high-quality research activities and promoting excellence (Hicks, 2012). The first experience of PBF can be traced back to 1986,[2] but since 2008 the use of performance-based elements in allocation schemes has expanded across the nation states of Europe – with the exception of Cyprus, Greece, Malta and Turkey, where universities receive public funding through line-item budgets (Estermann and Pruvot, 2011).

Eighteen countries have introduced some form of PBF, based on research output assessment oriented by peer review exercises and other metrics, except for the Scandinavian area where bibliometrics prevail (Jonkers and Zacharewicz, 2015). Also, several countries are in the process of incorporating more performance-based assessment into teaching funding decisions (i.e., Belgium, Poland and Italy). Performance agreements have been introduced in fifteen countries, mainly in Continental Europe, where they account for at the most 7 per cent of the overall block grant – the exception being Luxemburg and Austria where performance agreements represent the primary allocation mechanism.

Even in the absence of an explicit link between performance and funding, an increasing emphasis on output indicators can be observed. Although the most common – and most important – indicator of financing is represented by the number of bachelor and master students (input indicators), the number of output measures has grown dramatically to include fourteen dimensions against the five used as input criteria. The most recurrent output indicators are related to institutional competitiveness on funding markets especially in East and South Europe, where the number of output indicators is higher than the average. Other output indicators concern both doctoral degrees obtained/theses completed, research outputs regarding publishing activities and different kinds of public outreach. These indicators vary across disciplines for many reasons, such as the different priority given to doctoral activity and rates of completion, the variety of publication patterns and the impact of knowledge transfer and commercialization of research outputs.

Other indicators included in the funding formula are based on criteria linked to internationalization. Student and staff mobility have become a matter of growing importance on the agenda of both the EU and the EHEA, with a view to fulfilling the objective of sustainable and inclusive growth. This link has been translated into a new benchmark, that is, doubling the proportion of students completing their studies or training periods abroad as well as for financing opportunities of scholars' teaching and training within the Erasmus Plus programme. Criteria linked to internationalization are mostly present in Eastern and Southern countries, where the share of mobile students is lower than the EU average as is the perceived attractiveness of universities for international staff. Once again it is a matter of institutions' competitiveness, related to their reputation and networks.

The Organization for Economic Cooperation and Development (OECD) report on PBF for institutions of higher education shows a share of funding allocated by

---

[2] The first year of the UK Research Assessment Exercise (RAE) was 1986, which was replaced in 2014 by the Research Excellence Framework (REF).

performance indicators ranging from 2 per cent of total funding in Norway to 25 per cent in the United Kingdom (OECD, 2010). The same document reports a rising weight of performance indicators on funding mechanisms in Belgium, where the share of block funding allocated according to performance varies from 10 per cent to 30 per cent across the period 2003–06, and in the Slovak Republic, where the share ranges from 9.7 per cent to 23.1 per cent between 2002 and 2005. More recently, the Public Observatory on Public Spending on Higher Education has shown similar trends in the Czech Republic, where performance indicators have been introduced into the financing formula since 2009, accounting initially for 9 per cent of public funding and increasing to 20 per cent. Out of this 20 per cent, 39 per cent is allocated on the basis of research outputs (publications, patents, competitive grants obtained and the like).

In the meantime, public funding has been experiencing a substantial decrease since the financial crisis of 2007/08 – ranging from 10 per cent to 20 per cent between 2008 and 2014. Similarly, a huge decrease in public investment in higher education can be observed during the same period in Ireland. Such trends are also apparent in Eastern and Southern Europe, areas that have experienced the most substantial decrease in public spending on tertiary education during the period 2008–14. Such a decrease ranges from 5 per cent in Croatia, Slovakia and Slovenia to 40 per cent in Greece, Hungary and Latvia (EUA, 2015). The risk of sharpening the contexts and territorial divides between the more and the less developed and the wealthy areas becomes a severe threat, especially if, as frequently happens, allocation schemes represent a distribution mechanism based on the overall funding needs and allocations as determined by national governments. This risk is likely to occur within a regime of austerity, where the requirement to comply with PBF is not supported by any additional funding. The overall result is then increased competition for limited resources and increased inequalities between institutions.

However, performance indicators do not necessarily imply cuts in public expenditure in higher education. Positive funding trends in the field of higher education during the period 2008–14 can be observed in Continental and Northern Europe, although the European University Association (EUA) Public Observatory of Funding gives warning of a possible downturn in current and upcoming funding. These trends are certainly affected by the diverse effects of the financial crisis and of political choices involving (dis)investment in tertiary education, even if the influence exerted by these different factors is hard to disentangle.

Conclusions

The standardization of European higher education is an attempt at enacting a space of commensuration by using common standards. The fabrication of that space involves the adoption of a two main cycle system, the use of ECTS, the development of quality assurance systems, the mobility of students and researchers, the European dimension and later on the social dimension, and the internationalization of higher education. Standards permitted the consolidation of a governmental infrastructure of higher education in Europe and in all the countries that agreed to follow the Bologna Process. Standards established basic agreements on the main aspects of higher education and at the same time 'valuable' conditions of practice in the institutional fields. In adopting those standards, it was also possible to make visible the status of standardization and to understand the positioning of European member states against the agreed upon benchmarks. Data, reports, stocktaking exercises, visualization tools and colourful displays of performances are mobilized to perform the spectacle of comparisons, commensuration and competition in play.

Here, the project of standardization equates to Gottfried Wilhelm Leibniz's dream of *calculemus*:[3] the complexities of higher education are shifted to a list of measurable standards, and it is possible to calculate the distance and the range of accomplishments from the agreed objects without (apparently) being trapped in endless controversies about the differences and the similarities of higher education systems expressed through ordinary language. This simplification permits us to have an overview of higher education performances, to control at a distance and to elaborate policymaking on the basis of data and comparison.

Our scrutiny of the reports on the implementation of Bologna Process, and on the introduction of PBF reveals, however, a more complex scenario: a scenario in which Leibniz's dream appears far from being realized. Standards are malleable. They are incomplete over time, and the standardization in practice can be described more as a discovery than as an assessment of an a priori and once-and-for-all veritable accomplishment of stated benchmarks. Thus a comparative analysis of the scorecards from 2005 to 2015 has revealed refinements, substitutions, aggregations, abandonments, additions and subtractions of indicators and standards. The malleability maintains then a field permanently in tension. The effect is the enactment of multiple spaces of commensurability, that is, the installation of a regime of governance where higher education systems are heading towards moving targets. The malleability involves as well the translation of education standards at the national level. The fluidity of standards is stabilized by local translations that reinforce a standardized differentiation of the EHEA. As the harmonization of higher education is not driven by a 'philosophy of uniformity', it rather allows an ordered differentiation of the space, making the Europeanization of higher education a never completed fabrication.

In that respect, standards are the means of achieving a monitored coordination of the EHEA. They make visible the trajectories towards the implementation of the objectives of the Bologna Process and differentiate the member states according to their positions in meeting the benchmarks. The coloured maps are a soft mechanism for displaying the extent of implementation of the Bologna Process. They enact a scenario of differences among the member states and put in hierarchical order the stages of realization of the agreed standards so as to permit an assessment of the overall trajectory of each state in the implementation of the benchmarks.

Insofar as PBF is a standard aimed at relating outcomes to allocation, it provides a normative specification that recommends giving more weight to the outcomes of higher education by explicitly establishing a relationship between 'measuring' and the

---

[3] The reference is to the attempt by the German philosopher Gottfried Wilhelm Leibniz (1646–1716) to reduce logic to a kind of mathematical calculus, so that when disputes arose between persons they would declare *Calculemus* – or 'Let's compute!' – and employ that calculus to distinguish true from false statements. (Ed)

mechanism of financing. The suggestion is to shift attention from the inputs to the output indicators of research and higher education practice generally. However, our analysis illustrates that while the tendency towards PBF is clearly documented in the member states of the EU, the enactment of that standard is far from univocal. While there is a shared orientation of the regimes of accountability towards the outputs indicators, the range of those indicators in the formula is widening, with notable variations occurring in their composition and their relative load. There is clearly an attempt to relate the funding to the policy lines of the Bologna Process – but in practice the application of PBF highlights considerable variety.

The variability of solutions adopted at the national level shows how standardized differentiation opens the door to intensified stratification, especially with regard to the increasing emphasis on competition for resources within an austerity environment. The focus on competitiveness reproduces existing disparity across higher education systems. In addition it risks compromising the most competitive institutions of higher education by exhausting their capacity to perform well over time in the absence of additional resources. There are some concerns that while the introduction of PBF initially brings performance gains, improvements without funding increases are – after a few iterations – no longer possible. The costly exercises then return little or no benefit (Hicks, 2010). Furthermore, recent analyses show that concentrating research funds on the most excellent institutions does not increase research productivity overall. Rather, it is target diversity that is likely to prove more productive (Fortin and Currie, 2013).

References

Brøgger, K. (2016). The rule of mimetic desire in higher education: Governing through naming, shaming and faming, *British Journal of Sociology of Education* 37(1): 72–91. doi:10.1080/01425692.2015.1096191.

Bucharest Communiqué. (2012). *Making the Most of Our Potential: Consolidating the European Higher Education Area*. European Higher Education Area, http://www.ehea.info/.

Burke, J. C. (2002). *Funding Public Colleges and Universities for Performance: Popularity, Problems, and Prospects*. Albany: Rockefeller Institute Press.

Busch, L. (2011). *Standards: Recipes for Reality*. Cambridge, MA, and London: MIT Press.

Corbett, Anne. (2011). Ping pong: Competing leadership for reform in EU higher education 1998–2006. *European Journal of Education* 46(1): 36–53. doi:10.1111/j.1465-3435.2010.01466.x.

Council of the European Union. (2011). *Council Conclusions on the Modernisation of Higher Education* of the 3128th Education, Youth, Culture and Sport Council Meeting, 28–29 November 2011, Brussels. Consilium.europe.eu, http://www.consilium.europa.eu/uedocs/cms_data/docs/pressdata/en/educ/126375.pdf.

EC. (2011). *Supporting Growth and Jobs: An Agenda for the Modernisation of Europe's Higher Education Systems*. COM (2011) 567 final. Brussels: European Commission.

EC. (2012). *A Reinforced European Research Area Partnership for Excellence and Growth*. 392 final. Brussels: European Commission.

EC. (2014.) *Research and Innovation as Sources of Renewed Growth*. 339 final. Brussels: European Commission.

ENQA. (2005). *Standards and Guidelines for Quality Assurance in the European Higher Education Area 2005*. Brussels: European Association for Quality Assurance in Higher Education (ENQA).

ENQA. (2015). *Standards and Guidelines for Quality Assurance in the European Higher Education Area 2015*. Brussels: European Association for Quality Assurance in Higher Education (ENQA).

Estermann, T., and E. B. Pruvot. (2011). *Financially Sustainable Universities II European Universities Diversifying Income Streams*. Brussels: European University Association.

EUA. (2015). EUA Public Funding Observatory 2014. European University Association, http://www.eua.be/activities-services/projects/eua-online-tools/public-funding-observatory-tool.aspx.

Fortin, J. M., and D. J. Currie. (2013). Big Science vs. Little Science: How scientific impact scales with funding, *PLoS ONE* 8(6). doi:10.1371/journal.pone.0065263.

Gale, T. (2001). Critical policy sociology: Historiography, archaeology and genealogy as methods of policy analysis. *Journal of Education Policy* 16(5): 379–93. doi:10.1080/02680930110071002.

Gornitzka, A. (2010). Bologna in context: A horizontal perspective on the dynamics of governance sites for a Europe of Knowledge, *European Journal of Education* 45(4): 535–48. doi:10.1111/j.1465-3435.2010.01452.x.

Herbst, M. (2007). *Financing Public Universities: The Case of Performance Funding*. Dordrecht: Springer.

Hicks, D. (2010). Overview of models of performance-based research funding systems, in OECD (ed.), *Performance-Based Funding for Public Research*, Tertiary Education Institutions. Workshop proceedings. Paris: OECD Publishing. 23–52.

Hicks, D. (2012). Performance-based university research funding systems, *Research Policy* 41(2): 251–61. doi:10.1016/j.respol.2011.09.007.

Jonkers, K., and T. Zacharewicz. (2015). *Performance Based Funding: A Comparative Assessment of Their Use and Nature in EU Member States*. doi:10.2791/134058.

Knorr-Cetina, K. (2001). Objectual practice, in T. R. Schatzki, K. Knorr-Cetina and E. von Savigny (eds), *The Practice Turn in Contemporary Theory*. London and New York: Routledge. 184–97.

Miettinen, R. (2005). Epistemic objects, artefacts and organizational change, *Organization* 12(3): 437–56. doi:10.1177/1350508405051279.

Mulcahy, D. (2011). Assembling the 'accomplished' teacher: The performativity and the politics of professional teaching standards, *Educational Philosophy and Theory* 43(S1): 94–113.

OECD. (2010). *Performance-based Funding for Public Research in Tertiary Education Institutions: Performance-Based Funding for Public Research in Tertiary Education Institutions*. Paris: OECD Publishing. doi:10.1787/9789264094611-en.

Pépin, L. (2007). The history of EU cooperation in the field of education and training: How lifelong learning became a strategic objective, *European Journal of Education* 42(1): 121–32. doi:10.1111/j.1465-3435.2007.00288.x.

Pruvot, E. B., A.-L. Clayes-Kulik and T. Estermann. (2015). Strategies for efficient funding of universities in Europe, in A. Curaj, L. Matei, R. Pricopie, J. Salmi and P. Scott (eds), *The European Higher Education Area: Between Critical Reflection and Future Politics*. Dordrecht, Heidelberg, New York and London: Springer. 153–68.

Ravinet, P. (2008). From voluntary participation to monitored coordination: Why European countries feel increasingly bound by their commitment to the Bologna Process, *European Journal of Education* 43(3): 353–67. doi:10.1111/j.1465-3435.2008.00359.x.

Waldow, F. (2014). From Taylor to Tyler to No Child Left Behind: Legitimating educational standards, *Prospects* 45(1): 49–62. doi:10.1007/s11125-014-9334-x.

Part Two

Europe from the Inside

The impact of the 2007/08 financial crisis varied across the national regions of Europe and resulted in an economic landscape characterized by gross imbalances and inequalities between nation states. In many cases national governments had already adopted at least some of the measures associated with austerity – most notably the privatization of public assets – as key elements of the economic 'reforms' they were pursuing. In other national regions such measures were adopted by national governments – or were imposed upon them – following the crisis and the ensuing economic downturn or near collapse in the countries concerned. However, in all cases – as the following chapters suggest – the effect on higher education has been increased stratification across the sector as a whole, an intensification of competition within and between institutions and rising levels of job insecurity and professional uncertainty.

4

Higher Education in Poland: Budgetary Constraints and International Aspirations

Dorota Dakowska

In October 2015, the Crisis Committee of Polish Humanities organized a happening in front of the Academy of Science building in Warsaw. In a symbolic gesture, a few young researchers-activists burned their scientific output to the sound of a funeral march while some colleagues and trade unionists distributed an open letter and information material. This was a reaction to official communiqués published by the Ministry of Education and Science, which claimed that conditions of research were improving thanks to competition-oriented, market-friendly policies. The protesters countered that higher education in Poland was undergoing a deep crisis due to insufficient funding and low wages. A few weeks later, the electoral victory of the national-conservative Law and Justice party triggered mass demonstrations throughout the country following the new government's attempts to weaken the Constitutional Court and limit media freedom. As the neo-liberal policy discourse that had until then prevailed appeared to vanish, public discontent grew, and the very foundations of democratic institutions were called into question.

The case of Central and Eastern European countries (CEEC) invites us to reconsider the temporal and political aspects of the reconfiguration of higher education with regard to austerity measures. The new European Union (EU) member states have not been hit by the post-2008 financial and economic crisis in the same way as some of their Western counterparts. While Central and Eastern European universities have been affected by cuts in public expenditure and the privatization of higher education, it is worth recalling three facts. First, these countries were neither directly nor equally affected by the crisis (some of them were already eurozone members, others were not). Secondly, the major disruption of their higher education system occurred in the beginning of the 1990s after the communist regimes collapsed (Cîrstocea, Dakowska and Sigman, 2014; Sigman, 2014). Thirdly, the changes that affected the status and conditions of academic work resulted mainly from voluntary measures undertaken by governments in the region in the name of 'excellence', 'quality' and international 'competitiveness' of higher education and research institutions. Thus, the political materiality of austerity policies must be analysed case by case.

This chapter focuses on the Polish case, which has been characterized, since 1989, by a neo-liberal policy orientation.[1] Notwithstanding the small state ideology promoted by most governments, higher education policies were marked by ambiguity. On the one hand, the decision to give back autonomy to universities was intended to limit state control of academic governance. On the other hand, the state kept intervening in curricula, public financing and public steering of teaching and research (Dobbins, 2011; 2015). The Polish case, which is discussed here, is not an isolated example. It may be considered as a regional illustration of the CEEC as 'laboratories of reform' characterized by a strong openness to external reform recommendations, budgetary pressure and a policy preference for the competitive orientation of grants (Dakowska, 2015; Dakowska and Harmsen, 2015).

Following the general framework of this book, the Polish case exemplifies the way austerity has been applied to academia in the form of cuts in public expenditure, competitive financing and far-reaching privatization. This chapter focuses on different stages that led to the increasingly competitive orientation of higher education and research. Beyond policy conception and implementation, I consider how these competitive mechanisms of grant distribution are perceived by academics but also by the policy entrepreneurs who promote them. Following an interpretative policy inquiry, this chapter 'attempts to "understand" or "make sense of" social phenomena in terms of social actors' own motives, goals and explanations' (Fischer, 1995: 242).

The chapter is structured as follows. The first part examines the international dimension of Polish higher education redesign and documents the increasingly competitive orientation of the Polish academic sector. The second part looks into how budgetary constraints and the competitive orientation of teaching and research influence academic life. I ask how these new norms are perceived and interpreted both by users and those who are supposed to explain and enforce them. I conclude that the dividing line between the norm enforcers and the users is not as clear-cut as could be expected. This leads me to reconsider the commonly admitted distinction between the winners and losers of austerity reforms.

In the name of excellence: The competitive orientation of Polish higher education

In Poland, the eurozone crisis cannot be viewed as the main trigger of the higher education system's redesign, for two main reasons. First, the Polish economy has not been hit by economic turmoil to the same extent as some West European countries. Secondly, the main austerity measures affected the country's public sector following the fall of the Communist regime in 1989 and were due to the neo-liberal 'shock

---

[1] This analysis is based on different types of documents related to the reforms (legal acts, published and unpublished reports and communiqués as well as press articles) and on over eighty semi-structured interviews conducted between 2010 and 2016, mainly in Poland but also in France, Germany, Brussels and Ukraine with higher education experts, national and international civil servants and representatives of the academic community.

therapy' implemented by the first democratic governments. Like other countries of the region, Polish academia has experienced similar pressures to massify and privatize higher education (Levy, 2012; Slantcheva and Levy, 2007). However, these policy trends are connected to domestic political configurations. A study conducted by the Polish Rectors' Conference showed that while the higher education reforms of 1990, 2005 and 2011 were meant to strengthen the universities' autonomy, they also led to a degree of overregulation (Woznicki, 2013). Thus, the Rectors have asked for a deregulation of higher education, especially as far as higher education organization, internal fund distribution, research and staff policy are concerned.

While the number of competitive grants has steadily grown since 2010, this is largely due to the measures undertaken by the liberal governments in power from 2007 to 2015, which launched several major reforms of the academic sector. The Polish higher education system has been permeable to a reformist discourse based on neo-liberal ideas (which value the notions of competition and market orientation) and has sought international and European legitimation of the reform frameworks. Although this chapter focuses on education, I take into account policy instruments designed for the governance of the research sector, as they have affected the everyday life of academics and were designed by the same ministry.[2]

External inspirations in competitive policy measures

At the beginning of the 1990s, Central European higher education systems were recipients of the assistance programmes of institutions active in the field of education such as the Organization for Economic Cooperation and Development (OECD), UNESCO and the Council of Europe but also the World Bank and several private organizations. The first post-1989 Polish democratic governments adopted higher education and research reforms, whose international inspirations did not necessarily stem from Europe. For instance, the State Committee for Scientific Research (KBN), created in 1991, which institutionalized the principle of competition between researchers applying for grants, was inspired by the US National Science Foundation (NSF) (Jabłecka, 2009).[3] The main initiator of the KBN project was Stefan Amsterdamski (1929–2005), a professor of philosophy who accumulated outstanding academic, international and political resources.

The creation of the Committee for Scientific Research reflects the converging views shared both by opposition experts and representatives of the new democratic government. It aimed at creating a self-governing body made up of elected research community representatives and at setting up conditions for the allocation of public grants based on peer review. Several features of the system (peer review, goal-oriented

---

[2] The Polish academic system is characterized by a distinction between the universities and other higher education institutions on the one hand and the institutes of the Academy of Science on the other hand. The latter are more exclusively focused on research.

[3] Before the creation of the KBN the principle of competition for grants had been established, also based on the US example. The US embassy financed several study trips of Polish researchers and governmental advisers. These exchanges have inspired, among other things, the creation of accreditation bodies.

projects) were inspired by external models of research funding and organization (mainly from US agencies, but also Canadian, British, Dutch and German research councils) (Jabłecka, 2009).

The financing of higher education and research has been among the main interests of international organizations. In the first half of the 1990s, the advisers sent by the Council of Europe to CEEC noted that the higher education sector was underfinanced. They recalled that student fees and resources coming from the private sector had a limited contribution to the institutional budgets. The Council of Europe delegates demanded an increase to the percentage of state budget allocated to higher education. This demand was based on the claim that higher education institutions (HEIs) were leading drivers of economic development. In comparison with the Council of Europe, the World Bank promoted a more economically liberal vision of higher education. In a report on Polish tertiary education it called for the diversification of higher education revenues and the generalization of fees (World Bank, 2004). Although fee-paying courses mushroomed throughout the country in the 1990s, the recommendation concerning the generalization of fees has not seen any official policy translation so far, as higher education has remained constitutionally free of charge (even if in effect a high percentage of students do pay fees). This shows that the recommendations of international organizations may diverge.

At the beginning of the 1990s, EU programmes contributed to opening up Polish universities and researchers to international exchanges and organizational standards. The European Commission's Tempus programme allowed university instructors and managers to become familiar with Western European university systems during exchanges and site visits. Some of the participants in the Tempus mobility scheme were able to reinvest the knowledge of foreign higher education systems they had accumulated during the exchange programmes and become higher education experts. The launching of the EU accession process increased the receptiveness of political and academic elites to external incentives. After the accession, the EU funds contributed to the restructuring of the higher education sector. In the higher education modernization strategy published in 2011 the European Commission identified the necessity 'to increase investment in higher education and to diversify funding sources, drawing to a larger extent on private funding' and called for more flexible, results-based funding systems based on 'an element of competition' (2011). EU funds have not only facilitated the internationalization and reform of Polish higher education. They also contribute considerably to the higher education and research budget.[4] This has raised some concerns as to the post-2020 budgetary perspective, when the amount of structural funds allocated to Poland might decrease.

The Polish treatment of austerity in higher education

Due to the dramatic increase in student enrolment in the early 1990s, HEIs faced major funding problems. As high-level representatives of the Ministry of National Education

---

[4]   In 2013, 26.6 per cent of the overall budget for science came from EU funds. In 2014, the proportion reached 29 per cent. Author's calculations based on data from the 2014 budget report of the Ministry of Science, part 28, Science. Warsaw, May 2015, p. 10.

explained during an advisory mission of the Council of Europe in Warsaw, the increase in the number of students (by 70 per cent between 1989 and 1993) caused the annual budget per student to drop from USD $1,630 in 1989 to USD $1,100 in 1993 and under USD $900 in 1994.[5] The first major Higher Education Act, adopted in September 1990, included flexible regulations that ensured autonomy and collegiality for universities. One of the side effects of that law was a far-reaching privatization of higher education, due to the provisions on fee-charging courses, which introduced the distinction between full-time day studies, evening studies and extramural studies (Jabłecka, 2007). As the 1990 Higher Education Act limited the ministry's formal control, the development of an accreditation and quality evaluation system became a priority.

A key point in understanding the perception of austerity measures by the academic community is the fact that higher education policy was not so much based on radical budget cuts as on a new system for allocating funds. Compared to other European countries, the evolution of global expenditure on tertiary education in Poland falls within the average category. As far as the evolution of the share of public expenditure allocated to tertiary education between 2005, 2008 and 2011 is concerned, Poland belongs to the third group of countries where 'public expenditure on tertiary education increased at a slower pace than public expenditure (or decreased more rapidly than public expenditure)' (European Commission, 2015: 40). In these countries, the percentage of total public expenditure devoted to tertiary education was lower in 2011 than in 2005. Other members of this group are Norway, Iceland, Ireland and the United Kingdom. While between 2005 and 2011 the Polish per capita expenditure for tertiary students accounted for a decreasing share of the GDP, this is mainly because public expenditure increased at a slower pace than the GDP per capita. Regarding that indicator Poland was part of a group of countries that included Bulgaria, the Netherlands, Romania, Slovakia and Norway (European Commission, 2015).

Although the principle of competitive grant allocation was endorsed throughout the 1990s, the share of the budget distributed in such a form initially remained limited. The situation changed after 2007, especially with the 2010 law on research and the 2011 law on higher education (Dakowska, 2013).[6] These legal acts established new grant distributing agencies: the National Research Centre (NCN) for fundamental research and the National Centre for Research and Development (NCBiR), which supports applied research projects and cooperation with industry. Commenting on these legal acts, the higher education minister, Barbara Kudrycka, stated that she wanted to 'introduce a maximum of open competition mechanisms, also as far as fundraising is concerned' (Kudrycka, 2010: 6). In 2012, extra funds were earmarked for the so-called Leading National Research Centres (KNOW) selected upon parametric evaluation and quantitative indicators of 'scientific efficiency'. Prizes and scholarships were created to distinguish the best (especially young) scholars ('Diamond grant', 'The best of the best' and so on). As a result of these policy measures, the research budget, which, until 2010,

---

[5] Council of Europe, DECS LRP 95/19, Higher Education and Research Committee, *Legislative Reform Programme for Higher Education*. Poland, Report of the Advisory Mission on Quality Assessment and Accreditation, Warsaw, 26–29 September 1994, p. 4.

[6] Both acts have been amended several times since then.

was almost entirely distributed by the ministry, underwent a radical transformation. The share of this budget allocated to competitive grants has steadily grown in the past years, and now exceeds 50 per cent.

In order to differentiate the country's research units, these legal acts introduced a system of parametric evaluation, which pushes them to increase their publications in English-language, peer-reviewed journals. This measure of their scientific output introduced new hierarchies between and within research units. This evaluation draws heavily on international journal databases and citations as the ministry has established three categories of journal titles. The first and most rewarding includes journals with an impact factor from the Journal Citation Reports database (awarding up to fifty points per article published). The second contains mainly Polish journals (awarding up to ten points and, more recently, up to fifteen points per publication). The third one is the much-debated European Reference Index for the Humanities (ERIH).[7]

The heated debates on the low number of points attributed to Polish-language publications and the damage it could cause to the humanities led to the adoption of specific criteria to take into account the specificities of these disciplines. Yet, the distribution of public funds to research units has since been further regulated. According to the new algorithm, the basic allocation for category A+ research units must be multiplied by 1.5; category A units by 1.0; category B units by 0.7; and category C units by 0.4, which may force them to close (Ministry, 2015: 9). This policy has caused significant gaps to develop between HEIs, research centres and, last but not least, individual academics themselves. The next section examines how these measures were perceived by the academic community.

Co-producing and enduring reforms: the Polish case

There have been increasing numbers of comparative studies of the academic profession since the 1970s (Altbach, 1977; Clark, 1987). They were a major focus of higher education studies in the 1990s (Altbach, 1996; Boyer et al., 1994). Already at the time the idea of a perceived 'crisis' of the profession was advanced in the context of the massification of higher education, its loss of monopoly on knowledge production, the diversification of academic work and the contradictory pressures that affected it (Enders, 1999). The following section examines how domestic reinterpretations of international recommendations combined with austerity measures reflecting a neo-liberal conception of the managerial state affect academic work.

Focusing on internationalized academic entrepreneurs

Following a sociological-constructivist approach, I take into account the meso and even the 'micro' level, that is, the organized interest groups and academic experts

---

[7] Launched by the European Science Foundation (ESF), ERIH stagnated during the decline of the ESF. In 2014 it was overtaken by the Norwegian Social Science Data Services (NSD) and is now available as ERIH plus.

involved in public policy debates and reform design. The agency of higher education reform remains an underinvestigated research field. Usually the European Commission or international organizations as a whole are presented as actors. Sociological policy analysis calls for investigating contextual issues (the policy origin and main players), textual issues (who has advocated and promoted the policy and why? where are these advocates located?), policy structuring (focused on policy communities, the role of international agencies and policy borrowing) or policy implementation (Rizvi and Lingard, 2009: 54–5). Therefore I consider the transformations of the Polish higher education system by focusing on the individuals and groups involved in promoting external models of higher education management, engaging in international cooperation or explaining European policy frameworks to the academic community.

I focus on the individuals who have been involved in the internationalization strategies through their own practice at the HEI level and are familiar with the national and international policy levels. This population includes both academics involved in expert groups linked with the European Higher Education Area (EHEA) and those who have experienced the reforms through their everyday practice of academic international cooperation. While the former contribute to translating the frames and narratives developed abroad into domestic spaces, the latter struggle to apply them. Although a majority of these individuals have accumulated international experience, before 1989 or in its aftermath, their positions in the academic space vary. Some experts combine a traditional academic career with their expert activities. Others may hold an official position at the university but have invested more in their expert activities. Although the academic experts may have a more positive perception of international recommendations than the lecturers, both groups are aware of the side effects linked to their implementation.

The new academic life under the constraints of evaluation

While higher education reforms in Poland have been dominated by a neo-liberal approach, they initially affected mainly teaching through the expansion of fee-paying courses. The 2010–2011 reforms showcased a managerial approach to higher education and research policy. As the share of grants earmarked for competitive funding has steadily grown, obtaining a grant has become a condition sine qua non to carry on with academic activities such as participating in conferences or doing field research. At the same time, the competitive orientation of the grant-giving institutions has made access to them more and more difficult (the success rate of grant applications submitted to the NCN is currently about 15 per cent).

Since 2010 the evaluation of research has become a major component of academic life in Poland. While individual researchers are supposed to be evaluated every two years, their research institutes have to publish regular reports on their scientific productivity. The bibliometric measurement of published articles has become the basis for the allocation of grants. Thus, in the past few years, it has become clear to academics that their scientific output is directly correlated with the financing they are able to secure either individually or through their institute. This puts huge pressure on the academics themselves, on their relationships with their peers and on the organization of academic work. As they are drowning in paperwork and overloaded with teaching, university lecturers find it increasingly difficult to fulfil their traditional missions.

> We have to do with a real product whose position is measurable with a CV. I am the product. I have the impression that following this whole transformation I have become a product. I have some writing skills, some linguistic knowledge, which make me a decent quality product to sell on the international scientific market. Which means that I feel I am not doing science any more. There is frustration in me. If I had known I would live that way, that science would become an alibi. (Senior lecturer, M, Social science, University of South, 2014)

Facing the international academic competition has become a mantra for pro-reformist experts. This ubiquitous discourse has few open adversaries. But even scholars who do not oppose it openly and are used to publishing in English may express negative views.

> These points are so pervasive; even in the evaluation of employees everything is classified according to these points. How many reviews do I have from the ERIH list, how many from another list [. . .] Sometimes I don't even know, I have to look, because it changes from year to year. So this leads to specific choices and consequences. [. . .] There is a feeling of injustice. And we waste a lot of time on checking points, calculating, searching for data, filling forms. Now we have a new system where we have to put all our publications – how many points a given publication has and I think we have to attach the pdf. So this bureaucracy is thriving and I have to take care of it instead of writing, preparing courses, doing research – it's a kind of sick thinking. (Associate professor, F, Social science, University of West, 2015)

The feeling of competition between colleagues from the same unit – which grows as regular funding is shrinking – has become a major element of everyday academic life.

> In my view it is a worrying question because in the department where I am employed, also due to the great passivity of a large part of the academic staff, a considerable part of the points are produced by the doctoral candidates who are groomed to compete with each other while their publications are counted among the publications of the unit. This reflects a kind of paradox. The PhD candidates are not employees and the framework of points, which was initially not meant to evaluate employees, is used to quantify and to establish hierarchies in the doctoral population in the struggle for a very scarce amount of scholarships. (Junior researcher, M, Humanities, University of West, 2015)

Even among the younger generation of academics, who have been acquainted with foreign university systems and are supposedly more open to change (Kwiek, 2015), this situation may lead to frustration, a feeling of alienation or difficulties in coping with these new working conditions:

> I feel as if I have been hired under completely different conditions. Not for this kind of race [. . .] for always being compared [. . .] All this is sick and ridiculous,

right? But this system forces this kind of pushing and shoving [. . .] I mean some people do it, some don't. But we do not cooperate; it seems to me that people are increasingly rivals. (Associate professor, F, Social science, University of West, 2015)

Even if they care about their profession and consider their job as a vocation, the neo-managerial functioning of HEIs forces them to rethink their entire conception of academic work.

If we provoke a situation, in which the university, academia has become a corporation like any other in the sense that we have a client, we have a product', we have to fight for our international position, then I have to wonder whether this way of making money suits me. (Senior lecturer, Social science, University of South, 2014)

While academic instructors try to accommodate these new rules academic experts are unequally convinced of their fairness.

The higher education reformers under pressure

The competitive orientation of higher education reforms has been promoted by academic reformers who may be compared to Howard Becker's (1963) 'moral entrepreneurs'. On the one hand the 'rule creators', and especially 'crusading reformers', want to change the existing rules in which they see some evil. In the Polish case, this category may be applied to experts involved in the reform design, either by sketching the reform projects or by making public statements on the desired reform shape.

In order to create high quality HEIs, we need differentiation and competition. The main disease of public higher education is lack of competition. Only competition is able to boost initiative, to develop heterogeneity and to create conditions allowing the best to reach excellence. There is no better mechanism to eliminate faculties and professors who teach poorly. (Thieme, 2009: 10–11)

On the other hand, the 'rule enforcers' work in organizations that have been specifically set up to enforce the rule. They have 'no stake in the content of particular rules themselves' and may 'develop their own private evaluation of the importance of various kinds of rules and infractions on them' (Becker, 1963: 161). Experts who have been nominated to represent their disciplines in various evaluation bodies may be included in this category. However, unlike Becker's moral entrepreneurs, these experts who seek to enforce the new evaluation procedures are themselves bound by them, as they remain members of academic research units.

In order to better seize the tensions inherent in the implementation of new rules I have asked the rule enforcers themselves how they define, refine and deal with these rules. These experts act as brokers between the academic community and the ministry. They have been chosen for their technical knowledge in bibliometrics but also for their experience of representative functions in international academic bodies and European expert groups. Like Becker's crusaders they believe in the necessity to hierarchize the academic profession and to create mechanisms which trigger 'excellence'. At the same time, due to their position as users, that is, of academics, whose research centres are being evaluated under the new rules, they may assume a critical distance from the rules they have themselves helped elaborate. As they receive numerous complaints through their networks, they tend to consider parametric evaluation not as a panacea but as a lesser evil.

One way of expressing a critical distance from the new rules is to admit the side effects they may produce. The fact that the new evaluation rules largely privilege English-language journals and large publishing houses may cause some disillusion. A member of an expert group might get emotional talking about their own research field and the growing dominance of the Scopus database in the evaluation of research.

Awareness of the predominant market mechanisms and the editorial strategies of market leaders is another source of concern.

> I remember how shocked I was when I learned that the corporation Elsevier has a policy – as it picks up the journals which will integrate the Scopus list – a policy linked with its own distribution and sales market [. . .] I looked at the humanities as a whole and then I looked at specific disciplines. And it was all the same: United States, Great Britain and in third place, the Netherlands. The Netherlands as an editorial power. So this means they are promoting their own pool of journals, their own! Ukraine: Zero! Lithuania: Zero! Scandinavia: Zero. [. . .] So how can I consider such a list seriously? Why should a list shaped by a firm according to some market principles guide my scientific activities?? (Professor, F, Humanities, Academy of Science, 2015)

The experts who shape the bibliometric evaluation of research do not all share the same views. The hesitation expressed by some of them shed light on the tensions that may emerge between different disciplines or between the bibliometric hardliners and those who defend a softer approach. Beyond diverging views on the relative weight of different criteria, the material impact of evaluation on the research institutes has been debated. Parametric evaluation was intended to reward the most productive research institutions and to sanction the least efficient ones. However, the institutes of the Polish Academy of Science have been particularly hit by these new measures.[8] Contrary to university researchers, whose statutory funding relies mainly on a teaching mission, the Academy of Science institutes depend entirely on public subsidies for their research activity. The change in the grant distribution method has put some of the institutes in an extremely tense situation.

> The Institute where we stand is in the A category. According to the new algorithm, it got less money than in the previous year. Although as an A unit it shouldn't get

---

[8]   According to a table forwarded to the author by a leading member of the Academy of Science, out of fourteen institutes of the Academy, a vast majority (twelve) have been ranked A (eight) or A+ (four). Still, most of their budget endowments decreased between 2014 and 2016, and a further decrease due to the new algorithm is expected in 2017 and 2018. The overall budget of these research institutes is thus expected to decrease by 27 per cent between 2014 and 2018.

less. [. . .] Some social science and humanities units were, let us say, prejudiced by the new algorithm. In the sense that they got less because of the calculation method. Even in this building, there are institutes who are in the A+ category. And during the first round of funds distribution, [X] the director recalled that they have got 600,000 ZL less than in the previous year although they should have been rewarded. Probably this has been corrected but this does not mean [. . .] probably higher education did not get less in the end but did higher education get more? Rather not. So this distribution system is not perfect yet. (Professor, M, Social Science, Academy of Science, 2015)

This change shows that even the supposed winners of the race for excellence, who have obtained the maximum evaluation grades, do not necessary benefit from the new evaluation rules.

Conclusion

This chapter has been concerned with the domestic reinterpretation of external incentives for higher education reform in the context of post-communist transformation and EU accession. In Poland, austerity measures concerning higher education and research were overshadowed by other policy concerns. The sharp cuts in spending per student were considered, at the political level, as a necessary outcome of the sharp rise in student numbers and of GDP growth. Furthermore, the narrative concerning the desired effects of competitive grant distribution has legitimized the cuts that affected research units.

The conditions of academic work are changing rapidly. In Poland, the 2010–2011 legal acts have triggered major changes in how funds are allocated to universities and research units. As a result, universities and faculties have to struggle to secure external grants to survive. Academic writing has become a strategy to raise the number of points necessary to obtain grants. In this new situation, it is not always easy to distinguish between winners and losers. The academics who endorse the new competition and stratification logic may become grant-making entrepreneurs. For mid-career academics, following the point-gaining strategy is a way to remain loyal towards their home institutions or towards the professor they depend on. Those who do not have a chance to secure a grant because their publications remain too 'local' see their professional perspectives narrowing. In this way winning a grant has become a condition of academic survival.

The academic profession in Poland – as in other countries – is more and more stratified between those who benefit from the competitive grants and those who do not. But even the academic entrepreneurs who coproduce the new policy measures and enforce the competitive rules due to their participation in expert groups and evaluation bodies are aware of the side effects of the policy designed to bring about new hierarchies between researchers. In a situation where competitive measures may be a justification for further budgetary cuts, the losers can be easily identified. But it is not so clear who is really winning.

References

Altbach, P. G. (1977). Introduction: Notes on the study of the academic profession, *Higher Education* 6: 131–4.

Altbach, P. G. (2003). Introduction to *Higher Education* theme issue on the academic profession in Central and Eastern Europe, *Higher Education* 45(4): 389.

Becker, H. (1963). *Outsiders: Studies in the Sociology of Deviance*. New York: The Free Press.

Boyer, E. L., P. G. Altbach and M. J. Whitelaw. (1994). *The Academic Profession: An International Perspective*. Princeton, NJ: Carnegie Foundation for the Advancement of Teaching.

Clark, B. R. (ed.) (1987). *The Academic Profession: National, Disciplinary, and Institutional Settings*. Berkeley: University of California Press.

Cîrstocea, I., D. Dakowska and C. Sigman. (2014). Avant-propos, introduction to the special issue 'Transformations of Academic Fields in East-Central Europe since 1989', *Revue d'études comparatives Est-Ouest* 45(1): 5–19.

Dakowska, D. (2013). Polish higher education and the global academic competition: University rankings in the reform debates, in T. Erkkilä (ed.), *Global University Rankings: Challenges for European Higher Education*. London and New York: Palgrave Macmillan. 107–23.

Dakowska, D. (2015). Between competition imperative and Europeanisation: The case of higher education reform in Poland, *Higher Education* 69(1): 129–41.

Dakowska D., and R. Harmsen. (2015). Laboratories of reform? The Europeanization and internationalization of higher education in Central and Eastern Europe, *European Journal of Higher Education* 5(1): 4–17.

Dobbins, M. (2011). *Higher Education Policies in Central and Eastern Europe: Convergence towards a Common Model?*. Houndmills, Basingstoke: Palgrave Macmillan.

Dobbins, M. (2015). Exploring the governance of Polish public higher education: Balancing restored historical legacies with Europeanization and market pressures, *European Journal of Higher Education* 5(1): 18–33.

Enders, J. (1999). Crisis? What crisis? The academic professions in the 'knowledge' society, *Higher Education* 38(1): 71–81.

European Commission, *Communication from the Commission to the European Parliament, the Council, the European Economic and Social Committee and the Committee of the Regions of 20 September 2011: Supporting growth and jobs; an agenda for the modernisation of Europe's higher education systems* [COM(2011) 567].

European Commission/EACEA/Eurydice (2015). *The European Higher Education Area in 2015: Bologna Process Implementation Report*. Luxembourg: Publications Office of the European Union.

Fischer, F. (1995). *Evaluating Public Policy*. Chicago: Nelson-Hall Publishers.

Jabłecka, J. (2007). Legitimation of non-public higher education in Poland, in S. Slantcheva and D. C. Levy (eds), *Private Higher Education in Post-Communist Europe: In Search of Legitimacy*. Houndmills: Basingstoke, Palgrave Macmillan. 179–99.

Jabłecka, J. (2009). Revolution and evolution in the organization of public research funding in Poland between 1991 and 2007, in J. Jabłecka (ed.), *Public Research Funding: Research Councils, Funding Instruments, Evolution of the System in Poland*. Warsaw: Centre for Science Policy and Higher Education, University of Warsaw.

Kwiek, M. (2015). Academic generations and academic work: Patterns of attitudes, behaviours and research productivity of Polish academics after 1989, *Studies in Higher Education* 40(8): 1354–76.

Kudrycka, B. (2010). Uczelnie potrzebują konkurencji [HEIs need competition]. Interviewed by M. Suchodolska and K. Klinger, *Dziennik Gazeta Prawna*, 25 May 2010.

Levy, D. C. (2012). How important is private higher education in Europe? A regional analysis in global context, *European Journal of Education* 47(2): 178–97.

Ministry of Science and Higher Education. (2015). *11 September 2015 Regulation on the Calculation of Funding and Regulation of Financial Means for Maintaining Scientific Potential, Scientific Research and Tasks Supporting the Development of Young Researchers and Participants in Doctoral Studies.* Polish official journal, no. 1443, Warsaw, 22 September 2015.

OECD. (2006). *OECD Thematic Review of Tertiary Education: Country Background Report for Poland.* Warsaw: OECD.

Rizvi, F., and B. Lingard. (2009). *Globalizing Education Policy.* London and New York: Routledge.

Sigman, C. (2014). Les transformations de l'enseignement supérieur en Russie: Évolution du secteur public et stratégies d'établissements, *Revue d'études comparatives Est-Ouest* 45(1): 21–54.

Slantcheva, S., and D. C. Levy (eds) (2007). *Private Higher Education in Post-Communist Europe: In Search of Legitimacy.* Houndmills, Basingstoke: Palgrave Macmillan.

Thieme, J. K. (2009). *Szkolnictwo wyższe: Wyzwania XXI wieku. Polska, Europa, USA* [Higher education: challenges of the 21st century. Poland, Europe, USA]. Warsaw: Engram/Difin.

World Bank (2004). *Tertiary Education in Poland.* Warsaw: World Bank.

Woźnicki J. (ed.) (2013). *Financing and Deregulation in Higher Education.* Warsaw: Polish Rectors Foundation.

5

Compounded Inequalities in Croatian Higher Education: From Neo-liberalism to Austerity

Danijela Dolenec

Across former post-socialist Europe citizens have for the last two decades unwaveringly supported political and economic reforms in the hope of 'returning to Europe'. When they expressed their support for European integration, they did not have on their minds complex policy tools such as the open method of coordination or the European Semester, institutions like the Economic Monetary Union (EMU) or the intricate workings of the European Commission. Instead, Europe stood for – and still does – the most developed region in the world; it stands for human prosperity and quality of life, coupled with high levels of political and civil liberties. In other words, citizens across post-socialist Europe had on their minds the famous European social model. Using Polanyian (Polanyi, 1944) terminology, in the double movement between market efficiency and social equity, Europe for them represented societies which subordinated market principles to the social objectives of prosperity and quality of life. Alas, the Europe that they pictured exists no longer; today it is only a mirage, a reflection of what once was. Leaving no doubt about the profound shift that welfare states in Europe have undergone in the last twenty years, Mario Draghi, president of the European Central Bank (ECB), in an interview with the *Wall Street Journal* bluntly asserted that the European social model was gone (2012).

The political ascendency of neo-liberal ideas which undermined the welfare state in Europe goes back to the early 1980s, when this concept came under 'sustained intellectual attack' (Le Grand and Robinson, 1984) and European countries started implementing welfare state retrenchment (Schmidt and Thatcher, 2013). The belief that many of the economic, social and political problems of the period were attributable to welfare state growth was established as a dominant doctrine (Pierson, 1998). The public sector was accused as the main culprit for the sluggishness of Europe's economies and, as a result, government budgets sustained strong cutbacks (Le Grand and Robinson, 1984; Theisens, 2004). Margaret Thatcher's and Ronald Reagan's governments broke the post-war consensus according to which the state intervened in the market to provide security, prosperity and greater equality (Judt, 2010), and instead pushed for liberalization of trade and investment, public spending cuts, deregulation and privatization (Ayres, 2004). The result was a steady erosion of the welfare state (Bourdieu, 2003), while the new role of the state became the facilitating of competition and free trade, evaluating all state practices through a cost-benefit calculus (Brown, 2005).

Neo-liberal economic policies were taken up by the European Union (EU) in its reforms during the 1990s (Judt, 2010). As Peter Hall (2012) put it in a recent lecture, the guiding principle of the EU, which used to be 'peace for Europe', was with the 1987 Single European Act reformulated into 'prosperity for everyone via the Single Market'. The 1992 Maastricht criteria and the 1998 Stability and Growth Pact effectively closed a number of policy options available for pursuing social objectives (Esping-Andersen, 2001; Green et al., 2000). As a result, the EU's policy prescriptions since the 1990s increasingly resembled those of international financial organizations such as the International Monetary Fund (IMF) and the World Bank (Guillen and Palier, 2004). In a deliberate emulation of the US model of development, the Washington Consensus on deregulation, the minimal state and low taxation travelled to Europe (Judt, 2010).

However, during the 1990s and early 2000s criticisms of neo-liberal policies were fighting an uphill battle since at the time many European states seemed relatively prosperous. This situation has changed substantially since the start of the economic crisis in 2008. After the global financial meltdown, governments restored their economies by rescuing banks, and then passed the bill on to the average citizen, who is paying for this rescue with their savings while suffering cuts in public services and higher taxation (Streeck, 2011). The prospects for ordinary citizens today are frequently discussed within the context of a 'Lost Decade', so it is not surprising that neo-liberal economic policies are undergoing a renewed wave of criticism.

Having in mind this broader context, in this chapter the period of the last couple of decades is seen as one in which neo-liberal policies have pervaded all aspects of the welfare state, including higher education and research systems, creating a strong drive towards commodification. The austerity programmes implemented since 2008 onwards are understood as further amplifying these negative trends, both through further cost-cutting and by creating an atmosphere of emergency whereby policies are pushed through as imperatives – beyond democratic deliberation. The following sections first elaborate on the impact of neo-liberal policies in the field of higher education and then outline an empirical analysis of the impact of these policies in the case of Croatia.

Europeanization as a vehicle of neo-liberalism in higher education

The key shift towards the neo-liberal doctrine in higher education has been the assertion that its primary role is to drive economic progress and realize national economic interests (Jessop, 2008). Neo-liberal advocates criticized bureaucracy and 'producer capture' in education, arguing that efficiency and effectiveness are best achieved through market mechanisms (Green et al., 2000). The assumption is that a commodified higher education system brings increased efficiency, responsiveness to 'customers', innovation and revenue diversification (Brown, 2011). By advancing the assumption of individuals guided by self-interest, neo-liberal doctrine has shifted the definition of citizenship towards one of 'consumer citizen' (Lynch, 2006). Until the 1980s higher education was free or almost free for students across Europe, while today most countries charge for at least a proportion of the tuition fees (Eicher, 2000). Similarly, while before the 1980s governments provided support for students' living costs mainly in the form of grants, there has since been a shift towards the increased provision of loans for living costs. The sum effect of these reforms is the privatization of higher education – the shifting of the cost of higher education from public to private sources (Tilak, 2005).

For post-socialist countries, where the 'return to Europe' (Héritier, 2005) has been the pre-eminent political project during the last twenty-five years, the process of European integration has had a profound influence on all aspects of political and economic life, including higher education and research (Dolenec, Baketa and Maassen, 2014). During the 1990s key sources of international influence on higher education were the World Bank and the Organization for Economic Co-operation and Development (OECD) (Dobbins and Knill, 2009; Kwiek and Maassen 2012), but since 2000 the EU has become the dominant external force of change. In the field of higher education, the Bologna Process and the Lisbon Strategy were particularly important in introducing 'a new and spectacular dynamic into the affairs of higher education in Europe' (Neave, 2002: 186), carrying the potential of transforming 'the European states' higher education institutions as fundamentally as the nation state changed the medieval universities' (Corbett, 2005: 192).

The Lisbon Agenda aims to transform higher education into a strategic factor of European integration and a fundamental driver of competitiveness (Capano and Piattoni, 2011). The Lisbon policy recipe has been highly consequential for higher education and research policy in Europe, for at least three reasons: it reasserted the role of research and development for economic competitiveness and growth; it underlined the role of education as a core labour market factor; and it shifted the focus onto the European level of objectives and priorities, as opposed to national-level ones (Gornitzka, 2007). The reforms – made in an atmosphere of perceived crisis in which it was claimed that something must be done immediately in order for Europe to 'stay in the game' of global competition – use the language of modernization and emphasize the economic functions of the university and the need for adaptation to economic and technological change, while the university is envisioned as dynamic and adaptive to consumers, giving priority to innovation, entrepreneurship and market orientation (Olsen and Maassen, 2007).

Advancing such a functionalist conception, education is judged by its impact on labour markets and overall economic policy. Other roles of the university, such as in developing democratic citizens or social cohesion or in addressing the EU's democratic deficit are downplayed or ignored (Brown, 2015; Collini, 2012; Dolenec and Doolan, 2013; Nussbaum, 1998). Likewise, the democratic internal organization of the university and individual academic freedom are understood as obstacles to good performance (Olsen and Maassen, 2007). Furthermore, neo-liberal doctrine reconceptualizes the academic as a technoscientist, presuming a 'subjectivity that combines scientific rationality with instrumental and opportunistic sensibility' (Kenway, Bullen and Robb, 2007: 125). This creates pressure on academics to restyle themselves according to this image in order not to be perceived as redundant in the new order of things.

Echoing Maassen and Stensaker's (2011) observation that the buzzword of the knowledge economy plays 'panic football' by claiming that the university must be drastically reformed in order to stay in the game, the present analysis assumes that the post-2008 austerity period has created an atmosphere of emergency in which neo-liberal reform ideas, which have been around for a long time, assume a new urgency that more easily breaks down resistance. While before 2008 neo-liberal reform ideas were debated as one among several policy options, post-2008 they are presented in a 'there is no alternative' fashion, that is, as an imperative for restoring economic stability.

The next sections look at several long-term trends in Croatian higher education, aiming to support two main arguments. First, since the early 1990s when Croatia became an independent state, the dominant trend in higher education has been commodification. Second, the post-2008 period of austerity has further amplified this negative trend of commodification, leading to a compounding of social inequalities in the higher education system. The main sources of data and country analyses are research reports of the Institute for the Development of Education in Croatia, Eurostat educational statistics and the two rounds of Eurostudent surveys implemented in Croatia, in 2010 and 2014 respectively.

Massification and commodification of higher education in Croatia

Like many other regions of the world, in the last couple of decades Croatia has been characterized by the massification of higher education. Massification, or the dramatic expansion of student numbers across higher education systems, represents one of the most profound developments in higher education in the developed world (Theisens, 2004). Figure 5.1 shows the total enrolment rates in higher education institutions in Croatia between 1991 and 2014, the period between when Croatia became an independent state and the most recent data point available.

As can be seen from Figure 5.1, the student body in Croatia is today more than twice the size that it was in 1991, growing from a population of 68,720 students to 157,827. Despite this large expansion, Croatia currently remains below the EU average in terms of higher education attainment, with 24.3 per cent attainment in the twenty-five to thirty-four age group, while the average for EU27 is 35 per cent (File et al., 2013). Expressed as a proportion of the cohort enrolling in higher education, the proportion of eighteen-year olds increased from 42.1 per cent to 79 per cent in the period from 1994/95 to 2009/10 (ibid.). This increase in enrolment has resulted in a corresponding increase in graduation rates. Whereas in 1997 the proportion of twenty-five-year olds with a higher education degree was 14.7 per cent, it rose to 41.2 per cent in 2010 (ibid.). Assuming that these enrolment and graduation trends continue, by 2020 the higher education attainment of the twenty-five to thirty-four age group in Croatia will reach 40 per cent, bringing it in line with the EU 2020 strategy benchmark.

What happens when a system of higher education grows at this pace, but in a political environment in which the neo-liberal doctrine, buttressed by the process

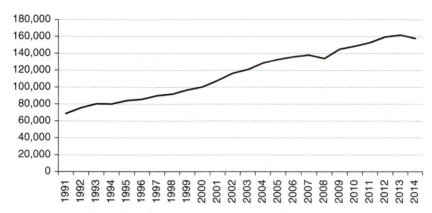

Figure 5.1 Total enrolment in higher education institutions in Croatia, 1991–2014

Source: Croatian Bureau of Statistics and Institute for Development of Education

of Europeanization, makes it impossible to implement significant redistributive policies? Either the government keeps expenditure constant while admitting more students, negatively affecting quality, or it increases the role of private funding, primarily by introducing tuition fees and loans (Barr, 1993). As we know, in the last couple of decades across Europe the dominant funding policy for higher education has been the introduction of private money, both via tuition fees and the reliance on so-called 'third-party' funding. The same story holds true for Croatia, which over the analysed period experienced stagnant public investment and the commodification of the higher education sector through increased reliance on tuition fees.

Figure 5.2 shows total public expenditure on higher education as a percentage of GDP for Croatia, Slovenia and the EU28 average. The comparison with Slovenia is instructive given that the two countries were part of the same federative state until 1990, and arguably share a number of political, cultural and economic features. Despite those similarities, as can be seen from Figure 5.2, in the post-2008 period Slovenia has managed to increase its total expenditure on higher education, reflecting an attempt to improve its economic competitiveness by investing in education. In contrast, Croatia, which maintained an already low level of public expenditure in higher education compared to the EU average, responded in the post-2008 period with a further downward trend in public investment, remaining at around 27 per cent below the EU average.

Figure 5.3, which shows total domestic expenditure on research and development, indicates an even more dramatic falling behind in the case of Croatia.

If we again focus primarily on the post-2008 period, it is visible on the level of the EU27 that member states have made efforts at increasing expenditure on research and development even in the context of fiscal consolidation and general austerity, relying on research and development as an engine of economic recovery. In contrast, in the post-2008 period Croatia has not yet recovered investment levels to its pre-2008 period. In 2013, it stood at 40 per cent of the EU27 average.

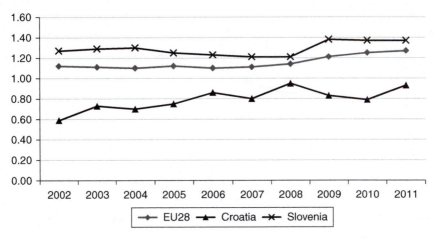

Figure 5.2 Total public expenditure on higher education as per cent of GDP, 2002–2011

Source: Eurostat

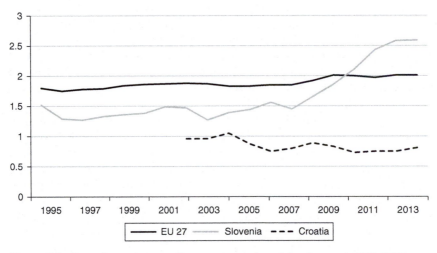

Figure 5.3 Gross domestic expenditure on research and development, 1995–2013

Source: Eurostat

Summarizing Figures 5.2 and 5.3, it seems safe to say that Croatia has failed to secure adequate funding for an expanding higher education sector and has particularly fallen back in the field of research and development, which is considered the primary driver of 'knowledge-based' economies. A recent monitoring report by the European University Association (2012) located Croatia in the group of countries that responded to post-2008 austerity by reducing funding for higher education up to 10 per cent. The study shows that in the period 2008–2012 many countries on the EU periphery reduced public spending on higher education, while the core EU countries responded to the crisis by increasing public funding.

Since student numbers are growing but public funding is not, the system relies increasingly on private investment. Based on available comparative data, it seems that private expenditure on higher education in Croatia is relatively high (File et al., 2013). For instance, as a proportion of GDP, private expenditure on higher education in Croatia was 0.28 per cent (in 2009), compared to Sweden (0.17 per cent), Austria (0.18 per cent) or Slovenia (0.19 per cent) (File et al., 2013). The largest proportion of private expenditure on higher education is composed of tuition fees. In 2014, 50 per cent of students enrolled in higher education institutions in Croatia paid tuition fees (CBS, 2015) – a substantial increase from 11.8 per cent of students who paid tuition fees during the academic year 1993/94 (Matković, 2009).

All students in part-time status pay tuition fees, and they comprise of 25.9 per cent of the total, while among full-time students 32 per cent pay tuition fees (Matković, 2009). For most higher education institutions in Croatia, income from tuition fees represents over 50 per cent of their overall own income (Doolan, Dolenec and Domazet, 2012). Income from other sources remains low, especially for activities such as research and development. In seven out of twenty-one countries with available data, the majority of bachelor students pay fees. This holds true for Switzerland, Bosnia-Herzegovina, Italy, Croatia, Slovakia, Armenia and Ireland (Hauschildt et al., 2015). The average tuition fee in Croatia for undergraduate studies in the year 2009 was 1.170 EUR per year (Farnell et al., 2012). Between 1994 and 2010, tuition fees in Croatia grew around 46 per cent[1] (Doolan, Dolenec and Domazet, 2012). By comparison, in 2009 the average tuition fees in those European countries that charge them were below 1,000 EUR per year, which reflects negatively on Croatia, which is among the poorest EU member states. Even before the post-2008 period of austerity, an OECD team that reviewed Croatia's higher education system warned that high tuition fees could become a major deterrent to higher education access (Duke et al., 2008).

An expanding system of higher education which is at the same time eroded by low public investment and growing commodification is bound to create inequalities, in relation to student access generally and to the streaming of students into higher- and lower-tier higher education institutions based on their socio-economic background. The following sections discuss inequalities of access, after which the multiple dimensions of compounding inequalities within the Croatian higher education system are analysed.

Inequalities of access in higher education in Croatia

Higher education systems which ensure equitable access to higher education have a student body whose composition mirrors the socio-economic structure of the given country's population as a whole. In international comparisons, one way of measuring

[1] This calculation is based on the lowest amount of fees paid in 1994 and 2010, given the very wide range and no cap on maximum fees that can be charged in Croatia.

this is by comparing the educational attainment of students' parents to the educational level of adults in the general population of corresponding age (Orr et al., 2011). No European country has succeeded in completely removing inequalities of access (Altbach et al., 2009; Bohonnek et al., 2010; Santiago et al., 2008), but large and politically consequential differences exist among EU member states. From a European perspective, Croatia is among the countries which display significant underrepresentation of students of parents with low levels of education and significant overrepresentation of students of parents with high levels of education (Orr et al., 2011).

Eurostudent's intelligence brief (2012) takes the share of students whose parents attained a certain level of education and the share of adults of the same age and educational attainment in the general population as a starting point in classifying European higher education systems. The premise is that higher education systems are socially exclusive if the share of students with highly educated parents is larger than the share of highly educated adults of the same age in the general population. Using as an indicator the highest educational attainment of students' fathers as a share of corresponding age group in the general population, they propose a fourfold typology of social inclusiveness of European higher education systems, ranging from exclusive systems, across two transitional types, to inclusive systems. In exclusive systems, low education groups are underrepresented and high education groups are highly overrepresented, while in inclusive systems low education groups are well represented and high education groups show representation. According to this analysis, Croatia is a socially exclusive system, together with Slovakia, Romania, Germany, Latvia, Turkey and France.

Compounding social inequalities in higher education in Croatia

In addition to inequalities of access, which have been convincingly demonstrated, additional inequalities stem from the availability (or absence) of financial support mechanisms available to students while they study as well as other features of the higher education system. The following paragraphs highlight some of the most prominent features of compounding social inequalities in the higher education system in Croatia. For data it relies primarily on the two rounds of the Eurostudent survey that Croatia took part in, implemented in 2010 and 2014 respectively. Analyses based on this recent data provide further support to the second argument advanced in this chapter, according to which the post-2008 period of austerity has further amplified already present negative trends in the higher education sector in Croatia.

It is uncontroversial to state that students of lower socio-economic status are exposed to greater financial difficulties than other students. Student self-assessments suggest that the lower the level of parental education, the lower the perceived adequacy of financial resources for students. In addition, in Croatia students of lower socio-economic status are also more likely to pay tuition fees than other students (Farnell et al., 2012). Next, the lower the level of parental education, the greater the likelihood that students will be employed full-time or part-time. Along the same lines, in Croatia students of lower socio-economic status have a more negative assessment of the burden of their workload compared to the time at their disposal (File et al., 2013). Furthermore, around 30 per cent of dropouts in Croatia mention the desire or need for employment, which is closely related to financial need or financial security, and over 15 per cent mention academic difficulties (UNDP Croatia, 2009). Each of these three factors is likely to be more pronounced among disadvantaged groups. Indeed, research by Doolan (2010), Matković, Tomić and Vehovec (2010) and Mihaljević Kosor (2010) shows that dropping out of higher education is more likely for students of lower socio-economic status, mature students and students who have completed vocational secondary schools.

In other words, Eurostudent survey data has helped expose consistent differences in the study experiences of these groups of students. For instance, full-time students who pay tuition fees have significantly less chance of being awarded scholarships or housing in student dormitories compared to full-time students who do not pay fees (File et al., 2013). In Croatia[2] the share of non-recipients of public support among fee-paying students is particularly high. If the number of fee-paying bachelor students were set at 100 per cent, more than 80 per cent of these students would belong to the group that does not receive public support. This is probably because in Croatia academic performance is the common criterion for achieving free-of-charge student status, for receiving a scholarship and for obtaining a place in a student dormitory. This compounding of privilege in the group of students who are already at an advantage results in greater financial burden for full-time, fee-paying students, who aside from higher costs due to fees also face higher accommodation costs.

Adding another layer of inequality, important differences exist between university and non-university students. Croatia belongs to a small group of European states where the average expense for fees paid by students at non-universities is at least twice as high as for students at universities (File et al., 2013). As a result of these multiple features that compound disadvantage, Croatia is in the group of countries where more than a third of students report either serious or very serious financial difficulties.

Relating these findings to Esping-Andersen's (1990) well-known typology of welfare states, it is useful to remember that in his conception decommodification, or the avoidance of full reliance on the job market for survival, may be accomplished by reliance on either state programmes in the form of public services or the family. The latter solution is characteristic of conservative welfare regimes, where the family is the primary social institution. This has important implications in the case of Croatia, which seems to have moved from a higher education system that primarily relied on state-funded public programmes towards a system of expanding commodification and increasing reliance on the family as economic institution – as the following paragraphs make clear.

Increasing reliance on family

Although across Europe families represent an important source of funding for students, providing an average of 47 per cent of their income (Hauschildt et al., 2015), important differences exist among European higher education systems in terms of how well they address disadvantages related to family circumstances and background.

---

[2] Also in Switzerland, Bosnia-Herzegovina, Italy, Slovakia, Serbia, Austria and the Czech Republic.

Importantly, only in some European countries do provisions from family or partner constitute the main source of student income – and this is predominantly the case in the region of former post-socialist Europe, including Croatia[3]. In these countries, the share of family or partner contributions accounts for more than 50 per cent of total income. In Croatia, currently 88 per cent of students report their family or partner as the main source of income (Šćukanec et al., 2015), which is an increase from an already high 82 per cent, reported a few years back (Farnell et al., 2012).

The final aspect of social inequality in the higher education system in Croatia that is considered here relates to the educational trajectories that lead into tertiary education. As numerous studies have shown, social inequalities in the higher education system are in large part generated at earlier levels of education, where family background plays an even more direct influence on educational outcomes. Orr et al. (2008) have established that a stratified system of secondary education leads to an underrepresentation of students from lower socio-economic backgrounds in the higher education system. Those secondary education systems where significant differences in educational attainment exist among schools, rather than at the individual level, are considered stratified. Causes for such school-level outcomes may vary, including the family socio-economic background of pupils, school location and other resources available (OECD, 2013). The last Programme for International Student Assessment (PISA) analysis confirms that in the case of Croatia differences in educational attainment are largely attributable to socio-economic distinctions among schools. In other words, in Croatia the choice of secondary school is by itself a good predictor of educational attainment at tertiary level of education (Šćukanec et al., 2015).

Before moving on to data that links prior educational attainment to types of student status, a brief clarification regarding the structure of the higher education system is necessary. Croatia has a binary higher education sector, which means that in addition to academic study programmes, professional study programmes are also offered. Such programmes are usually more vocationally oriented and generally provided by professional higher education institutions such as polytechnics (Shavit et al., 2007, in Doolan, Dolenec and Domazet, 2012). In addition, Croatia has two types of higher education institutions: universities and professional higher education institutions, but the particularity of the Croatian system is such that professional studies are not offered only at professional higher education institutions but at universities too. In other words, there is a binary system of study programmes as well as a binary system of higher education institutions, with the two systems not linked in all segments (Cvitan et al., 2011).

This detour into features of the Croatian higher education system is crucial for understanding the ways in which the higher education system reproduces socio-economic inequalities established at earlier levels of education. Grammar school pupils comprise 65 per cent of university studies, in comparison with 32 per cent of vocational school pupils (Šćukanec et al., 2015). In professional studies the situation

---

[3] This is the case in Serbia, Bosnia-Herzegovina, Montenegro, Croatia, Slovakia, Lithuania, Latvia, Hungary, Germany, Slovenia, Armenia, Georgia, Italy, France and Ireland (Hauschildt et al., 2015).

is reversed: the ratio is 22 per cent to 78 per cent, with the majority being vocational school pupils. Furthermore, not only do pupils from better-off families more frequently study university programmes but they form 60 per cent of the group that does not pay tuition fees. Unsurprisingly, they are also the minority among part-time students – at 43 per cent compared to 66 per cent of former vocational school pupils, who more often come from underprivileged families.

Conclusion

Summarizing these findings, the parallel with Esping-Andersen's (1990) welfare regime typology seems particularly pertinent. If the purpose of the welfare state is to decommodify people from total wage dependence and ensure a decent living irrespective of their position in the labour market, then arguably in the case of young people the key role of the state is to decouple educational attainment from family background and circumstances. As this chapter has amply evidenced, in Croatia the state has over time been abandoning this function. Starting from the 1990s when the system was overwhelmingly publicly financed, it has allowed for a massification of entry into the higher education system without increasing public funding. The result has been an ever stronger reliance on tuition fees and broad family support for student living expenses, thereby creating over time an education system that compounds social inequalities rather than decoupling them. Apart from the obvious problem with this kind of public education system from the perspective of social justice, it is also important to stress that such outcomes have been used as arguments for the further dismantling of the public education system. The Thatcherite argument brought up in the mid-1980s, according to which tuition-free higher education is a regressive policy because it subsidizes the rich, thereby becomes a self-fulfilling prophecy which works to undermine the already crumbling public education sector.

References

Altbach, P. G., L. Reisberg and L. E. Rumbley. (2009). *Trends in Global Higher Education: Tracking an Academic Revolution. A Report Prepared for the UNESCO 2009 World Conference on Higher Education*. Paris: United Nations Educational, Scientific and Cultural Organization.

Ayres, Y. M. (2004). Framing collective action against neoliberalism: The case of the 'anti-globalization' movement, *Journal of World-Systems Research* 10(1): 11–34.

Barr, N. (1993). Alternative funding resources for higher education, *Economic Journal* 103(418): 718–28.

Bohonnek, A., A. F. Camilleri, D. Griga, K. Muhleck, K. Miklavić and D. Orr. (2010). *Evolving diversity: An overview of equitable access to Higher Education in Europe*, EURASHE. Available at: http://www.eurashe.eu/library/equnet_report_1_evolving-diversity_overview-pdf/.

Bourdieu, P. (2003). *Firing Back: Against the Tyranny of the Market 2*. London: Verso.

Brown, R. (ed.) (2011). *Higher Education and the Market*. New York: Routledge.

Brown, W. (2005). *Critical Essays on Knowledge and Politics*. Princeton and Oxford: Princeton University Press.

Brown, W. (2015). *Undoing the Demos*. Cambridge, MA: MIT Press.

Capano, G., and S. Piattoni. (2011). From Bologna to Lisbon: The political use of the Lisbon 'Script' in European higher education policy, *Journal of European Public Policy* 18(4): 584–606.

CBS (2015). Croatian Bureau of Statistics Report, No. 8.1.7. *Students Enrolled on Professional and University Study Winter Semester of 2014/2015 Academic Year*, (August). Zagreb: Croatian Bureau of Statistics. Available at: http://www.dzs.hr/Hrv_Eng/publication/2015/08-01-07_01_2015.htm

Collini, S. (2012). *What Are Universities for?* London: Penguin.

Corbett, A. (2005). *Universities and the Europe of Knowledge: Ideas, Institutions and Policy Entrepreneurship in European Union Higher Education 1955–2005*. Basingstoke: Palgrave MacMillan.

Cvitan, M., K. Doolan, T. Farnell and T. Matković. (2011). *Social and Economic Conditions of Student Life in Croatia: National EUROSTUDENT Survey Report for Croatia*. Zagreb: Institute for the Development of Education.

Dobbins, M., and C. Knill. (2009). Higher education policies in Central and Eastern Europe: Convergence toward a common model, *Governance* 22(3): 397–430.

Dolenec, D., and K. Doolan. (2013). Reclaiming the role of higher education in Croatia: Dominant and oppositional framings, in P. Zgaga, U. Teichler and J. Brennan (eds), *The Globalisation Challenge for European Higher Education. Convergence and Diversity Centres and Peripheries*. Frankfurt a/Main: Peter Lang. 225–346.

Dolenec, D., N. Baketa and P. Maassen. (2014). Europeanizing higher education and research systems of the Western Balkans, in J. Branković, M. Kovačević, P. Maassen, B. Stensaker and |M. Vukasović (eds), *The Re-Institutionalization of Higher Education in the Western Balkans*. Frankfurt: Peter Lang. 61–89.

Doolan, K. (2010). 'My dad studied here too': Social inequalities and educational (dis)advantage in a Croatian higher education setting. PhD diss., University of Cambridge, UK.

Doolan, K., D. Dolenec and M. Domazet (2012). *The Croatian Higher Education Funding System in a European Context: A Comparative Study*. Zagreb: Institute for the Development of Education.

Draghi, M. (2012). Q&A: ECB President Mario Draghi, *Wall Street Journal*, 23 February. Available at: http://blogs.wsj.com/eurocrisis/2012/02/23/qa-ecb-president-mario-draghi/.

Duke, C., A. Hasan, R. Cappon, W. Meissner, H. Metcalf and D. Thornhill. (2008). *OECD Reviews of Tertiary Education: Croatia*. Paris: OECD.

Eicher, J.-C. (2000). The financing of education: An economic issue?, *European Journal of Education* 35(1): 33–44.

Esping-Andersen, G. (2001). A welfare state for the 21st century, in A. Giddens (ed.), *The Global Third Way Debate*. Cambridge: Polity Press. 134–56.

European University Association. (2012). *The EUA Public Funding Observatory*. Available at: http://www.eua.be/eua-workand-policy-area/governance-autonomy-and-funding/public funding-observatory.aspx.

Eurostudent Intelligence Brief. (2012). *Is Higher Education in Europe Socially Inclusive?* Eurostudent. Available at: http://www.eurostudent.eu/download_files/documents/IB_HE_Access_120112.pdf

Farnell, T., K. Doolan, T. Matković and M. Cvitan. (2012). *Social and Economic Conditions of Student Life in Croatia: National EUROSTUDENT Report for Croatia.* Zagreb: Institute for the Development of Education.

File, J., T. Farnell, K. Doolan, D. Lesjak and N. Šćukanec. (2013). *Higher Education Funding and the Social Dimension in Croatia: Analysis and Policy Guidelines.* Zagreb: Institut za razvoj obrazovanja.

Gornitzka, Å. (2007). The Lisbon Process: A supranational policy perspective, in P. Maassen, and J. P. Olsen (eds), *University Dynamics and European Integration.* Dordrecht: Springer. 155–78.

Green, A., A. Wolf and T. Leney. (2000). *Convergence and Divergence in European Education and Training Systems.* London: Institute of Education, Bedford Way Papers.

Guillen, A., and B. Palier. (2004). Introduction: Does Europe matter? Accession to EU and social policy developments in recent and new member states, *Journal of European Social Policy* 14(3): 203–9.

Hall, P. (2012). Trouble in the eurozone: Views on the once and future crisis, Director's Seminar, Harvard University, Minda de Ginzburg Center for European Studies, 18 October 2012, YouTube. Available at: https://www.youtube.com/watch?v=vwWTMdTlRq0.

Hauschildt, K., C. Gwosc, N. Netz and S. Mishra. (2015). *Social and Economic Conditions of Student Life in Europe. Synopsis of Indicators, EUROSTUDENT V 2012–2015.* Bielefeld: W. Bertelsmann Verlag.

Héritier, A. (2005). Europeanization research East and West: A comparative assessment, in F. Schimmelfennig and U. Sedelmeier (eds), *The Europeanization of Central and Eastern Europe.* Ithaca: Cornell University Press.

Jessop, B. (2008). A cultural political economy of competitiveness and its implications for higher education, in B. Jessop, N. Fairclough and R. Wodak (eds), *Education and the Knowledge-based Economy in Europe.* Rotterdam: Sense. 13–39.

Judt, T. (2010). *Ill Fares the Land.* London: Penguin.

Kenway, J., E. Bullen and S. Robb. (2007). The knowledge economy, the techno-preneur and the problematic future of the university, in S. Marginson (ed.), *Prospects for Higher Education.* Rotterdam: Sense Publishers.

Kwiek, M., and P. Maassen. (2012). Introduction: Changes in higher education in European peripheries and their contexts: Poland, Norway, and Europe, in M. Kwiek and P. Maassen (eds), *National Higher Education Reforms in a European Context: Comparative Reflections on Poland and Norway.* Oxford: Peter Lang. 11–40.

Le Grand, J., and R. Robinson (eds) (1984). *Privatization and the Welfare State.* London: George Allen and Unwin.

Lynch, K. (2006). Neo-liberalism and marketisation: The implications for higher education, *European Educational Research Journal* 5(1): 1–17.

Maassen, P., and B. Stensaker. (2011). The knowledge triangle, European higher education policy logics and policy implications, *International Journal of Higher Education Research* 61(6): 757–69.

Matković, T. (2009). Pregled statističkih pokazatelja participacije, prolaznosti i režima plaćanja studija u Republici Hrvatskoj 1991–2007, *Revija za socijalnu politiku* 16(2): 239–50.

Matković, T., I. Tomić and M. Vehovec. (2010). Efikasnost nasuprot dostupnosti? O povezanosti troškova i ishoda studiranja u Hrvatskoj, *Revija za socijalnu politiku* 17(2): 215–37.

Mihaljević Kosor, M. (2010). Rani odlazak sa studija: determinante nezavršavanja studija u hrvatskom visokom obrazovanju, *Revija za socijalnu politiku* 17(2): 197–213.

Neave, G. (2002). Anything goes: Or, how the accommodation of Europe's universities to European integration integrates – an inspiring number of contradictions, *Tertiary Education and Management* 8(3): 181–97.

Nussbaum, M. (1998). *Cultivating Humanity*. Cambridge, MA: Harvard University Press.

OECD. (2013). *PISA 2012 Results: Excellence Through Equity: Giving Every Student the Chance to Succeed (Volume II)*. Paris: PISA, OECD Publishing. Available at: http://dx.doi.org/10.1787/9789264201132-e.

Olsen, J. P., and P. Maassen. (2007). European debates on the knowledge institution, in P. Maassen and J. P. Olsen (eds), *University Dynamics and European Integration*, Dordrecht: Springer. 3–22.

Orr, D., C. Gwosć and N. Netz. (2011). *Social and Economic Conditions of Student Life in Europe: Synopsis of Indicators; Final Report; Eurostudent IV 2008–2011*. Bielefeld: W. Bertelsmann Verlag. Available at: http://www.felvi.hu/pub_bin/dload/eurostudent/EUROSTUDENT_IV.pdf.

Pierson, C. (1998). *Beyond the Welfare State*. Cambridge: Polity Press.

Polanyi, K. (1944). *The Great Transformation*. Boston: Beacon Press

Santiago, P., K. Tremblay, E. Basri and E. Arnal. (2008). *Tertiary Education for the Knowledge Society: OECD Thematic Review of Tertiary Education. vol. 2*. Paris: OECD.

Schmidt, V. A., and M. Thatcher. (2013). *Resilient Liberalism in Europe's Political Economy*. Cambridge: Cambridge University Press.

Šćukanec, N., M. Sinković, R. Bilić, K. Doolan and M. Cvitan. (2015). *Socijalni i ekonomski uvjeti studentskog života u Hrvatskoj: Nacionalno izvješće istraživanja EUROSTUDENT V za Hrvatsku za 2014*. Zagreb: Institut za razvoj obrazovanja.

Shavit, Y., R. Arum and A. Gamoran (eds) (2007). *Stratification in Higher Education: A Comparative Study*. Stanford: Stanford University Press

Streeck, W. (2011). The crises of democratic capitalism, *New Left Review* 71: 5–29.

Theisens, H. (2004). *The State of Change: Analysing Policy Change in Dutch and English Higher Education*. Enschede: Center for Higher Education and Policy Studies (CHEPS).

Tilak, J. B. G. (2005). Global trends in the funding of higher education, *IAU Horizons* 11(1): 1–2.

UNDP Croatia. (2009). *Survey: Educational and Employment Careers of Youth in Croatia*. Zagreb: UNDP Croatia

6

Austerity Ireland and the Neo-liberal University: Hollow Enterprise

Marnie Holborow and John O'Sullivan

The effects of austerity measures, despite what their promoters say, are not just temporary, while crisis conditions prevail. They alter permanently the structure and distribution of public services and direct them towards new goals. In the case of Irish higher education, the shrinking of public funding for universities and colleges, forced through under the conditions of one of the costliest banking crises in history (Browne, 2011), has allowed a new, mutually reinforcing dependence on private funds and on employers' needs. Critics of austerity tend to dismiss it as 'perverse madness' because, from a Keynesian perspective, it kills market demand and is self-defeating (Blyth, 2013; Krugman, 2012). Some trade union leaders in Ireland also see austerity as 'irrational' (while, incidentally, having supported its implementation) and criticize its continuance in the midst of economic contraction (O'Connor, 2013). Within the ranks of the Irish Universities Association, the representative body of Ireland's seven universities, spending cuts in higher education are deemed not 'sustainable' and it is argued that what is needed is a sensible balance between public and private investment (Humphries, 2014).

These observations miss the point: that austerity constitutes 'the rationality in an irrational system' and flows logically from both the capital-labour relations and competition between capitalist states (Dunn, 2014). Austerity policies in higher education, this chapter argues, are no different: they carry a certain logic from the point of view of specific class interests. Public policy in Irish higher education, which closely follows what has been laid down by the European Union (EU) institutions, sees as its main goal to produce a suitably prepared potential workforce – flexible, highly skilled and even, as the Irish employers association stipulates, with the 'right attitude' (IBEC, 2012) – ready to slot into the national economy, which needs to be ever more competitive on the global stage. We suggest that recent developments in Ireland show how austerity, pushed through amid the 'uninterrupted disturbance' (Fraser et al., 2013) of a severe economic crash, has become the cover for replacing state support in higher education with a privatized regime operated at the behest of corporate and neo-liberal imperatives.

Austerity, spending cuts and the banking crisis

In the backdrop to these changes are unprecedented cutbacks in public spending in Irish higher education. Between 2007 and 2014, state funding to universities was cut by 26 per cent, while student numbers surged by over 16 per cent and staff numbers declined by 4,500 (Jennings, 2016). As a result, there has been a sharp increase in the staff-student ratio, which, at 20:1, now falls second highest amongst Organization for Economic Cooperation and Development (OECD) and EU countries (HEA, 2015). From 2006 to 2014, the real value of public expenditure per student in higher education fell sharply, from just over €11,000 to just over €8,000. This shortfall has been picked up, in part, by the individual student: what was once a 'registration' charge of €150 has ballooned into a crushing €3,000 fee in 2016 (see Figure 6.1).

Spending cuts have also been absorbed by the impact of centrally imposed large pay cuts for public sector employees, which, in the university sector, delivered savings of €80m between 2008 and 2014 (IUA, 2014). Successive pay cuts and recruitment and promotion embargoes were imposed under coercive national agreements. All institutions of higher education are, as a result, under severe pressure, with some institutes of technology (IOTs), at the beginning of 2015, running deficits and universities desperately seeking ways to plug gaps in funding, mainly through extra income from private sources. The crisis is set to intensify as high birth rates will raise student numbers, projected to grow by almost 30 per cent by 2028 (O'Brien, 2016a). The austerity agenda has fallen heavily on higher education in Ireland with disturbing results, both social and ideological, as we shall see.

It should be remembered that Irish austerity stems directly from the decision of the government on 30 September 2008, to issue a blanket guarantee for €440 billions worth of Irish banking debt. The cost of the eventual bailout of the most indebted bank, Anglo Irish, was €29.3 billion, and of another, Irish Nationwide, €5.4 billion. Over time and including interest, the bailout for the banks is estimated to have cost the public exchequer €64 billion, more than 40 per cent of GDP, or €35,000 for every household in the country (McCabe, 2015). It was this that led to a sharp increase of the budget deficit.[1] The severity of the Irish crash, and the fear in Brussels that it could spread across the banking system, led the International Monetary Fund (IMF), the European Commission and the European Central Bank (ECB) (the Troika) to put in place the bailout. The loan as stipulated by the ECB president was to be contingent on spending cuts and tax increases which would be strictly monitored by representatives of the Troika. Thus, decisions about Irish state spending were now to be tightly directed from Europe (Allen and O'Boyle, 2013). Five regressive budgets were duly implemented in the years that followed and hit the poorest and most vulnerable in society hardest. Education's share of public expenditure dropped to the ninth lowest in Europe, at the very time when, beyond the sharp rise in college students, an additional 44,000 places were needed at primary level and an additional 25,000 places at second level (Social Justice Ireland, 2016).

---

[1]   Before the crash government debt stood at 25 per cent of GDP; after the crisis, it increased to 118 per cent of GDP, or €192 billion.

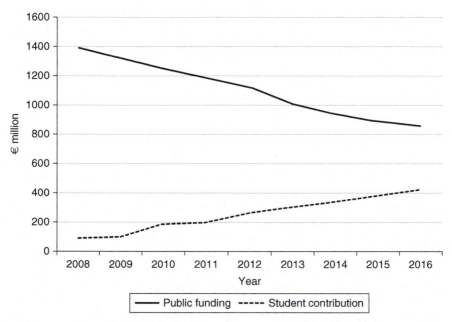

Figure 6.1 Declining public expenditure and rising student contribution 2008–2016 (€ million)
Source: Mercille, 2015a

In public discourse, the causal link between protecting the banks and austerity often has been buried under descriptions of the debt as 'national' or 'sovereign' debt, a rhetorical ruse which simultaneously socialized the cost and shifted responsibility. For example, the majority of articles on the subject in the print media, between 2008 and 2012, put the case that profligate government spending prior to the crash was at the origin of the crisis, and that austerity was vital to maintaining 'economic sovereignty' (Mercille, 2014). It has been noted that the discursive strategy that has marked the Irish crisis consisted of the narrowing down of the field of political possibility, with the problem repeatedly reduced to the simple question 'how can the fiscal crisis be fixed?' (Allen and O'Boyle, 2013: 30; Coulter and Nagle, 2015).

In effect, the government versions[2] were that sacrifices from the majority were necessary to set the population on the path to market recovery, and that fixing the deficit required both mending our spending ways and paring back the market-shy public sector. This led to a badgering and denigration of public sector workers in the print media (Cawley, 2012). Ironically, it was many of the 'expert' economists in the universities who, having spectacularly failed to foresee the crash, maintained their unwavering belief in the market and enthusiastically joined in the pro-austerity chorus

---

[2] There have been three Irish governments post-crash, one led by Fianna Fáil in coalition with the Green Party, who agreed to the bank guarantee, and the other, led by Fine Gael in coalition with Labour, whose policies were based on accepting its terms. At the time of writing, post the 2016 election, a third Fine Gael minority government appears to be likely.

(O'Dowd, 2012). The degree of acceptance and conformity to this narrative was striking, particularly across the Irish academy. A handful of voices expressed an opposing view, but official policy and university managements accepted that public funding was set to decline for the foreseeable future and that the issue was how to attract private income to replace dwindling state funds, and what legacies and cultures in higher education needed to be altered to effect that change.

The neo-liberal restructuring of academic work

Most – though certainly not all – of those working in universities have experienced, as we have already stated, the sharp end of the cuts and suffered dramatic drops in staff-student ratios. Burgeoning class sizes have brought pressures on resources and supports such as physical space and equipment, tutoring backup and administrative help. A recent survey of academic staff across universities and institutes of technology documented, alongside changing demands in teaching and research, deteriorating working conditions with less time for research (despite the fact that the latter continues to be highly privileged as the basis for career progression); longer hours and heavier, non-productive administrative burdens; and greater exclusion from decision-making processes. Other issues identified were the increased pressure to drum up external funding and to conform with research agendas that otherwise might not fit with academics' primary interests, and additional difficulties in teaching connected with the poor literacy skills of students (Clarke, Kenny et al., 2015). A survey in which a majority of Dublin City University (DCU) staff participated identified broadly similar issues, especially marked isolation of part-time or temporary staff, favouritism concerning promotions, lack of transparency and communication from management, gender and disability discrimination and, in some cases, bullying (SIPTU, 2015). This followed an earlier informal survey, carried out by the authors as SIPTU committee members, in which staff articulated anxieties over the operation of unilaterally imposed metrics in the Faculty of Humanities and Social Sciences, at the vanguard of the new, top-down managerialism (DCU SIPTU, 2013), in tune with wider trends towards control mechanisms (Burrows, 2012; Clancy, 2007).

While zero-hour or 'flexible' contracts recently have emerged as topics of wide debate, exploitative, precarious employment has long been a feature of academic life in Ireland, predating austerity. A study of non-permanent academics has revealed a nightmarish 'hamster wheel' in which individuals, whose average age is 39, are trapped in a cycle of shouldering much of the burden of increased workloads, with little credit and with diminishing prospects for conventional employment (Courtois and O'Keefe, 2015). In one case at DCU, a temporary part-timer who had 24 separate casual contracts lost his appeal to the Labour Court, only to be appointed soon after when he applied for a permanent post, becoming one of the lucky few to achieve the transition.

Concerns for stable and inclusive working conditions and academic freedom hardly resonate with the establishment of the entrepreneurial university (Slaughter and Rhoades, 2004), with its always-on streams of emails and tweets from the corporate offices, individual research centres and enterprise centres urging positioning for funding-friendly projects, advertising one-off competitions or celebrating successes for individual academics or their teams. Just as students are nudged towards entrepreneurship, so staff are jostled and cajoled to compete for scarce funding to conduct research or to implement ever more novel teaching methods. In this way, academics, who once had been organized collegiately, if not professionally, are set against one another in the struggle merely to do their work, much of which is hardly likely to qualify as innovative or enterprising within official prescriptions. As academic and administrative salary scales have stretched upward, corporate style, in recent years, with the top pulling away dramatically from colleagues and university presidents on €200,000 a year (Drennan and McCormack, 2014; Flynn and McGuire, 2010), the winners in the 'game', the connected hustlers and adroit self-promoters in an already markedly careerist environment, are massively rewarded, not only financially but also with further institutional resources and research breaks with which to cement their positions. Elsewhere, such processes of segmentation have been described as favouring science and engineering, and disadvantaging low-resource humanities departments (Rosinger et al., 2016). It is clear that, after a perhaps slow start, the trend elsewhere of the 'slicing and dicing' of staffs, already naturally divided by closer identification with their own disciplines than with the general role of an academic (Clarke, Drennan et al., 2015), has begun in earnest in Ireland too.

Parallel to the redefining of relations among academic staff and with their employers, the marketized university increasingly positions students as customers exercising consumer choices. Such logic follows clearly from the breakup of degree programmes into readily commodifiable modules and 'learning outcomes' expressing measurable, instrumental 'doing' values at the expense of quality of education (Brancaleone and O'Brien, 2011), offered to disparate cohorts, who are invited to express their satisfaction or otherwise in anonymous surveys conducted, in contrast to previous practice, for the benefit of management.[3] Academics are further aligned to the discipline of the market through exhortations to increase engagement or to protect revenue and institutional reputation through student retention, translating in practice into disincentives to register failing marks and to fuel grade inflation (O'Grady, 2013).

Serving business and the enterprise agenda

Dogma's role in Irish education primarily has been associated, from a liberal perspective, with the state ceding control of schooling to religious interests. This long-standing narrative is accurate as far as it goes, although often overlooked is the residual connection of religious authorities with public higher education, whose largest institution, University College Dublin, began with the purpose of countering the historical dominance of Anglo-Irish Protestantism (Walsh, 2013). In the more recent case of Dublin

---

[3] Advertising a new referencing system service, ProQuest provides a blunt insight on its vision of academic relationships, thus, *'Need to fire your advisor? ... Find answers, advice, and more at Revise and Resubmit, a new academic community, brought to you by the makers of Flow.'* See http://prep. refworks.com/refworks/.

City University, a merger of the existing entity with a number of religious teacher training institutions has proceeded with little or no institutional or public concern, the secular spirit of marketized education being presumed sufficiently established to take care of itself.[4]

Such insouciance can be understood in light of the robustness of the neo-liberal doctrine that, coexisting comfortably with corporate authoritarianism, and reinforced by austerity, has come to pervade higher education in Ireland. Profound changes have been implemented with little controversy, with most press coverage of higher education devoted to the anxious topics of career choices and competition for college places. More widely, austerity has wreaked havoc in health and housing, and has triggered widespread protests over the funding of water. Education has been subjected to less starkly relatable but equally fundamental processes of reform, motivated by a similar desire to shift the burden from public to individual funding.

The far-reaching restructuring in higher education in recent years largely has been executed under the banner of a keystone document, The National Strategy for Higher Education to 2030, notorious for having been produced by a committee that included no Irish academic, and known as the Hunt Report, after the Australian economist chair of its authoring committee (DES, 2011). Hunt had worked in Irish banking and as an adviser to government in the period prior to the collapse of 2008, and subsequently for an Australian capital group that successfully bid for participation in public-private partnership education projects in Ireland (Coulter, 2011; Department of Education and Skills, 2011). The strategy was positioned as a response to the country's economic predicament. It re-cemented the notion, already formally in place in Ireland since the 1960s, of education as serving the economy. While this overarching theme was not new, the report drew heavily on British and Australian practice, adapted in tone, perhaps, to what had been a more consensual culture in Ireland, and introduced elements of new public management, performance auditing, competition, mergers and an emphasis on research outputs, with business influence hardwired into institutional structures and underpinned through wider networks (Walsh and Loxley, 2014). However, it was not considered radical enough for the news media, overwhelmingly adherents to the new dogma, in a phase of post-crash news coverage located in a 'discourse of derision' of higher education and the wider public sector (ibid.). While Irish policy largely has been in lockstep with EU and OECD policy for many decades (Mercille and Murphy, 2015), Hunt has become the key instrument through which higher education, increasingly driven by and for business interests, is being reformed in line with neo-liberalism (Heffron and Heffron, 2013; Holborow, 2012a).

One aspect of this is how enterprise, with very little public debate, has been put by official policy at the heart of post-crash education policy. In the Hunt Report, mentioned above, the term 'enterprise', used across the document, becomes indistinguishable

---

[4] We give many examples from our own university, Dublin City University. While we set our data and arguments in the broader Irish context, and give examples also from other Irish universities, we believe that in order to foster the necessary critical debate within our institutions, it is important to be specific about individual institution's neo-liberal practices.

from the goals of education itself and a main plank of the economic priority to attract foreign investment, as one paragraph makes clear.

Ireland's long-term enterprise strategy of investing in increasing levels of educational attainment has yielded clear returns to individuals, to enterprises and to the State. IDA Ireland (Industrial Development Authority) sees continual enhancement of our education and research system and training programmes as key to our capacity to attract foreign investment, and has highlighted the need 'to ensure we have a workforce with relevant skills and that supports advanced research, development and innovation activities' (DES, 2011: 34). Ireland's long-term enterprise strategy is to achieve sustainability through commercializing and exporting goods, services and ideas. The current economic downturn must not deflect attention from the necessity of ensuring that the right infrastructure is in place to develop the increasingly high skills required by Ireland's enterprise base (DES, 2011)

Enterprise has now expanded to stand for commercialization, succeeding in the market, personal initiative, innovation, creativity and a host of other things too. It has come to have specific ideological inferences as well: a driver of the digital economy and the ultimate expression of 'free market' individualism. The spirit of enterprise as embedded across higher education has considerable ideological effects, for academics and students within the institutions and for society at large. Its widespread and unthinking adoption reinforces a set of solutions within an accepted logic and certain unspoken parameters, in this case the workings of the capitalist market and individual initiative as the driver of social change. Thus, DCU sees fit to adopt the learning of 'enterprise skills' in its curricula, to promote the widespread commercialization of intellectual property and entrepreneurial start-up companies for staff and students and, as if to prove its unreserved commitment to the new culture, to add *University of Enterprise* to its title. As its website makes clear, at DCU,

> the focus is not solely on academic learning; students get the opportunity to spend time in real world professional environments as part of their studies, and they also get to work with innovators on their own ideas, setting up enterprises and exploring their own social and commercial ideas. (DCU, 2016)

The pages of the website market the university as a set of different units selling their own unique product to potential student *entrepreneurs*. For example, the DCU Ryan Academy of Enterprise is described as a bridge between 'academia and entrepreneurial practice' and a 'unique partnership' between 'Ireland's leading young university, Dublin City University and the family of one of our greatest entrepreneurs, Tony Ryan' (one of the founders of Ryanair). The connection between a big profitable business and what goes on in a university is never quite spelled out, but the assumption, via a cluster of accompanying words such as 'innovative' and 'creative', is that new ways of thinking, whatever the discipline, involve new ways of making money. DCU is not alone in the widespread use of entrepreneur. Entrepreneurial skill training now forms the necessary component of all subjects in university education (as well as for 'life skills' for the population at large). State agencies sponsor plans to upskill lecturers so they can 'teach entrepreneurship' and 'give our children the toolkit they need to design their own future' (NUIG, 2014).

Post-crisis, the institutions of the EU have been the prime movers of embedding the enterprise philosophy in universities across its member states. The European Commission for Industry and Enterprise, now an unapologetically neo-liberal institution, has played a lead role. Its 2012 *Survey of the Effects of Entrepreneurship Programmes in Higher Education in Europe,* for example, declares that 'the primary purpose of entrepreneurship education at university is to develop entrepreneurial capacities and mindsets'. While 'the teaching of entrepreneurship has yet to be suf-ficiently integrated into university curricula', the study reaffirms its commitment 'to make entrepreneurship education accessible to all students as innovative busi-ness ideas may arise from technical, scientific or creative studies' (EC Industry and Enterprise, 2012). Enterprise acts as a normalized point of reference upon which education performance is measured. Following this template, the Irish Higher Education Authority (HEA) report reaffirms the need for universities to interact with enterprises and, in support of this argument, highlights the achievements of 'university-enterprise partnerships' across Europe (2013: 26). The new entrepreneur-ial buzzwords of higher education, first coined in Brussels, are slavishly adopted and locally promoted through official policy channels in the member state (Holborow 2012b; 2013; 2015).

The new entrepreneurial ethos rests on the notion that education is about people accruing human capital, another core term in the neo-liberal lexicon. Articulated first in the 1960s by the Milton Friedman Chicago School of economics, human capital encapsulates the notion that individuals can increase their job prospects and their 'earnings premium' by taking full responsibility for their own education and upskill-ing. One strident proponent of human capital theory, Gary Becker (2002), has claimed that the contemporary world is the 'age of human capital' because this is by far the most important form of capital in modern economies, and that education at all levels should enable this form of 'investing in yourself'. The prevalence of this notion, coin-ciding with massive expansion, was one marker of the social shift of higher education in capitalist societies, being now no longer mainly for those who will rule and manage people in society but also for those who will work in it.

In Ireland, what is sometimes referred to as the 'massification' of higher education (Woolridge, 2005) has been significant. In 1960, just 5 per cent of Irish students who completed secondary education went on to college. Twenty years later it was still only 20 per cent (DES, 2011: 35). The official view of a university then was that it should provide a liberal education, a place where what Cardinal John Henry Newman had called 'universal knowledge' should be acquired by students who would be conscious of the social and economic role expected of them. Today, however, as capitalist pro-duction grows more sophisticated and intercapital competition more intense, over and above more specialized managers an ever more sophisticated workforce is required. In Ireland, increased participation in higher education has been striking: in 2016, two out of three school leavers enter a third-level institution before the age of twenty-three. Higher education has become the new educational norm for young people (Delaney and Healy, 2014) with the ethos promoted in universities reaching to an ever wider segment of the population.

Inequality reinforced

Authors of the many strategy documents typified by the Hunt Report always are careful to box-tick education goals beyond the economic, not least equality and social mobility (Higher Education Authority, 2014). Actual outcomes, however, expose the weakness of such aspirations: access to college remains stubbornly unequal, with significant sections of the population excluded while others, most notably pupils in elite fee-paying schools, are privileged (Kennedy and Power, 2010; Lynch, 2014; McCoy and Byrne, 2011; Walsh et al., 2015) to the extent that education has been described as a long-embedded 'caste system' (Courtois, 2013; Jones, 2014). The failure of the abolition in the 1990s of university fees, since partially restored, to address problems of access (Denny, 2010), points to wider, more profound patterns of inequality that have never receded, even in prosperity.

The notion that society and its policymakers cherish the goal of equality is dispelled in the annual scramble for college places, with media coverage bordering on hysteria as second-level students weigh options based on the apparent meritocracy of anticipated points achieved in the Leaving Certificate. In addition to structural factors affecting socio-economic class divisions, the frenzied pitch of the 'points race' is most exemplified by the remarkable rise of grind schools in the shadow education sector. Even if aggregate outcomes are little changed by the use of such tactics (Smyth, 2009), the Irish middle classes have embraced the ultracompetitive maintenance of privilege, and such institutions are advertised and promoted heavily in the news media with which they closely partner (Kearns, 2015). In a period in which many occupations have been subjected to the weakening of conditions under internationally sponsored reforms, the protected professions, heavily reliant on the state as client, have secured immunity from such processes, even when liberalization of legal services was demanded by the IMF during the country's bailout (Cahill, 2014). Subsequently, competition for entry to courses in law or medicine, constituting reservations free of the effects of neo-liberal austerity, remains especially intense, while the promotion of STEM (science, technology, engineering, and mathematics) subjects also feeds into demand (Mooney, 2015). If the imposition of austerity has worked to frustrate any change in patterns of educational and wider inequality, neo-liberal rigour has been applied selectively enough to protect the elite and to solidify their position.

At this point, belated recognition of the collapse in public funding for higher education has prompted more urgent discussions on the subject of the reintroduction of full fees – students in approved public colleges, other than those on means-tested assistance, currently pay roughly a third of the cost – and the possibility of movement to a loan scheme or graduate tax (RIA, 2016), with a government-appointed working group led by a prominent trade union leader, due to report its findings in 2016

(Heaphy, 2015). Fees became a political issue in the 2016 election, with particular attention given to the reneging on a previous election pledge not to impose them. Beyond direct charges and the prospect of loans, however, private finance already has begun to play a role. A foretaste of the distortion that this may bring is the offering by (nationalized, state-owned) Allied Irish Banks (AIB) of interest-free loans confined to students on cherry-picked courses including law, medicine, veterinary, science, architecture and computing, with, predictably, most humanities subjects excluded (AIB, 2015).

Hip to the corporate groove

If Irish higher education has conformed to imposed international templates for some time, another dimension, based on a relatively recent economic exceptionalism, has been in play. In addition to its controversially low gross corporate tax rate of 12.5 per cent, one of Ireland's most cited selling points in the battle for foreign investment has been its young population. This accident of demographics has translated in official rhetoric into a ready supply of human capital, young, flexible, suitably educated and skilled 'digital native' knowledge workers (Prensky, 2001). It has provided fertile soil for the cultivation of the values of the US tech sector, with its fundamental faith in the self-correcting market, notions of frictionless business and a gung-ho celebration of 'disruption' (Christensen, 1997; Lapore, 2014), the successor-ally to Joseph Schumpeter's creative destruction, as a progressive force. The presence of large operations, often European or European, Middle East and Africa (EMEA) headquarters of totemic multinational corporations (MNCs) such as Apple, Google, Microsoft, Facebook and Twitter, encouraged to settle here not least by enthusiastic facilitation of tax avoidance schemes, is a matter of national pride in a state with historically underdeveloped industry. As traced by Angela Nagle (2015), Ireland's self-depiction as Europe's Silicon Valley is carefully cultivated to follow the 'Californian ideology' of a digital utopia, in which 'everybody will be both hip and rich' (Barbrook and Cameron, 1996), even if such role playing is hardly unique internationally (Accenture, 2014) and if employment numbers realized in the post-industrial economy are relatively modest. Reliance on the information and communications technology (ICT) and pharmaceutical industries has become central to the strategy for GNP recovery, and it has been argued that exports from foreign firms, rather than austerity measures and attendant structural 'reforms', have given the country its remarkable headline growth rates in recent years (Guider, 2016; Regan, 2016).

Tech industry values are sometimes forthrightly expressed in the discourse on education, with interventions such as that by PayPal's vice president of global operations, who accused Irish graduates of laziness and of lacking interest in learning new skills (Flanagan, 2013), or by the American Chamber of Commerce in Ireland which conversely has talked up the 'can-do' attitude of Irish labour (Burke-Kennedy, 2014). The staple concern, however, is to address a perceived skills deficit by steering second-level students towards STEM subjects, seen as serving employability (Accenture, 2014; Mooney, 2015) to the extent that the Leaving Certificate (the final examination at post-primary level) was adjusted in 2012 to give additional points to honours maths, with qualified success (Hayes, 2015).

At the time of writing, a government-commissioned report by a committee chaired by DCU's president, who is a director of the Irish employers' representative group, and including a representative of IBM, has yet to be published, though advance comment indicates that it will promote STEM education as 'necessary to drive our economic ambitions' (MacCraith, 2014). Alongside the STEM project, universities in Ireland, as part of the connected international drive to embed the spirit of commerce in higher education structures and processes (Benneworth and Osborne, 2015), have moved to steer graduates directly towards the 'smart' economy (Department of the Taoiseach, 2008). At Trinity College, Dublin (TCD), the US capital fund Blackstone is established on campus to encourage start-ups. TCD, despite its classical education reputation, has been quick to embrace the education-enterprise model. In April 2016, it announced plans to expand its output of skilled graduates by building its campus 'enterprise centre' next door to Google, Facebook, Twitter and Airbnb's offices in Dublin's hi-tech hub of Grand Canal Dock (O'Brien, 2016b). Meanwhile, the flip side of the juggernaut that is the digital sublime is that academics, in common with educators generally, are now seen participants in an industry that itself is a massive market for software, as they have become accustomed to working with and constantly adopting a panoply of 'solutions' in everything from email to message boards, virtual learning environments, library and database services, and, of course, data entry and management, all part of a push towards exploiting opportunities in the promising 'edtech' sector (Johnson et al., 2015). On the publishing front, completing the digital colonization of education, in common with trends internationally, research indices operated by private interests such as Elsevier's Scopus or Google's Scholar measure and regulate academic endeavours and reinforce the dominance of established publishers.

Saturation talking up of enterprise and entrepreneurial education (American Chamber of Commerce Ireland, 2015; IBEC, 2015) and softer 'nudge' incentives rooted in neo-liberal behavioural economics (Bradbury et al., 2013) run in tandem with more conventionally direct appeals to the interests of the MNCs. The IDA has won its foreign investment coups based on pitches such as one boasting of a 20.5 per cent return on investment for US firms in 2009, 'full political unanimity' on continuation of the 12.5 per cent gross rate on profit, with additional credits for research and development and 'high-quality human capital'. The document's author exults in reporting that the cost of Irish human capital was forecast to 'improve', by 13 per cent relative to the European competition, with salaries for new hires in Irish companies down by up to 22 per cent, and a 14 per cent cut in public pay, with additional cuts for new employees, while 'a major public sector transformation is under way' (IDA, 2011).[5] Thus, the radical potential of the originally countercultural,

---

[5] The Irish Congress of Trade Unions presented the erosion of pay and conditions for public sector workers in bleaker terms: 'If you are a Public Sector worker, you will have experienced a basic pay reduction (including the pension levy) of between 9 per cent and 19.5 per cent since 2009. You will also have lost allowances, had your overtime rates cut, your increments deferred or frozen, your hours of work increased by up to 3 hours per week, your annual leave adjusted and your sick pay

anti-establishment spirit of the software movement in the United States has been appropriated, via networked individualism and the export of Silicon Valley culture (Harris and Alter, 2014), so that it squares fully with conventional corporate agendas. Materially and symbolically, this contradictory elevation of business interests dovetails seamlessly with the reconstruction of the university, and all of its constituents, staff and students, as market players.

Reality and resistance

Recent data on graduates' employment patterns shows modest improvement in their prospects, largely limited to the in-focus disciplines around computer science and ICT, and with poor outcomes especially in arts and humanities (HEA, 2016). For all the talk of education for employment and the need to promote enterprise culture, Irish graduates over the post-crash period have faced an uncertain future. First, youth unemployment remains one of the most enduring and destructive legacies of the financial crash and the great recession that followed it. Rates of unemployment among young people (those aged under twenty-five) increased dramatically over the 2007–2009 period. In 2015, youth unemployment in Ireland still stood at 20.7 per cent, well above the EU average (MacFlynn, 2015). Secondly, emigration, not entrepreneurship, has become the norm. In 2008, just 13,000 Irish emigrated, but this figure climbed to 50,000 in 2013. In 2014, despite the talk of recovery, 35,000 people emigrated – three times pre-recession levels. Indeed, graduates have been over-represented amongst those leaving, with 62 per cent of emigrants in 2013 holding a tertiary qualification of three years or more (Glynn et al., 2013). 'Generation emigration' is the title of a regular series in *The Irish Times* whose featured young Irish people, now based in London, Berlin, Boston, Australia or the United Arab Emirates, are often graduates forced to seek to earn their living abroad.

Thirdly, start-up businesses have hardly taken off in the numbers that the official enterprise craze indicated. Such initiatives are often short-lived, employ on average just one person and, during the recession, have not been an option open to many people. Where they have been successful they often end up being taken over by larger corporations (White, 2014). Fourthly, where graduates find jobs, they find them in places where their skills and knowledge are not being used to the full. The trend in employment in the recession has been towards deskilling and new kinds of repetitive work. Bobek and Wickham, in their study of jobs, employment and working conditions in Irish financial services, note how banks are setting up customer service centres to replace the more demanding job of bank official, and that such routine jobs are having a stronger presence in Ireland. They remark that graduates increasingly find themselves in unpaid internships or poorly paid jobs

entitlement halved. The mantra of "do more with less" was rampant and public sector job numbers decreased by 30,000 in the period' (see http://www.ictu.ie/download/pdf/patricia_king_irn_speech_march_12_2015.pdf).All these dimensions of work-related conditions would apply to those working in higher education.

with few prospects of long-term security or a career structure (2015). This echoes a study that found that, across the EU, graduates post-2008 are generally overqualified for the jobs that they do, increasingly occupying roles previously filled by non-graduates – a process called occupational filtering down (Holmes and Meyhew, 2015). Despite the increase in the number of students, higher education is simply being used as a new job filtering system, replacing others such as apprenticeships, and is leading to the high skills of these graduates being underutilized. Holmes and Meyhew's (2015) data shows Irish graduates to be near the top of the list of other EU graduates in having qualifications above what their occupation requires or pays for (ibid.).

Finally, with large corporations dominating the economy, the likelihood is that graduates will either be working for them under strict regimes, with little room for entrepreneurship, or even finding that they are losing out to other EU graduates who have the skills and languages required. In sum, while graduate employment has rarely been such a fraught question, the education-to-entrepreneurial-employment pathway sold by the neo-liberal university blithely ignores the reality of overqualification and unemployment.

Dashed expectations can lead to resistance. While, overall, Irish colleges and universities have been sullenly quiet throughout the post-crash period, there are signs that this might be changing. In 2015, the National College of Art and Design (NCAD) conducted a one-day sit-in and demanded that students, not revenue management, to be at the centre of education (Mercille, 2015b). Furthermore, in 2012 a campaign to defend the public university attracted support from academics and students. It continues to gain traction around its comments on the erosion of academic freedom and the commercialization of education, even if it has remained at the level of statements and meetings rather than organized action.[6] Widespread opposition among public servants to pay cuts in 2012 singling out new staff, including those in higher education, have succeeded in overturning this basic inequality, according to press reports.

In 2016, strike action by a lecturers' union (the Teachers Union of Ireland) over the Technological Universities Bill, which proposes to merge ten institutes of technology into 'technological universities', arose from fears of further cutbacks and loss of resources. In a reference to the militancy of the mass anti-water charges movement that has rocked the political establishment, lecturers have warned that this issue could become the 'Irish Water of higher education' (McGuire, 2016). Whether that will be the case remains to be seen. But what can be said is that, alongside this institution-based controversy, proposals for the introduction of student loans to cover the cost of higher fees, worsening conditions for academic staff, a growing criticism of the commercialization agenda and future financial crises impending with perhaps further cutbacks in public spending, the road ahead for Ireland's neo-liberal experiment in higher education is unlikely to be free of contestation.

---

[6]　See *Defend the Irish University* website at http://defendtheuniversity.ie/.

Conclusion: private ends

Patrick Prendergast, provost of TCD, in April 2016 summed up the changes that have occurred in Irish higher education in recent years:

> I think higher education is a mixture of a public and private good. Society needs the engineers, doctors, dentists and social workers, who are all educated in university. But it's also a private good in that individuals benefit from higher salaries over their lifetimes. If you accept that, you don't need to go to an ideological extreme for a solution ... If we're good at anything, it's finding a balance. So let's find that. (O'Brien, 2016c)

Prendergast's acceptance of the dilution of the concept of a public university and his embracing of the human capital agenda is an explicit articulation of the degree to which the neo-liberal view of education has become common sense, so natural that it appears to contain no ideological positioning. Similarly, an uncontroversially reported announcement of large-scale borrowing, departing from conventional, on-the-books public investment, by DCU to fund campus expansion (O'Brien, 2016d), gives immediate and concrete expression to the positioning of Irish higher education within the realm of the market.

This chapter has argued that developments, both institutional and ideological, changes to funding and the drastic narrowing of content are motivated by the social interests of the corporate elite, who, under an appeal to business efficiency, competition and entrepreneurialism, seek to direct Irish university education ever closer to the needs of capital. We have shown how austerity policies, imposed in the aftermath of economic collapse in Ireland, have enabled an alarming intensification of the privatization of the university, even as we recognize that that entity in Ireland has never conformed to the ideal, and how its promised outcomes have not only not been realized but have created something of a crisis in higher education in Ireland, for its students, graduates and staff. Our chapter is written in the spirit of contributing to and developing further a much-needed challenge to this state of affairs.

References

Accenture. (2014). *Powering Economic Growth: Attracting More Young Women into Science and Technology*. Dublin: Accenture. Available at: http://www.accenture.com/SiteCollectionDocuments/Local_Ireland/PDF/accenture-STEM-powering-economic-growth.pdf.

AIB. (2015). Education Loans. *AIB Personal Banking*. Available at: http://personal.aib.ie/our-products/loans/education-loans. Accessed 23 February 2016.

Allen, K., and B. O'Boyle. (2013). *Austerity Ireland: The Failure of Irish Capitalism*. London: Pluto.

American Chamber of Commerce Ireland. (2015). *Submission with Regard to the Formulation of a National Skills Strategy Department of Education and Skills Ireland: A Global Centre for Talent.* Dublin. Available at: http://www.amcham.ie/Amcham/media/SiteMedia/ Submissions/Submission-on-a-National-Skills-Strategy.pdf

Barbrook, R., and A. Cameron. (1996). The Californian ideology, *Science and Culture* 6(1): 44–72.

Becker, G. S. (2002). The age of human capital, in E. P. Lazear (ed.), *Education in the Twenty-First Century.* Palo Alto: Hoover Institution Press.

Benneworth, P., and M. Osborne. (2015). 'Understanding universities and entrepreneurship education: towards a comprehensive future research agenda'. CHEPS-CRADALL Working Paper CHEPS 08/2015; CR&DALL 101/2015, CHEPS: Enschede (NL) and CR&DALL, Glasgow (UK). Available at: http://cradall. org/sites/default/files/CRDALL-WP101-2015-SR002_0.pdf.

Blyth, M. (2013). *Austerity: The History of a Dangerous Idea.* Oxford: Oxford University Press.

Bobek, A., and J. Wickham. (2015). *Working Conditions in Ireland Project: Employment in the Financial Services Sector.* Dublin: Irish Congress of Trade Unions/ TASC / Foundation for European Progressive Studies. Available: http://www.tasc.ie/download/ pdf/20150929160149.pdf. Accessed 4 April 2016.

Bradbury, A., I. McGimpsey and D. Santori. (2013). Revising rationality: The use of 'Nudge' approaches in neoliberal education policy. *Journal of Education Policy* 28(2): 247–67.

Brancaleone, D., and S. O'Brien. (2011). Educational commodification and the (economic) sign value of learning outcomes, *British Journal of Sociology of Education* 32(4): 501–19.

Browne, V. (2011). Let's own up to our part in the burst bubble. *The Irish Times,* 6 April. Available at: http://www.irishtimes.com/opinion/let-s-own-up-to-our-part-in-the-burst-bubble-1.564844. Accessed 10 May 2016.

Burke-Kennedy, E. (2014). Flying the flag for US business as tax dominates the agenda. *The Irish Times,* 5 September. Available at: http://www.irishtimes.com/business/ economy/flying-the-flag-for-us-business-as-tax-dominates-the-agenda-1.1917894. Accessed 10 April 2015.

Burrows, R. (2012). Living with the h-index? Metric assemblages in the contemporary academy. *Sociological Review* 60(2): 355–72.

Cahill, A. (2014). IMF denies undermining Irish legal system. *Irish Examiner,* 26 March. Available at: http://www.irishexaminer.com/ireland/imf-denies-undermining-irish-legal-system-263170.html. Accessed 9 May 2016.

Cawley, A. (2012). Sharing the pain or shouldering the burden? News-media framing of the public sector and the private sector in Ireland during the economic crisis, 2008–2010, *Journalism Studies* 13(4): 600–15. doi:10.1080/1461670X.2011.629108.

Christensen, C. M. (1997). *The Innovator's Dilemma: When New Technologies Cause Great Firms to Fail.* Boston: Harvard Business School Press.

Clancy, P. (2007). Resisting the Evaluative State: Irish academics win the battle but lose the war, in J. Enders and F. van Vucht (eds), *Towards a Cartography of Higher Education Policy Change: A Festschrift in Honour of Guy Neave.* Enschede: CHEPS, University of Twente, 111–18. Available at: papers2://publication/uuid/ C9F44015-843E-4221-99E6-C7E45D9CF5AE.

Clarke, M., J. Drennan. D. Harmon, A. Hyde and Y. Politis. (2015). *The Academic Profession in Ireland.* Dublin. Available at: http://irserver.ucd.ie/handle/10197/7204.

Clarke, M., A. Kenny and A. Loxley. (2015). *Creating a Supportive Working Environment for Academics in Higher Education: Country Report Ireland.* Dublin: The Teachers' Union of Ireland and The Irish Federation of University Teachers.

Coulter, C. (2011). Factory Farms for the Mind. *Politico.ie*, January. Available at: http://
    politico.ie/archive/factory-farms-mind.
Coulter, C., and A. Nagle. (2015). *Ireland under Austerity: Neoliberal Crisis, Neoliberal
    Solutions.* Manchester: Manchester University Press.
Courtois, A. (2013). Becoming elite: exclusion, excellence and collective identity in
    Ireland's top fee-paying schools, in J. Abbink and T. Salverda (eds), *The Anthropology
    of Elites: Power, Culture, and the Complexities of Distinction.* New York: Palgrave
    Macmillan, 163–83.
Courtois, A., and T. O'Keefe. (2015). Precarity in the ivory cage: Neoliberalism and
    casualisation of work in the Irish higher education sector, *Journal for Critical Education
    Policy Studies* 13(1): 43–66.
DCU. (2016). University of Enterprise. Available at https://www.dcu.ie/university-of-
    enterprise.shtml. Accessed 6 May 2016.
DCU SIPTU. (2013). *Survey Shows Serious Concerns over Workload System.*
    DCU Union. Available at: https://dcuunion.wordpress.com/2013/04/19/
    survey-shows-serious-concerns-over-workload-system/.
Delaney, A., and T. Healy. (2014). *NERI Working Paper No. 15: We Need to Talk about
    Higher Education.* Dublin. Available at: http://usi.ie/wp-content/uploads/2014/02/
    NERI-Paper-We-need-to-talk-about-Higher-Education-28Mar14-1.pdf.
Denny, K. (2010). What did abolishing university fees in Ireland do? *UCD Geary Institute
    Discussion Papers Series.* Available at: http://www.ucd.ie/geary/static/publications/
    workingpapers/gearywp201026.pdf.
Department of Education and Skills (2011). *National Strategy for Higher Education.*
    Dublin: Department of Education and Skills. Available at: http://www.education.ie/en/
    Publications/Policy-Reports/National-Strategy-for-Higher-Education-2030.pdf.
Department of the Taoiseach. (2008). *Building Ireland's Smart Economy: A Framework
    for Sustainable Economic Renewal.* Dublin. Available at: http://www.taoiseach.gov.ie/
    BuildingIrelandsSmartEconomy_1_.pdf.
Donnelly, K. (2015). 'Study now pay later': Considered to tackle crisis in third level
    funding, *Irish Independent*, 29 October. Available: http://www.independent.ie/
    irish-news/education/study-now-pay-later-considered-to-tackle-crisis-in-thirdlevel-
    funding-34151230.html. Accessed 4 January 2016.
Drennan, J., and C. McCormack. (2014). 25pc of university academics earn more
    than €100k, *Sunday Independent*, 3 November, p. 23. Available at: http://www.
    independent.ie/irish-news/education/25pc-of-university-academics-earn-more-than-
    100k-30766334.html. Accessed 4 May 2016.
Dunn, B. (2014). Making sense of austerity: The rationality in an irrational system, *ELRR
    (The Labour Relations Review)* 25(3): 417–34.
European Commission Industry and Enterprise. (2012). *A Survey of Entrepreneurship
    in Higher Education in Europe.* Brussels. Available at: http://ec.europa.eu/enterprise/
    policies/sme/promoting-entrepreneurship/education-training-entrepreneurship/
    higher-education/index_en.htm.
Flanagan, P. (2013). PayPal boss says graduates are not hungry enough to succeed, *Irish
    Independent*, 12 March. Available at: http://www.independent.ie/business/irish/paypal-
    boss-says-graduates-are-not-hungry-enough-to-succeed-29123273.html. Accessed 9
    May 2016.
Flynn, S., and P. McGuire. (2010). The top 100 best paid in education, *Irish Times*, 9
    November. Available at http://www.irishtimes.com/news/education/the-top-100-best-
    paid-in-education-1.674554. Accessed 3 May 2016.

Fraser, A., E. Murphy and S. Kelly. (2013). Deepening neoliberalism via austerity and reform: The case of Ireland, *Human Geography* 6(2): 38–53.

Glynn, I., T. Kelly and P. McÉinrí. (2013). *Emigration in an Age of Austerity*. Department of Geography and the Institute for the Social Sciences in the 21st Century, University College Cork. Available at: https://www.ucc.ie/en/media/research/emigre/Emigration_in_an_Age_of_Austerity_Final.pdf.

Guider, I. (2016). Election 2016: Recovery nothing to do with government – ex-IMF mission chief, *Sunday Business Post*, 23 February. Available at: http://www.businesspost.ie/election-2016-recovery-nothing-to-do-with-government-says-former-imf-mission-chief/. Accessed 24 February 2016.

Harris, J. G., and A. E. Alter. (2014). California dreaming, *Outlook: The Journal of High Performance Business (Accenture)* 1: 1–8. Available at: https://www.accenture.com/t20150522T061601__w__/ie-en/_acnmedia/Accenture/Conversion-Assets/Outlook/Documents/1/Accenture-Outlook-California-Dreaming-Corporate-Culture-Silicon-Valley.pdf#zoom=50.

Hayes, K. (2015). Minister may review Leaving Cert maths bonus points, *Irish Times*, 12 August. Available at: http://www.irishtimes.com/news/education/minister-may-review-leaving-cert-maths-bonus-points-1.2314596. Accessed 2 October 2015.

Heaphy, E. (2015). Peter Cassells: 'We will have a final report by the end of the year', *University Times*, 23 September. Available at: http://www.universitytimes.ie/2015/09/peter-cassells-we-will-have-a-final-report-by-the-end-of-the-year/. Accessed 26 October 2015.

Heffron, J. A., and R. J. A. Heffron. (2013). Institutional governance in Irish higher education, *Studies: An Irish Quarterly Review* 102(405): 68–80.

Higher Education Authority. (2013). *Towards a Performance Evaluation Framework: Profiling Irish Higher Education*. Dublin: HEA. Available at http://www.hea.ie/sites/default/files/evaluation_framework_long.pdf.

Higher Education Authority. (2014). *Consultation Paper: Towards the Development of a New National Plan for Equity of Access to Higher Education*. Dublin: HEA. Available at: http://www.hea.ie/sites/default/files/consultation_paper_web_0.pdf.

Higher Education Authority. (2015). *Key Facts and Figures 2014–15*. Dublin: HEA. Available at: http://www.hea.ie/sites/default/files/hea-key-factsfigures-2014–15.pdf.

Higher Education Authority. (2016). *What Do Graduates Do? The Class of 2014*. Dublin: HEA. Available at: http://www.hea.ie/sites/default/files/hea-whatgraduatesdo-the_class_of_2014-final.pdf.

Holborow, M. (2012a). Austerity, capitalism and the restructuring of Irish higher education, *Irish Marxist Review* 1(2): 24–36.

Holborow, M. (2012b). Neoliberal keywords and the contradictions of an ideology, in D. Block, J. Gray and M. Holborow (eds), *Neoliberalism and Applied Linguistics*. Abingdon, Oxford: Routledge.

Holborow, M. (2013). Applied linguistics in the neoliberal university: Ideological keywords and social agency, *Applied Linguistics Review* 4(2): 227–55.

Holborow, M. (2015). *Language and Neoliberalism*. London: Routledge.

Holmes, C., and K. Mayhew. (2015). *Over-qualification and Skills Mismatch in the Graduate Labour Market*. London: CIPD. Available: https://www.cipd.co.uk/binaries/over-qualification-and-skills-mismatch-graduate-labour-market.pdf. Accessed 23 April 2016.

Humphries, J. (2014). Universities seek action on 'crisis in funding', *Irish Times*, 29 September. Available at: http://www.irishtimes.com/news/education/universities-seek-action-on-crisis-in-funding-1.1944706. Accessed 22 April 2016.

IBEC (Geraldine Anderson and Kara McGann). (2012). *National Survey of Employers Views of National Educational Outcomes*. Dublin: HEA. Available at: http://www.hea.ie/sites/default/files/national_employers_survey_pilot_report.pdf. Accessed 19 March 2016.

IBEC. (2015). *Entrepreneurial Education: Policy Recommendations to Deliver the Skills Needed for the Workplace of the Future*. Dublin: IBEC. Available at: /IBEC/Press/PressPublicationsdoclib3.nsf/vPages/Newsroom~time-to-promote-entrepreneurial-thinking-in-education-20-08-2015/$file/Entrepreneurial+Education.pdf.

IDA. (2011). *Ireland and US Investment*. Available at: http://merrionstreet.ie/en/wp-content/uploads/2011/05/ida-ireland-and-us-investment.pdf.

IUA. (2014). *Issues Facing Higher Education in Ireland*. Available at: http://www.iua.ie/wp-content/uploads/2014/09/Issues-Facing-Higher-Education-in-Ireland-an-IUA-paper-for-Symposium-Sept-2014-embargoed-Monday-29th.pdf.

Jennings, M. (2016). Funding third level education, *Irish Times*, 25 January, 15.

Johnson, L. et al. (2015). *2015 NMC Technology Outlook for Higher Education in Ireland: A Horizon Project Regional Report*. Austin, TX. Available at: http://cdn.nmc.org/media/2015-nmc-technology-outlook-ireland-higher-ed.pdf.

Jones, J. (2014). Second opinion: Ireland's educational caste system affects all aspects of life. *Irish Times*, 3 September. Available at: http://www.irishtimes.com/life-and-style/health-family/second-opinion-ireland-s-educational-caste-system-affects-all-aspects-of-life-1.1909807. Accessed 9 May 2016.

Kearns, P. (2015). Welcome. *Exam Times*. Available at: http://studyzone.ioe.ie/wp-content/uploads/2015/02/EXAMTIMES_Science_2015.pdf. Accessed 9 May 2016.

Kennedy, M., and M. J. Power. (2010). The smokescreen of meritocracy: Elite education in Ireland and the reproduction of class privilege, *Journal for Critical Education Policy Studies* 8(2): 222–48.

Kennedy, S. (2015). A perfect storm: Crisis, capitalism and democracy, in C. Coulter and A. Nagle (eds), *Austerity Ireland: Neoliberal Crisis, Neoliberal Solutions*. Manchester: Manchester University Press.

Krugman, P. (2012). Europe's austerity madness, *New York Times*, 27 September. Available at: http://www.nytimes.com/2012/09/28/opinion/krugman-europes-austerity-madness.html. Accessed 7 January 2016.

Lapore, J. (2014). The disruption machine, *The New Yorker*, 23 July. Available at: http://www.newyorker.com/magazine/2014/06/23/the-disruption-machine. Accessed 5 July 2015.

Lynch, K. (2014). Economic inequality creates educational inequalities and class-based cuts to education, an engine for equality, subvert other rights and goods for the most vulnerable, *Village Magazine*, 8 February. Available at: http://www.villagemagazine.ie/index.php/2014/02/by-kathleen-lynch-economic-inequality-creates-educational-inequalities-and-class-based-cuts-to-education-an-engine-for-equality-subvert-other-rights-and-goods-for-the-most-vulnerable. Accessed 20 May 2015.

MacCraith, B. (2014). Opinion: It's time to get serious about STEM education in Ireland, *Silicon Republic*, 11 November. Available at: https://www.siliconrepublic.com/portfolio/2014/11/19/opinion-its-time-to-get-serious-about-stem-education-in-ireland. Accessed 3 March 2016.

MacFlynn, P. (2015). Youth unemployment: A broader view, *Nevin Economic Research Institute*, October. Available at: http://www.nerinstitute.net/blog/2015/10/29/youth-unemployment-a-broader-view/. Accessed 23 April 2016.

McCabe, C. (2015). False economy: The financialisation of Ireland and the roots of austerity, in C. Coulter and A. Nagle (eds). *Ireland under Austerity: Neoliberal Crisis. Neoliberal Solutions*. Manchester: Manchester University Press.

McCoy, S., and D. Byrne. (2011). 'The sooner the better I could get out of there': Barriers to higher education access in Ireland, *Irish Educational Studies* 30(2): 141–57.

McGuire, P. (2016). Technological universities: Are they really such a good idea?, *Irish Times*, 15 March. Available at: http://www.irishtimes.com/news/education/technological-universities-are-they-really-such-a-good-idea-1.2567757. Accessed 23 April 2016.

Mercille, J. (2014). The role of the media in fiscal consolidation programmes: The case of Ireland, *Cambridge Journal of Economics* 38: 281–300.

Mercille, J. (2015a). Students loaded with loans are less free to conduct their lives in the way they wish: It's a bad idea, *Journal.ie*, 21 December. Available at: http://www.thejournal.ie/author/julien-mercille-/3954/. Accessed 5 January 2016.

Mercille, J. (2015b). Students rising, *Broadsheet.ie*, 20 April. Available at: http://www.broadsheet.ie/2015/04/20/mercille-on-monday-students-rising/. Accessed 23 April 2016.

Mercille, J., and E. Murphy. (2015). The neoliberalization of Irish higher education under austerity, *Critical Sociology*. Available at: http://crs.sagepub.com/content/early/2015/10/07/0896920515607074.

Mooney, B. (2015). Focus on STEM subjects at school leads to high points for college, *Irish Times*, 17 August. Available at: http://www.irishtimes.com/news/education/minister-may-review-leaving-cert-maths-bonus-points-1.2314596. Accessed 2 October 2015.

Nagle, A. (2015). Ireland and the new economy. In C. Coulter and A. Nagle (eds), *Ireland under Austerity: Neoliberal Crisis, Neoliberal Solutions*. Manchester: Manchester University Press, 110–30.

NUIG (2014). *Irish Higher Education Institutes Partnership Leading a National Education Revolution*. Available at: http://www.nuigalway.ie/about-us/news-and-events/latest-news/irish-higher-education-institutes-partnership-leading-a-national-education-revolution.html. Accessed 4 July 2014.

O'Brien, C. (2016a). Funding cuts putting Irish third level sector under pressure as never before, *Irish Times*, 4 January, 8.

O'Brien, C. (2016b). Trinity College Dublin eyes up 'silicon docks' expansion, *Irish Times*, 19 April. Available at: http://www.irishtimes.com/news/education/trinity-college-dublin-eyes-up-silicon-docks-expansion-1.2615364. Accessed 20 April 2016.

O'Brien, C. (2016c). *Trinity's provost: 'Irish universities have been resilient but it isn't sustainable'*, *Irish Times*, 19 April. Available at: http://www.irishtimes.com/news/education/trinity-s-provost-irish-universities-have-been-resilient-but-it-isn-t-sustainable-1.2610916. Accessed 23 April 2016.

O'Brien, C. (2016d). DCU plans €230m expansion across four Dublin campuses, *Irish Times*, 4 May. Available at: http://www.irishtimes.com/news/education/dcu-plans-230m-expansion-across-four-dublin-campuses-1.2629183. Accessed 4 May 2016.

O'Connor, J. (2013). SIPTU's President Jack O'Connor's speech on the economy at ICTU conference. Available at: http://www.siptu.ie/media/pressreleases2013/fullstory_17410_en.html. Accessed 7 January 2016.

O'Dowd, L. (2012). Public intellectuals and the crisis: Accountability, democracy and market fundamentalism, in M. P. Corcoran and K. Lalor (eds), *Reflections on the Crisis: The Role of the Public Intellectual*. Dublin: Royal Irish Academy.

O'Grady, M. (2013). *Paper 10: Updated Analysis of Grade Inflation in the University Sector in Ireland (Including 2005–2009 data)*. Tralee. Available at: http://www.stopgradeinflation.ie/Universities_update_05-09.pdf.

Prensky, M. (2001). Digital natives, digital immigrants part 1, *On the Horizon* 89(5): 1–6.

Regan, A. (2016). Why austerity and structural reforms have had little to do with Ireland's economic recovery, *Social Europe*. Available at: https://www.socialeurope.eu/2016/02/why-austerity-and-structural-reforms-have-had-little-to-do-with-irelands-economic-recovery/. Accessed 3 February 2016.

RIA (2016). *Royal Irish Academy Advice Paper on the Future Funding of Higher Education in Ireland*. Dublin: Royal Irish Academy. Available at: https://www.ria.ie/sites/default/files/royal-irish-academy-advice-paper-on-the-future-funding-of-higher-education-in-ireland.pdf.

Rosinger, K. O., B. J. Taylor, L. Coco and S. Slaughter (2016). Organizational segmentation and the prestige economy: Deprofessionalization in high- and low-resource departments, *Journal of Higher Education* 87(1): 27–54.

SIPTU. (2015). *A Survey of Academic Staff on Working Conditions at Dublin City University*. Dublin. Available at: http://www.siptu.ie/media/media_19532_en.pdf.

Slaughter, S., and G. Rhoades. (2004). *Academic Capitalism and the New Economy: Markets, State, and Higher Education*. Baltimore, MD: JHU Press.

Smyth, E. (2009). Buying your way into college? Private tuition and the transition to higher education in Ireland, *Oxford Review of Education* 35(1): 1–22.

Social Justice Ireland. (2016). *Budget 2016 Analysis and Critique*. Dublin: Social Justice Ireland. Available at: http://www.socialjustice.ie/sites/default/files/attach/publication/4051/sjibudget2016analysis.pdf.

Walsh, J. (2013). The problem of Trinity College Dublin: A historical perspective on rationalisation in higher education in Ireland, *Irish Educational Studies* 33(1): 5–19.

Walsh, J., and A. Loxley. (2014). The Hunt Report and higher education policy in the Republic of Ireland: An international solution to an Irish problem?, *Studies in Higher Education* 40(6): 1128–45.

Walsh, S., D. Flannery and J. Cullinan. (2015). Geographic accessibility to higher education on the island of Ireland, *Irish Educational Studies* 34(1): 5–23.

White, B. (2014). The Sunday interview; Chris Horn: You may not be able to define an entrepreneur, but you'd recognise one if you saw one, *Sunday Business Post*, 4 May, 15.

Woolridge, A. (2005). The brains business, *The Economist*, 23 April. Available at: http://www.economist.com/node/4339960. Accessed 23 April 2016.

7

Greek Political Turbulence and Its Aftermath: A Lost Generation

Daphne Kyriaki-Manessi

Greece has been experiencing the consequences of an economic crisis since 2008, and every year the crisis deepens leaving more people unemployed and diminishing the funds spent on education. During the period 2009–2012, the GDP of Greece shrank by approximately 18 per cent. The following years (2013 and 2014) it continued to shrink by a further 6 per cent and 4 per cent respectively, thereby reaching a ten-year low (Trading Economics, 2016). This contraction is the largest in the history of the modern Greek economy in times of peace. In 2008 the budget deficit and sovereign debt reached unsustainable levels. By 2009 and 2010 Greece needed financial assistance, which was acquired by joint International Monetary Fund (IMF) and European Commission mechanisms. Greece was faced with the worst political and economic crisis since 1974, and tough reforms were enforced by the IMF and the European Commission as part of three consecutive bailout programmes (2010, 2012 and 2015).

All three bailout programmes had a serious impact on the finances of higher education as well as on salaries and resources for universities and higher education institutions. However, most importantly, the economic environment had an adverse effect on employment. The economic crisis led to the worsening of employment conditions and an increase in unemployment. The unemployment rate in Greece rose to 26.5 per cent in 2014, while youth unemployment (fifteen to twenty-four years old) went up to 52.4 per cent (OECD, 2016b). The prospects for university graduates now look better, since the Organization of Economic Cooperation and Development (OECD) has estimated a 19.4 per cent unemployment rate for graduates of tertiary education (OECD, 2016b). Nevertheless, that unemployment rate is deeply concerning and is likely to have a long-term economic and social impact.

The impact of the economic crisis

In this economic environment, Greece has had a very low budget for education. General government expenditure on education as a proportion of GDP is among the lowest in the European Union (EU). For 2013 government expenditure for education amounted to 4.5 per cent, whilst the EU average rose to 5.0 per cent. In addition, the lowering of GDP by approximately 28 per cent during the period 2009–2014 has in fact created a reduction in real funds for education. Greek authorities report a 36 per cent drop in funding for education during the 2009–2015 period (Hellenic Government, 2015). Finally, the proportion of spending on education out of a total public expenditure is the smallest in the EU, at 7.6 per cent compared to an EU average of 10.2 per cent (Directorate-General of Education and Culture (DG EAC), 2016). Furthermore, Greece spends only 0.8 per cent of its GDP on research and development, which is well below the 2.5 per cent average for OECD countries. The largest share of research and development expenditure (around 37 per cent) occurs in universities whose links with industry are actually weak in Greece (OECD, 2016a). This weak link has been identified through the evaluation procedures of higher education institutions in Greece, and is considered to be one of the key elements in the failure to connect education to the labour market and thus as contributing to the unemployment of young graduates.

Higher education institutions are affected by the social and political contexts within which they are continuously evolving. A university is an open system in constant dialogue with society and in Greece's case in constant dialogue with the state. Universities and higher education institutions generally are publicly funded and are in effect state universities. The economic crisis and the stringent mechanisms related to financial support that have been imposed upon Greece (Koulouris, Moniarou-Papaconstantinou and Kyriaki-Manessi, 2014) have taken a deep toll on both its economy and its society and had a great impact on all institutions of higher education. As the state is responsible for providing financial resources and personnel to all such institutions, substantial cuts have been made over the past five years. Budget cuts regarding regular expenditures, funds for covering the cost per student, utilities, research funding, and so on, have resulted in a tremendous stain on regular day-to-day operations. In addition, although personnel for higher education are selected independently by the institutions themselves, they are subject to the authorization of the central government. Similarly, ministerial authorities are responsible for their salaries, in accordance with their status as employees within the broader public sector (Koulouris, Moniarou-Papaconstantinou and Kyriaki-Manessi, 2014). Salary reductions imposed by the Greek government at the end of 2012 on all government employees impacted most significantly on academic staff. Enforced restrictions on the recruitment of new academic staff worsened the situation and created higher student/professor ratios and an overload of administrative tasks.

Since 2009 there has been a reduction in faculty positions, which reached its lowest point in 2013. The freeze on all hiring and the non-replacement of retired faculty members have depleted departments still further. During this period, due to radical and continuous pension reforms, a large number of public employees (including faculty members) rushed into retirement. A sudden wave of retirements in 2013 following the signing of the second bailout left higher education institutions with a fraction of their academic staff.

The following table (Figure 7.1) clearly illustrates the shrinkage of academic staff of the Technological Educational Institute of Athens (TEI of A) over the past five years

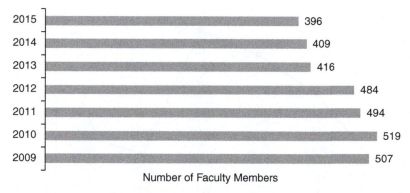

Figure 7.1 Decrease of academic staff within the TEI of A (2009–2015)

of recession. The TEI of A suffered an overall 23.7 per cent reduction in academic staff from 2009 to 2015 (data derived from the Institute's External Evaluation Report, Dec. 2015).

Interestingly enough, funded research has increased over the years of the economic crisis. Figure 7.2 below presents the actual funds per year which came to the TEI of A over the past five years. Although Greece spends less on research and development compared to the rest of Europe, most research programmes occur within higher education institutions. Projects funded by the National Strategic Reference Framework (NSRF) 2007–2013 resulted in universities and technological educational institutions providing a reliable source of incoming funds.

More than in the years prior to the crisis, faculty members did get involved in securing research projects. One should consider this as a positive effect of the economic crisis. It should be mentioned, though, that the complex bureaucracy imposed by EU research-funded projects – the continuously changing Greek legislation regarding the management of funds, the overtaxation of those funds and the never-ending delays – has placed a tremendous burden on these activities (Koulouris, Moniarou-Papaconstantinou and Kyriaki-Manessi, 2014). It has also acted as a restraining mechanism on the possibility of creating development, research and professional jobs. This activity is represented in Figure 7.3. Data were collected from the Institute's Evaluation Report (TEI of Athens, Quality Assurance Committee, 2015) and Research Committee Annual Reports (TEI of Athens, Research Committee, 2015).

Figure 7.2 illustrates the noticeable increase in research projects and their corresponding funds in 2011 and 2012, which reached a peak in 2013. There is a decline in 2014 as many national projects funded by the EU (National Strategic Reference Framework (NSRF) 2007–2013) ended the previous year. However, the number of projects in 2014 is still higher than in 2010, and again increased in 2015, although the new national project (new NSRF) has not yet been launched. We can assume that research activity has increased as a result of faculty members' efforts to boost incoming funds. One should also consider this as a positive result of the financial crisis and as an opportunity arising from the economic constraints.

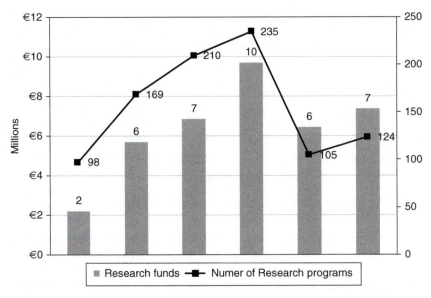

Figure 7.2 Research activity within the TEI of A (2009–2015)

The reform agenda

Financial pressures on non-academic expenditures have led institutions of higher education to operate with a minimum of resources. As a result, institutions have explored all possibilities for raising funds – mainly through the funding of research projects (international, European and state ones) and the exploitation of existing infrastructures, such as facilities, labs and so on. These practices have had some results and have actually boosted research activity. Overall, however, usage of facilities and infrastructure has had very limited results.

While some countries in Southern Europe have addressed these issues by increasing, or even imposing for the first time, tuition fees (Douglas, 2010), Greece has not followed this route. Education in Greece continues to be tuition free, at all levels of the system, including higher education. The issue of imposing fees is a hot topic on the political agenda. The right to equal access to all levels of education is included in the Greek constitution (Greek Parliament, 2008) and is considered to be one of the fundamentals of a democratic society.

The recently opened (January 2016) 'National Dialogue for Education' by the Greek Ministry of Education is incorporating all major issues regarding higher education, including the discussion of fees in tertiary education (see Ministry of Education, 2016). The 'Dialogue' deals not only with issues regarding the framework and basic axes of higher education in the country but also with finances, accessibility, the influx of refugees and the role of existing structures. It also aims at reshaping the map of higher education in Greece. It is no coincidence that all issues regarding education are currently under review and that a long postponed discussion on its predicament has now been initiated – a reflection of the importance of the concerns and issues that have long awaited serious discussion regarding the underlying issues. What is most encouraging is that the government itself has started a dialogue and is looking at the problem in a holistic manner. Whilst this discussion is still in its early stages, the axes have emerged and there seems to be a common understanding that things really need to change. Higher education has a key role to play in this deliberative process and is itself central to the reform process.

These changes are not independent of what is happening in the country in general. Rather, they are a reflection of the general financial strain and the geopolitical turmoil of the area we live in. In this respect, one has to point out that the issue of imposing fees at the graduate level (leading to a master's degree) was addressed and discussed extensively. The latter is already common practice in most higher education institutions, in which the assumption is that a master's degree is beyond the absolute right of all but rather a choice of the few to further educate themselves. In addition to this, the oddity of PhD students paying no fees at all can be explained only by the fact that there are many fewer of these students than master's students; thus, the imposition of fees would produce no substantial income for the university and it is therefore in its interests not to disturb the principle of no fees at this level.

Furthermore, one should also take into account that the country's significant shortage of funds is leading the Dialogue to address issues regarding the actual geographic and thematic dispersion of institutions of higher education generally across the country. The relative cost to the state of maintaining a large number of departments in various smaller or larger cities, islands and remote areas has been expressed and is being debated.

This is not the first attempt at such a dialogue. In 2013 the Ministry of Education created a plan (named *Plan Athina*) in an attempt to minimize the number of higher education departments from 534 to 384 and the number of actual institutions from forty to thirty-four. In this context, many departments, particularly in the technological sector, were merged to form a larger department or institution that could be financially sustainable in the long term. *Plan Athina* (now termed *Athina 1*) in anticipation of a forthcoming *Plan Athina 2*, was not welcomed by the universities or the technological institutions, and its impact was minimal. The plan was criticized for the lack of real evaluation criteria and the uneven treatment between universities and technological institutions. At the end of *Athina 1* – in late 2013 – Greece still had 440 departments of higher education in higher education institutions, with 271 located in universities and 169 in technological educational institutions (State Gazette, Ministry of Education, 2014). Meanwhile, the aim of reducing the actual number of higher education institutions (both university and technological institutions) from forty to thirty-four resulted in reducing the number to thirty-eight, thereby closing down two universities (the University of Central Greece and the University of Western Greece) (Ministry of Education. Greece, 2013).

Athina 1 reduced the number of higher education departments by 123, with a much stronger impact on the technological institutions, but still did not meet its target. *Athina 1*'s main objective was to upgrade higher education institutions by rationalizing scientific fields and strengthening leading departments and institutions, making them more innovative and creating centres of excellence (Ministry of Education. Greece, 2013). However, there is a lot to be implemented and reach the aforementioned objective.

At the same time, it is widely predicted, that the shortfall and decline in financial resources for public education will continue in the foreseeable future. As a result the 'map' of higher education in Greece is again under review. The amount of funds available for public education is small, and the more it is divided, the smaller the portions become. Indeed the funds are barely sufficient to sustain the system as a whole. Difficult decisions are required regarding, for example, the quality of the infrastructure and the critical mass of human resources required to boost research and educational activities. In this sense, the economic crisis is resulting in the stripping away of all the supposedly excess departments which are located in a variety of smaller cities at the Greek periphery and the consolidation human resources in larger cores that are deemed to be more effective and that create strong foci for research activity.

However, while several voices addressed the issue within the National Dialogue (Gavroglou, Georgatos and Makatsori, 2016), there no definite plan has been produced as yet. Legislative act 4009/2011 (State Gazette, 2011) and 4076/2012 (State Gazette, 2012) mostly targeted the organization and governance of higher education institutions along with quality assurance issues relating to key elements. As a result, during the period 2012–2015 external evaluations of both universities and technological institutions were carried out by the Hellenic Quality Assurance Authority. In 2014 new organizational charts were drawn up and university councils were established.

Law 4327/2015 seems to suggest a re-examination of issues relating to the governance and functioning of the higher education sector – including the powers of university councils – is in order. The reinstated time limits for retaining student status are expected to have an impact on evaluation criteria: indicators of number of years of study, ratio of professors to students, overload of administrative work and so on) (Hellenic Parliament, 2015) Furthermore, new legislation regarding higher education is in process, and the aforementioned Dialogue is expected to feed into this legislative process. The Memorandum of Understanding of August 2015 includes higher education reform and points to legislative changes which were to be made by June 2016 (Directorate-General of Education and Culture (DG EAC), 2016).

At the same time, the Greek government continues to produce, on an annual basis, the lists of all universities and technological institutions and their respective departments and to designate the number of incoming students for the next academic year (2016–17) through the statewide exams taking place in late May (Panhellenic exams). Increased numbers of students – often exceeding the capabilities of the hosting institutions' infrastructure – impose an additional strain. The aforementioned Dialogue for Education is also exploring solutions and ways for changing the methods of access to higher education. This is expected to relieve the stress for candidates, establish fair evaluation criteria and lead to a re-examination of the numbers of incoming students on the basis of infrastructure capabilities, socio-economic conditions and relevance to the demands of the job market.

The government's intention with the legislative acts of 2011 and 2012 was to better connect the academic sector with regional and statewide development needs.

However, this is not something that can happen overnight, and it continues to be one of the aims of the new Dialogue for Education. This is a crucial issue as the uncontrolled number of incoming students, especially at professional schools, has contributed to the increase in the number of unemployed graduates and has fed a growing 'brain drain'.

Graduate unemployment and the 'brain drain'

When *The Guardian* published an article last year entitled 'Young, Gifted and Greek: Generation G – the World's Biggest Brain Drain' (Smith, 2015), nobody in Greece was surprised. The 200,000 plus young university graduates who have left the country just over the past five years constitute the largest emigration wave since the 1950s. A similar article entitled '"Brain Drain": Greece's Future Is Walking Away', by Ivana Kottasova, published in June 2015 on the website *CNNMoney* said it all. Table 7.1 draws on data from the Hellenic Statistical Authority (2015).

To this grim picture we can add older age groups, as shown in Table 7.2:

What is clear from this evidence is the dramatic growth of emigration in 2011, 2012 and 2013, with the highest movement in 2012 but with a strong flow continuing in 2014 (see Figure 7.3).

Moreover, while the 'brain drain' is been most marked in the twenty-five to twenty-nine age group, it is by no means restricted to this group and remains a significant factor among older graduates (see Figure 7.4).

It should be noted that the professions have been hit particularly hard by the recession, and it is estimated that migration rates are higher among these occupational groups. While earlier emigration waves, in the 1950s, 1960s and 1970s, tended to involve those with lower education profiles, the post-2008 emigration surge has

Table 7.1 Graduates in the 25–34 age group leaving Greece in the period 2008–2014

Age Group	2008	2009	2010	2011	2012	2013	2014	Total per annum
25–29	10.434	10.029	13.998	20.210	24.435	23.812	18.688	121.606
30–34	5.931	5.819	8.962	14.480	18.583	17.810	13.974	85.559

Table 7.2 Graduates in the 35–54 age group leaving Greece in the period 2008–2014

Age Group	2008	2009	2010	2011	2012	2013	2014	Total per annum
35–39	3.662	3.925	5.139	10.117	13.107	12.274	9.662	57.886
40–44	2.894	2.761	4.499	7.560	11.136	10.185	7.981	47.016
45–49	2.077	2.044	2.732	5.904	9.034	8.130	6.415	36.336
50–54	1.393	1.651	2.381	4.864	7.302	6.689	5.867	30.147

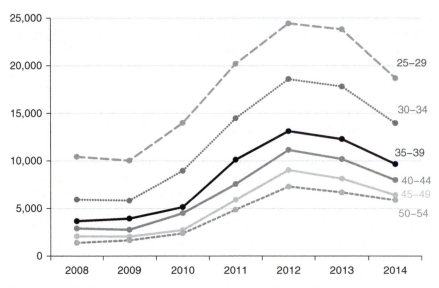

Figure 7.3 'Brain drain' from Greece by age group (2008–2014)

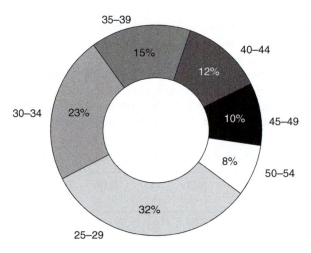

Figure 7.4 Share of 'brain drain' from Greece by age group (2008–2014)

consisted almost entirely of tertiary education graduates. For example, migration is particularly high among young engineers since construction has been one of the areas hardest hit by the economic recession. In addition, doctors, nurses, computer scientists and other graduates of professional schools are also a significant part of the migration wave.

In order to ascertain how the 'brain drain' is impacting at precise points within the higher education sector, we examine in the following section the situation within a particular department. Although not among those departments with the highest migration rates, it is particularly vulnerable given that it lies within the technological domain.

The post-2008 graduate experience

When I started researching to write this chapter, I already had a survey underway relating to graduates within my department (Library Science and Information Systems, Technological Educational Institute of Athens). The survey was designed to ascertain the employment opportunities available to these graduates and the professional pathways undertaken during one of the major financial crises in the country. My survey targeted those who had graduated during the past six years, thus highlighting the crisis years.

It is important to bear in mind that before the crisis (i.e., before 2008), 96 per cent of our graduates found work in their field within the first year of graduation. After 2008, and increasingly over the past five years, there has been an observable increase in graduate 'brain drain', unemployment and contract work, and an observable reduction in levels of remuneration. Overall, Greece now has very low levels of employability for recent tertiary education graduates, at only 47.4 per cent in 2014, in comparison with an EU average of 80.5 per cent (Directorate-General of Education and Culture (DG EAC), 2016).

An analysis of statistical, financial and other official documents regarding education data for Greece was conducted as part of a literature review in an effort to explain the general socio-economic setting of the country. In addition, legislation, discussion papers and policy documents relating to the work of the Ministry of Education were included. Indicative data and field research methodologies were employed as a case study of the Technological Educational Institute of Athens in order to report the imposed cuts in expenditure and personnel in higher education. Furthermore, in order to provide an indicative account of the effects of unemployment among young graduates of tertiary education and the consequent 'brain drain' a questionnaire was developed. This was uploaded to the Web using open source software (*Google docs*) in the Spring semester of the academic year 2015–16, and was concluded in February 2016. It targeted those who graduated between June 2009 and June 2015.

The first part of the questionnaire asked for participants' demographic characteristics such as gender, age and year of graduation, along with educational data such as knowledge of languages, communication and information technologies, other degrees and so forth. The second part focused on employment details, plans and ambitions, and the respondents' educational career and professional trajectories. An open-ended question was also included for remarks regarding employability and related issues. The participants were asked to respond to questions on a 5-point Likert scale that ranged from 1 (negative, or not at all) to 5 (positive or very much), or to choose an answer for multiple choice questions, or to respond to 'yes' and 'no' questions. A total of 125 graduates returned the questionnaire. No questionnaires were excluded as all of them were complete and valid.

Figures 7.5, 7.6 and 7.7 present the demographic characteristics of the graduates: age distribution, educational qualifications and other credentials.

The twenty-two to twenty-four age group, which is the most likely age for completing a bachelor's, accounted for 86 per cent. The majority of respondents across all age groups (88 per cent) were bachelor's graduates; 8.8 per cent also had a master's degree; and another 13.2 per cent had obtained a second bachelor's (see Figure 7.6).

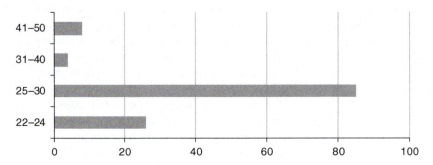

Figure 7.5 Age distribution among respondents

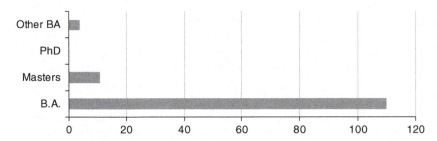

Figure 7.6 Degrees obtained by respondents

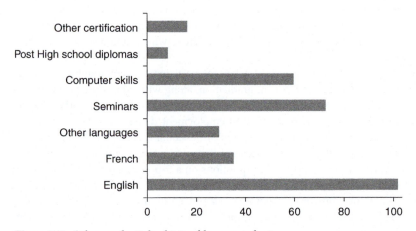

Figure 7.7 Other credentials obtained by respondents

Graduates tend not to rely exclusively on their first degree, but complement this with languages, information technology skills, additional field seminars and forms of training (see Figure 7.7).

Clearly the graduates who were surveyed constitute a highly qualified labour force of which a significant proportion nevertheless remains unemployed or underemployed. Figure 7.8 shows the pattern of labour force participation among the respondents.

Only 55 per cent of respondents reported were working full-time, with a further 16 per cent employed only part-time. Part-time employment is usually not a choice but is due to the lack of full-time employment. A significant proportion of respondents, therefore, were underemployed in terms of their work status.

Moreover, among the 72 per cent who were employed on either a full-time or part-time basis, only 46 per cent were employed in areas of work relating to their field of study (i.e., information science). The majority (i.e., 54 per cent) were employed in areas of the labour market – chiefly in the food or hospitality industry – that often demand fewer skills or a lower skills base. Although not underemployed in terms of time, they are likely therefore to be underemployed terms of the skills required (see Figure 7.9).

Given the high unemployment rate among young people nationally – 24.5 per cent for 2012; 27.5 per cent for 2013; and 26.5 per cent for 2014 (Eurostat, 2016) – the

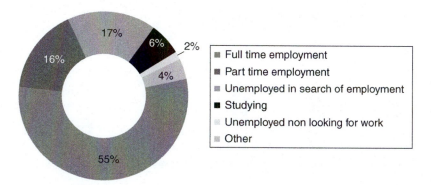

Figure 7.8 Labour force participation among the respondents

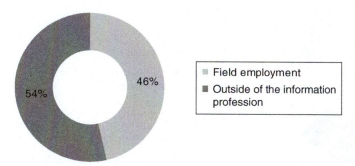

Figure 7.9 Proportion of respondents employed within and outside their field of study

situation of the respondents is better than might be expected. However it should be borne in mind that a significant proportion (just over 78 per cent) of those employed are on fixed-term contracts ranging from a few months to two years. Contract work is regarded as a means of providing young graduates a means of entry into the labour market and some initial work experience, but is usually lower paid, lacks job security and does not allow for long-term career planning and development either by the employee or the hiring organization.

For employees, contract work makes for a difficult and stressful working situation and a sense of insecurity regarding the future. Figure 7.10 presents the satisfaction levels of the respondents with particular reference to remuneration.

Not surprisingly remuneration is one of the reasons respondents gave for seeking alternative employment. But the most significant factor would seem to be the desire among many of them to gain employment in an area more closely related to their field of study (see Figure 7.11).

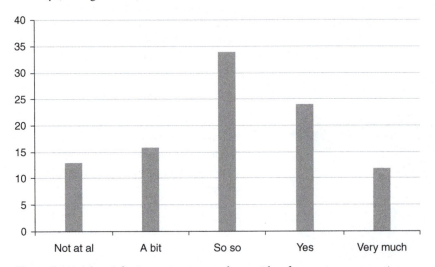

Figure 7.10 Job satisfaction among respondents with reference to remuneration

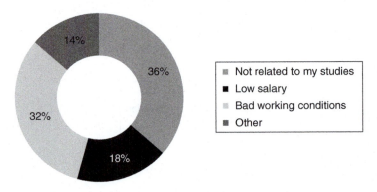

Figure 7.11 Factors affecting search for alternative employment

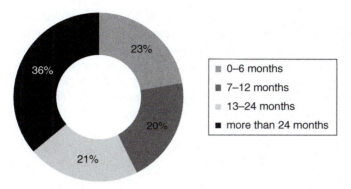

Figure 7.12   Time spent by respondents searching for employment

The search for employment can be an extremely time-consuming and protracted process, which is discouraging to those seeking employment and which depletes the dynamics of the labour force. Thirty-six per cent of all respondents had spent more than two years looking for employment; 21 per cent had been looking for work for between one and two years; and 20 per cent spent between six and twelve months looking for work (see Figure 7.12).

For this particular group of graduates, obtaining employment in their specialized field and within a reasonable period of time after graduation proved an extremely daunting and arduous task. It required the acquisition of additional skills, qualifications and credentials; repeated job applications; and the willingness to accept job insecurity and – very often – low salaries. Added to this is the fact that many of the respondents are likely to have had other family members who were facing the same hardships. Traditional family support networks were therefore not always available or were already under considerable strain. Such was the situation they found themselves in that 13 per cent of the respondents had decided to seek work in Canada or the United States, thereby leaving Greece depleted of its most educated and better qualified labour force. Given that the vast majority of respondents were under thirty years of age – and that a significant proportion were either unemployed, underemployed or were potential or actual emigrants – we can without exaggeration characterize them as members of a lost generation.

Conclusion

The reform agenda for higher education in Greece is much talked about but requires urgent and coordinated action. Previous attempts at reform have had some results, but much still needs to be done if we are to reclaim at least some of the lost generation and ensure that the skills and talents of future generations are not similarly squandered. In spite of the many strains and hardship that the economic crisis has occasioned, it could yet provide an opportunity for achieving a more efficient, innovative and focused system of higher education. There is a pressing need across the higher education sector to target the available human and infrastructure resources through the creation of dedicated centres of teaching and research that would provide continuity and develop strong and vibrant links with the labour market. The financial constraints are severe, but depriving higher education of the basic elements that will enable it to meet the necessary quality standards is a sure way of stalling recovery and denying young people a future. Unless urgently and seriously tackled, the 'brain drain' among young graduates in particular will have an irreversible effect on the socio-economic fabric of Greece.

References

Directorate-General of Education and Culture (DG EAC). (2016). *Education and Training Monitor 2015, Greece*. Luxembourg: Publications Office of the European Union, 2015. doi:10.2766/872466.

Douglas, J. (2010). *Higher education budgets and the global recession: Tracking varied national responses and their consequences*. Research and Occasional Paper Series: CSHE. 4.10.

Eurostat. (2016). *Unemployment statistics*. Eurostat: Statistics explained, http://ec.europa.eu/eurostat/statistics-explained/index.php/ Unemployment_statistics#Youth_unemployment_trends.

Gavroglou, K., S. Georgatos and D. Makatsori. (2016). *The Unified Area for Tertiary Education*. Retrieved from National Dialogue for Education, http://dialogos.minedu. gov.gr/wp-content/uploads/2016/03/eniaios_xwros_tritovathmias_kai_erevna.pdf.

Greek Parliament. (2008). Greek Constitution.

Hellenic Government. (2015). *National Reform Plan: Educational Reform* [in Greek], European Commission, http://ec.europa.eu/europe2020/pdf/csr2015/ nrp2015_greece_el.pdf.

Hellenic Statistical Authority. (2015). *Estimated Migrantion Movements Per Year (Men And Women) by Age Groups 2008–2014*. Hellenic Statistical Authority, http://www.statistics. gr/el/statistics/-/publication/SPO15/-

Kottasova, I. (2015). Brain drain: Greece's future is walking away. *CNNMoney*, 24 June, http://money.cnn.com/2015/06/24/news/economy/greece-europe-brain-drain/.

Koulouris, A., V. Moniarou-Papaconstantinou and D. Kyriaki-Manessi. (2014). Austerity measures in Greece and their impact on higher education, *Procedia – Social and Behavioral Sciences* 147: 518–26. doi:10.1016/j.sbspro.2014.07.147.

Ministry of Education. (2016). *National Dialogue for Education*. Dialogos, Greek Ministry of Education, https://dialogos.minedu.gov.gr/.

Ministry of Education. Greece. (2013). *Athina Plan (Shedio Athina)*. Greek Ministry of Education, http://www.minedu.gov.gr/publications/docs2013/130305_telikh_protash_ athhna.pdf.

OECD. (2016a). *Basic Statistics of Greece, 2014*. OECD Economic Surveys: Greece 2016. Paris: OECD Publishing, http://dx.doi.org/10.1787/eco_surveys-grc-2016-1-en.

OECD. (2016b). OECD Data, Unemployment rates by education level, https://data.oecd. org/unemp/unemployment-rates-by-education-level.htm#indicator-chart.

Smith, H. (2015). Young, gifted and Greek: Generation G – the world's biggest brain drain, *The Guardian*, 19 January, http://www.theguardian.com/world/2015/jan/19/ young-talented-greek-generation-g-worlds-biggest-brain-drain.

State Gazette. (2011). Law 4009/2011. *FEK 195 A/6-9-2011*.

State Gazette. (2012). Law 4076. *FEK A 159. 10/8/2012*.

State Gazette, Ministry of Education. (2014). *F.253.1/46539/B6, FEK7 68, vol. B*, March 28, http://edu.klimaka.gr/arxeio/nomothesia-fek/fek-768-2014-arihtmos-eisakteoi-tritovathmia-ekpaidevsh-klimaka.pdf.

TEI of Athens, Quality Assurance Committee. (2015). *Internal Evaluation Report 2009*, http://modip.teiath.gr/wp-content/uploads/2015/12/10.12.15_%CE%99%CE%94%CE%A1%CE%A5%CE%9C%CE%91%CE%A4%CE%99%CE%9A%CE%97-%CE%95%CE%9A%CE%98%CE%95%CE%A3%CE%97-%CE%A4%CE%95%CE%99_%CE%91_.pdf.

TEI of Athens, Research Committee. (2015). *Annual Report 2013–2014*, http://www.teiath.gr/userfiles/khitas/documents/2015/eee/apologismos_eee_2013_2014.pdf.

Trading Economics. (2016). *Greece GDP 1960–2016*, http://www.tradingeconomics.com/greece/gdp.

8

Attempts at Reshaping Lithuanian Higher Education: Austerity in Disguise

Almantas Samalavičius

In contrast to other (mostly Western or so-called Old) European countries that experienced an impressive wave of student unrest over the last ten years, there were actually no mass protests against the continuous shift in largely unpopular state policies in Lithuania. Since 2009 such policies have been aimed at transforming higher education into an assuredly neo-liberalist mode. A repertoire of austerity measures has been implemented by several succeeding governments with seemingly different ideological orientations, despite the fact that neither society at large nor students and professors seem to be satisfied with the current course of action. Those uninitiated into local political culture might be inclined to assume that the lack of public protest against state policies means that Lithuanian higher education is not suffering from any serious controversies, or that the system is performing, if not as well as it might, then at least satisfactorily. Such an assumption would be unfounded. The fact that the country has not yet witnessed a large wave of popular discontent taking the form of mass rallies or continuous protests – in a form, for example, of the 'Occupy' movement that emerged in various parts of the globe – does not mean that the present neo-liberal trend towards reshaping the Lithuanian system of higher education and its institutions is hailed and supported by the academic community, students and other segments of society. Far from it.

Recent policy developments were and continue to be criticized by a large number of higher education analysts, leading academics and public intellectuals, but dissenting opinions on how Lithuanian higher education should be transformed and managed for society's benefit have so far made very little impact, if any, on state policies that continue to follow the neo-liberal agenda. While agreeing with Chris Newfield (2008: 272) that university education should not and 'cannot be captured in economic terms', I fully accept Philip G. Altbach's (1997: 333) diagnosis that 'increases in student numbers have not been accompanied by growth in the professoriate, and the conditions for teaching and learning are declining. Few jobs are available for younger scholars, and research funding has been cut or at least has not kept up with costs.' This observation – made before the turn of the millennium and with reference to the Western European context – now applies to the general situation in Eastern Europe and, more specifically, to the situation within Lithuania.

This particular chapter focuses on the Lithuanian case in an attempt to analyse how austerity measures have been applied to Lithuania's higher education system and the form these measures have taken, for example, imposing repeated cuts in public expenditure on higher education, forcing universities to merge or in some cases close, making them compete endlessly for public funds, pushing individual scholars into a competitive game of winners and losers and undermining the values traditionally associated with a university culture by inculcating an ethos more appropriate to business corporations. Though the very notion of 'austerity' remains largely outside public discourse and is often avoided in local political vocabulary, its recognizable measures are systematically applied to institutions of higher education. The state has in effect refused to be the sole provider of funds for higher education, demanding that these institutions seek alternative sources of funding in order to ensure their existence. This situation is by no means exclusive to Lithuania. As Boaventura de Sousa Santos (2011: 10) has observed, 'for the last thirty years, the university's institutional crisis in the great majority of countries was provoked or induced by the loss of priority of the university as a public good and by the consequent financial drought and disinvestment in public universities.' Nevertheless, the Lithuanian case has some notable and distinctive features.

The assimilation of neo-liberal reform

As soon as Lithuania gained its independence in 1990 – thereby triggering the fall of the Soviet empire – its economic and social system underwent rapid and undeniably epochal transformation that had a huge impact on many sectors of society that previously belonged exclusively to the sphere of state regulation. The privatization of former state property at the time was seen both as a goal and a tool for reshaping the outdated, largely compromised and ineffective 'planned economy' that had stopped working long before the national resurgence movement that finally brought independence had taken root. A large and ideologically driven programme of privatization was carried out with enormous enthusiasm through the introduction of a market economy into most sectors of social life. The market in those early transition days was generally seen as a magic instrument capable of creating – almost ex nihilo – prosperity and welfare for all. As a result the privatization of former state property that started soon after the declaration of independence was in the main chaotic, ill-prepared, poorly managed and sometimes openly corrupt.

For a number of years these processes had very little impact – if any – on higher education and its institutions. Higher education continued to exist without any significant institutional or structural changes. Indeed, in many ways it began to stagnate: universities and other institutions of higher education continued to be poorly funded, academics were largely underpaid and many younger and promising faculty members as well as more ambitious doctoral students left the academy in search of more rewarding commercial activities and business employment. Those who opted to continue their careers in higher education had either to settle for a meagre and marginalized existence, combining teaching and research with a number of other part-time jobs, or gain employment in several institutions of higher education at the same time. For some, teaching in three or four state institutions was the only viable means of maintaining a satisfactory standard of living.

During this early post-Soviet period, a number of specialized institutions of higher learning – previously called 'institutes' or 'academies' – changed their academic 'brand' to that of university in the hope of gaining greater social and intellectual capital and institutional prestige (Samalavičius, 2003). (Throughout the Soviet period Lithuania had only one university – Vilnius University – that in the early post-war years was renamed after a local the Communist icon, Vincas Mickevicius Kapsukas.) A few private universities eventually came into being and, though they grew in number, they remained relatively small and their employees – though generally enjoying a better income than the faculty of state colleges and universities – were far from being overpaid. The first post-Soviet decade also witnessed an expansion of higher education through the transformation of former technical and vocational schools (providing three-year, post-secondary education) into four-year colleges providing higher education. For some time universities as well as other institutions of higher education were fully financed by the state, but as the funding mechanisms diversified and students who failed to gain a place on courses that were publicly funded had to rely increasingly on their own private resources or on banks loans.

Because of these and other factors some ten universities and almost forty colleges providing higher education finally became fierce competitors fighting endlessly for state provisions. Since the controversial 2009 reforms and the introduction of so-called student vouchers, some universities have been able to expand their study programmes, while other programmes have been forced to shrink or shut down because of unprofitability. These tendencies suggest that Lithuanian politicians and university administrators alike have fallen under the spell of neo-liberalism: 'as a form of public pedagogy and cultural politics neoliberalism casts all dimensions of life in terms of market rationality' (Giroux and Samalavičius, 2016: 12). The principles of Darwinian competition – already deeply established within the UK and US higher education systems – now inform and shape the Lithuanian academic context and have been assimilated into its evolving reform agenda (see Geiger, 2004: 133).

Shifts in funding policy

Since 2000, when the Lithuanian parliament adopted its Law on Higher Education, a further source of higher education funding has been established: a fixed amount of tuition costs paid by the students themselves. Prior to the introduction of the voucher system about half of the students – those whose grades were lower than average – had to pay this fee (Želvys, 2013: 11). At the time it was relatively small and more or less affordable for the majority of students or their families (being equal to 1000–1040 litas, i.e., approximately 280 euros, per year). As Jonas Balčiūnas and Aušra Turčinskaitė-Balčiūnienė argue,

> To the student, it was more convenient to deal directly with the institution, while the institution acquired the right to take in as many students as it wanted. This

was particularly important when the number of students declined. Seeking to attract them, the required qualifications and the cost were constantly reduced. Conditions for study were created for those who had finished their general education with poor grades. (2015: 40)

This situation came to be interpreted by some influential political parties as outdated and inefficient. Similarly, a number of researchers and analysts argued the need for some form of private funding of university studies. Zita Tamašauskienė, Algis Šileika and Fausta Smolenskienė (2008: 182), for example, contended that there was a clear choice between increasing public expenditure on higher education and attracting more private funds. Since the state was – as they saw it – unable to bear the full cost of higher education and research, it would be necessary to rely more heavily on private sources of funding in order to ensure quality while at the same time widening participation. On the basis of their analysis they proposed that 'expenditure on higher education should be connected to a review of student fees and an increase in the availability of student loans.'

Responding to growing popular and political concern about the future of higher education – and to the kinds of analyses being developed by, for example, Tamašauskienė, Šileika and Smolenskienė – the Lithuanian Ministry of Education and Science drafted a project proposal in 2007 entitled *Reform of Higher Education: Financing the Studies*. The concerns and issues highlighted in this proposal were echoed throughout the parliamentary election of 2008. Both major political parties claimed that, although the state was granting more funds to the higher education sector over time, higher education remained inadequately funded, particularly so, since the existing financial regulations demanded an increase in student numbers at a time when financial resources per student were falling (Babravičius and Dzemyda, 2012). The principles of future reform had been discussed and drafted by the Liberal Movement as early as 2006, and the concept was based on establishing a student voucher (analogous to the one existing in the sector of public secondary education). A further move was made in 2007 when an agreement between the main parliamentary parties regarding guidelines for the reform of Lithuania's higher education was reached.

The introduction of student vouchers had serious implications in that money moving with each student who received state support weakened some universities (namely those with study programmes which failed to attract a sufficient number of voucher holders). As Burton R. Clark had earlier observed,

> subsidy by means of grants to individual students strengthens the hands of consumers: it helps more of them to come into the market and choose among institutions. This method of spending state funds is the antithesis of institutional aid, where monies go directly to institutions in either block or restricted form. Institutional subsidy strengthens the place of institutions in the consumer market, freeing them somewhat from the dependency on consumers. (1986: 170)

In the Lithuanian context this shift in policy meant that smaller and regional universities became more financially vulnerable immediately after the voucher reform was implemented and their futures became uncertain.

During the first post-Soviet decade the number of students entering university was constantly growing, and this process reached its climax in the year 2000 after which it began to decline (Želvys, 2013: 12). This decrease in student numbers meant that under the new system fewer students required vouchers and that the state was therefore able to reduce its expenditure. As Rimantas Želvys has noted,

> the main motif while minimizing the number of students whose education was covered by the state is the annually decreasing number of students occurring for demographic reasons. Of course, one has to bear in mind that when student vouchers were introduced the price of many study programs went up, thus the rise in study costs performed a sort of regulative function and because of it the number of those individuals willing to pay for studies on their own allocations decreased. Institutions of higher education can theoretically regulate the price of studies for those willing to pay from their own resources. But practically they are constrained, because when they announce prices that are lower than those established by the state the state takes actions to reduce the value of the state voucher. (2013: 13)

Thus, the policies relating to the development of higher education after the introduction of the voucher system have been subject to well-grounded criticism. In the words of one of its most persistent critics, Vytautas Daujotis,

> the 2009 higher education reforms have had one clearly visible result – the sharp increase in the flow of students from Lithuania. Students seeking cross-border education migrate to countries with more equitable higher education systems than Lithuania's. Many graduates of Lithuanian secondary schools, hesitating over their chances to gain admission to fee-free higher education, apply for admissions both at home and to foreign universities. If both admissions are approved, they usually prefer cross-border education ... Studying abroad will always be beneficial to the student. Will it be beneficial to their home country, which has denied equity to them and treated them as surplus people not qualified for the state orders for specialists? (2015: 82)

This process can be characterized as a 'brain drain'. It is a process that in Lithuania can be clearly traced back to the introduction of student vouchers in 2009.

The rise of entrepreneurialism

During the first post-Soviet decade and even later, business did not take an interest in Lithuanian higher education as this sector seemed to be outside the realm of significant financial profits. However, in recent years leaders of various business structures have realized that institutions of higher education, associated with the production and distribution of knowledge, possess considerable economic potential. Abstract discourse urging universities to establish closer relations with business and industry has – as a consequence – become more focused and gained greater currency in the eyes of politicians and government officials. The fact that business has changed its attitude towards higher education is evident in the themes covered by the media. Whenever problems of higher education are discussed one can expect to hear the voice of some important business spokesman (less often spokeswoman). In one of his articles published in the popular media Robertas Dargis, president of the Confederation of Industrialists and also head of the Real Estate Development Association, articulates the growing interest of Lithuanian big business in the higher education sector.

According to Dargis (2015), the most essential investments bypass Lithuania because of a lack of cooperation between business and research structures:

> While trying to attract these investments we constantly encounter the same challenges as fifteen or twenty years ago: co-operation between politicians, business and research not yet started; an obscure environment for investments; insufficiently clear and competitive labour relations, an education system not oriented towards human autonomy and creativeness ... Now co-operation between research and business is fragmented and weak, thus we cannot feel assured that we will be competitive in the technological world of the future.

This appeal to relations between business and knowledge-producing institutions of higher education is echoed by some university leaders. One of the most ambitious and outspoken recent reformers in the sphere of higher education – Petras Baršauskas, rector of Kaunas University of Technology (ranked among one of the three to four largest and leading Lithuanian universities), seems to echo the plea of Dargis in arguing that

> research is looking for business, while business is looking for research. I am guided by a principle that a university has to be an international and interdisciplinary and should co-operate with business. There was a lack of such co-operation because both partners were not ready. I also believe that the interested parties did not see a lot of synergy and profit in co-operation. Now, however, the situation has significantly shifted – co-operation between research and business is a mutual necessity. (Baršauskas, 2015)

Market rationality has finally captured the imagination of the Lithuanian elites.

Too many universities?

No sooner had Lithuanian institutions of higher education been designated university status than the more significant structural changes that were expected to follow this conversion were either delayed or remained unimplemented. Of course, there had been numerous internal changes: in each particular university some schools merged, some departments were closed and at the same time some new ones came into being. We have witnessed, in particular, a proliferation of departments and even schools of so-called 'creative industries' that are seen as having the potential to attract large numbers of state-supported and self-supporting students (as well as their vouchers).

Similarly, questions regarding the optimum number of universities – although a subject of debate for the last fifteen years – have risen to the top of the agenda and are now hotly debated. Such questions are continually raised – and policy responses continually revised – by outgoing and incoming governments, politicians, top officials of the Ministry of Education and Science, higher education analysts and most recently by those speaking on behalf of large and influential business structures that have cast their eyes on the higher education sector.

In 2009 a call to merge the existing universities was made by Giedrius Viliūnas (vice rector for studies at Mykolas Romeris University, prior to which he had served as a secretary at the Ministry of Education and Science and briefly as head of the Department of Research Policy at the Research Council of Lithuania). Viliūnas (2009) claimed that merging universities was a timely option, arguing that Lithuanian universities were too small to fulfil their research potential, develop a national and international image and maximize the impact of their study programmes (see also Viliūnas, 2015). Despite the fact that there were many other voices urging a major revision of the network of universities and other institutions of higher education, as well as groups lobbying to reduce the number of universities, the author's call was generally ignored at the time.

However, during the last couple of years the call for a reduction in the number of universities has increasingly gained support from politicians, business people and others who have become convinced – in part through the intervention of various media sources – of the supposed underperformance of the higher education system within Lithuania. Here, for example, are some public statements made by influential figures on the issue of Lithuanian higher education:

> I have been repeating on many occasions that the present situation is dangerous to the future of the state: the goal of education is to educate specialists of a certain quality … There should be fewer universities and the decision should be political. (Saulius Jurkevičius, director of Vilnius Lyceum, while participating in a debated mediated by Lithuanian National TV. Quoted in Samalavičius 2015c: 16)
>
> While speaking of institutions of higher education we have four times more per million inhabitants than the average European state … I am not insisting we should close universities, but they should be incorporated, their programs should be shared. (Robertas Dargis, one of the most influential figures in Lithuanian business circles. Quoted in Samalavičius, 2015c: 16)
>
> Such a higher education system – where there are fifteen schools providing higher education while the EU countries on average have five – cannot be competitive by any means. Have you ever yourselves given a thought to what is the difference between district hospitals and institutions providing higher education? First of all, we have too many of both … And this happens because most establishments of higher education do not care about the quality of knowledge they provide. To the contrary, the establishments of higher education – and we have as many as 47 all in all – are fishing for imbeciles who should not study at all and educate them only because they can pay money and after a few years award them with graduation diplomas. (Rimvydas Valatka, one of Lithuania's most famous journalists and political commentators, whose opinions on this issue were broadcast by national media. Quoted in Samalavičius 2015c: 17)

Valatka – well-known in Lithuania for his strong opinions on each and every issue and his not so delicate vocabulary – is echoing comments that are widely expressed across the Web: in the main anonymous comments that chime well with Valatka's views if expressed in even more 'colourful' vocabulary. These comments – to the effect the number of higher education institutions is too high for a small and young EU member – build on the assumption that a state should reduce the number of institutions and provide more space for competition, private funds, bank loans for fees and so forth. Austerity, suitably disguised, is advocated as a social remedy.

Responding to these claims that the main problems of higher education are related to the number and size of its institutions – the repeated claim that some institutions are too small to perform well –Želvys has argued that these assumption are largely mythological:

> During the 2008–2009 school year … when Lithuania's student population reached a record high, there were 49 schools of higher education with an average of 4,300 students in each school. Theoretically, it looks like there was a decrease in the size of schools of higher learning. However, it should be remembered that 27 of them are colleges, which in 2000 were restructured *en masse* from schools of higher education without much critical analysis … 22 universities had 149,000 students. However, 7 of them were non-state schools. The government cannot consolidate or reorganize non-state schools. Thus there remain 15 university-level schools of higher education which have a total of 141,000 students – on average 9,400 students for each school. In the same 2008–2009 school year, six universities in Lithuania had more than 10,000 students, and the largest of them, the Vilnius University, had 24,500 students. (2015: 19)

The claim that the abundance of Lithuanian universities is an obstacle to improving their quality would seem to be based on the neo-liberal assumption that issues relating to educational quality can be reduced to a matter of cost effectiveness. It is interesting, therefore, that the claim is supported by some of those affiliated to political parties belonging to the Left. For example, Benediktas Juodka (2009), former rector of Vilnius University and an active member of the Lithuanian Social Democracts, has advocated a reduction in the number of Lithuanian universities as a means of raising their standards. His supporting argument – that in Europe normally there is one university for every one million inhabitants – has however recently been debunked as misleading and inaccurate by other Lithuanian experts on higher education (see, e.g., Želvys, 2015; Samalavičius, 2015d).

Equally unconvincing are local appeals based on the size of those universities considered to be most successful. After all, some such institutions, say, Cambridge, Harvard, Massachusetts Institute of Technology and Oxford, can hardly be considered large with enrolment figures varying from 11,000 to 28,000 students. Those figures are not significantly larger than many of the research universities in Lithuania with the exception of a few regional universities based in Klaipėda or Šiauliai cities. Although all too often based on misleading information, inaccuracies, speculation and self-perpetuating myths, the claim that Lithuanian institutions of higher education are too small to perform well is constantly repeated across the mainstream Lithuanian media with a view to strengthening the widespread – if misplaced – belief that there are just too many universities.

Austerity and commodification

Almost three decades ago, in his book *University in Ruins*, Bill Readings (1996: 11) observed that 'the contemporary university is busily transforming itself from an ideological arm of the state into a bureaucratically organized and relatively autonomous consumer-oriented corporation'. Although the commodification and commercialization of higher education is hardly an exclusively European phenomenon, it has recently become an international and, some would argue, global phenomenon, having been imposed on the higher education sector by different governments subscribing to a broadly neo-liberal agenda. As Derek Bok observed a decade earlier than Readings, while commenting on the development of higher education within the North American context, the market strategies associated with this agenda have severe limitations:

> Many social ends cannot be achieved through the operation of market forces. Better information about job opportunities may help women and minorities to locate academic posts, but it will hardly do away with the need for the rules outlawing discrimination. Nor will market forces ensure that handicapped students achieve full access to higher education or that laboratories observe a due regard for public safety. Furthermore, because universities do not constitute a free market in the ordinary commercial sense, efforts to rely on market forces will often prove impossible or prohibitively expensive. (1982: 46)

In *Universities in the Marketplace* Bok (2003: 107) warned of the dangers of commercialism and of the adoption by universities of corporate business models: 'Universities should likewise be cautious in looking to corporate models to achieve greater efficiency in their operations. Business methods can offer useful clues for cutting expenditures on building maintenance or support services. But efficiency is not a very helpful guide for teaching and research.' Yet this is precisely the direction in which present higher education policy is taking universities in Lithuania and elsewhere in Europe: an institutional dead end towards which Lithuanian universities have been pushed by the state following the neo-liberal turn of 2009.

In his overview of the consequences of the 2009 reforms sociologist Gediminas Merkys has argued that this policy shift

> has created a dangerously explosive mixture that will soon exhaust our higher education system. In an attempt to survive in these circumstances, institutions of higher education ... are combining some perverse escape mechanisms: first, accepting anyone who is capable of paying their own student fees; second, not removing regressive students from the student roll for fear of financial loss; third, constantly introducing a variety of eccentric specialities for the sole purpose of

marketing. Schools should never have started this trade in qualifications. Our higher education system has been forcefully subjected to an apparently vicious model of administration and finance. (2015)

Conclusion

It remains to be seen whether this gloomy prognosis will be confirmed by further developments within Lithuania's higher education system. Will austerity – 'a habitual form of discourse for international leaders and creditor nations' and 'an excuse *not to think*' (Jabko, 2013: 706–7; italics in original) – continue to prevail in the increasingly transnational contexts of higher education? So far, austerity measures – frequently introduced in the guise of financial incentives and disincentives – have had one undeniable effect on Lithuanian higher education: they have pushed public universities to adopt a market mentality, to establish market relations with great rapidity and little forethought and to ignore or give up many of their previous social and cultural commitments. In their increasing reliance on market regulation universities have become knowledge-producing factories preoccupied with marketing and selling their products – something that European universities were never meant to be.

References

Altbach, P. G. (1997). An international academic crisis? The American professoriate in comparative perspective, *Dedalus* 126(4): 3 15–38.

Babravičius, J., and I. Dzemyda. (2012). Naujosios viešosios vadybos elementai ir,,studijų krepšelio' modelio diegimas Lietuvoje, *Viešoji politika ir administravimas* 11(2): 260–71.

Balčiūnas, J., and A. Turčinskaitė-Balčiūnaitė. (2015). Lithuanian universities: Threshold of change, or decline, *Lituanus: The Lithuanian Quarterly* 61(3): 30–46.

Baršauskas, P. (2015). Petras Baršauskas: Mokslo ir verslo bendradarbiavimas reikalingas apibusiškai. Apzvalga. www.apzvalga.eu/petras-barsauskas-mokslo-ir-verslo-bendradarbiavimas-reikalingas-abipusiskai.html.

Bok, D. (1982). *Beyond the Ivory Tower: Social Responsibility of the Modern University*. Cambridge, MA: Harvard University Press.

Bok, D. (2003). *Universities in the Marketplace: Commercialization of Higher Education*. Princeton and Oxford: Princeton University Press.

Clark, B. R. (1986). *The Higher Education System: Academic Organization in Cross-National Perspective*. Berkeley; Los Angeles: University of California Press.

Dargis, R. (2015). Intelektinio kapitalizmo pradžia: ar esame tam pasiruošę? http://www.i5min.lt/../robertas-dargis-intelektinio-kapitalizmo-pradzia-ar-esame-tam-pasiruose-18-503858.

Daujotis, V. (2015). The rise and the legacy of the dual-fee-track system: A case study of the 2009 Higher Education Reforms in Lithuania, *Lituanus: The Lithuanian Quarterly* 61(3): 63–84.

de Sousa Santos, B. (2011). Universitetas XXI amžiuje: Demokratiškos ir išlaisvinančios universiteto reformos link, *Kultūros barai* 9: 9–18.

Geiger, R. L. (2004). *Knowledge and Money: Research Universities and the Paradox of the Marketplace*. Stanford: Stanford University Press.

Giroux H., and A. Samalavičius. (2016). Higher education and neoliberal temptation, *Kultūros barai* (4): 11–14.

Jabko, N. (2013). The political appeal of austerity, *Comparative European Politics* 11: 705–12.

Juodka, B. (2009). Į universitetus įstoja 'dundukai'. *Delfi*. http://www.delfi.lt/news/daily/education/bjuodka-i-universitetus-istoja-dundukai.d?id=18479465.

Merkys, G. (2015). Aukštosios mokyklos miršta stovėdamos ir tylėdamos. Ekspertai.eu. http:/www.ekspertai.eu/aukstosios-mokyklos-mirsta-stovedamos-ir-tyledamos86323.

Newfield, C. (2008). *Unmaking the Public University*. Cambridge, MA: Harvard University Press.

Readings, B. (1996). *University in Ruins*. Cambridge, MA: Harvard University Press.

Samalavičius, A. (2003). *Universiteto idėja ir akademinė industrija*. Vilnius: Kultūros barai.

Samalavičius, A. (2015a). Universitetas vartotojiškoje monokultūroje, *Nepriklausomybės sąsiuviniai* 1(11): 62–7.

Samalavičius, A. (2015b). Universitetas ir verslas: pavojingi ryšiai?, *Kultūros barai* 10: 2–6.

Samalavičius, A. (2015c). Užkalbėtojų ir šundaktarių vaistai aukštojo mokslo negalavimams gydyti, *Kultūros braai* 11: 16–20.

Samalavičius, A. (2016). Kokių universitetų reikia Lietuvai? *Kultūros braai* 5: 2–7.

Tamašauskienė, Z., A. Šileika and F. Smolenskienė. (2008). Lietuvos aukštojo mokslo finansavimo problemos, *Ekonomika ir vadyba: Aktualijos ir perspektyvos* 1(10): 175–85.

Viliūnas, G. (2009). Kodėl dabar reikia sujungti Lietuvos universitetus? *Delfi*. http://www.delfi.lt/news/ringas/lit/gviliunas-kodel-dabar-reikia-sujungti-lietuvos-universitetus.d?id=23274605.

Viliūnas, G. (2015). Liberalisation and the establishment of disciplinary policies in Lithuania's higher education, *Lituanus: The Lithuanian Quarterly* 61(3): 48–63.

von Osten, M. (2010). The Bologna paradox, *Kultūros braai* 9: 7–9.

Želvys, R. (2013). Lietuvos aukštojo mokslo studijų finansavimo politika: Istorinė raida ir 'studento krepšelio' modelio įdiegimo padariniai, *Acta Pedagogica Vilnensia*, 9–18.

Želvys, R. (2015). The mythology of higher education and its regional context, *Lituanus: The Lithuanian Quarterly* 61(3): 8–29.

Part Three

Beyond Austerity Europe

Policy is never ideologically neutral and the economic policies associated with austerity are no exception. 'Austerity Europe' may be characterized by a particular set of practices and organizational structures, but it is also is an ideological construct based on highly contested assumptions. To challenge these assumptions is to think against the economic policies that comprise 'austerity Europe'. But that can only be achieved through the gathering of alternative conceptual and intellectual resources, i.e. new frameworks for thinking about and doing higher education and remaking the institutions that support it. That is the prime purpose of the following three chapters. They are a call to hope but also a reminder that hope requires conceptual clarity and intellectual substance if it is to achieve fulfilment. In order to move forward we must first – to evoke Hannah Arendt's famous dictum – 'stop and think'.

9

The Politics of Austerity and Entrepreneurialism: Reflections on the Role of the Humanities

Ari-Elmeri Hyvönen and Esko Harni

[A] great deal will depend on how [...] above all, we prevent the reduction of all education to the purely technological. Which is very tempting because it becomes increasingly difficult even to run the machinery of modern life and keep it functioning.

Hannah Arendt to Karl Jaspers, 11 August 1959
(Arendt and Jaspers, 1992: 375)

In September 2015, a group of students, teachers, researchers and staff occupied the Porthania building of the University of Helsinki. The general assembly of the occupation reached consensus on three basic demands. The occupiers opposed austerity (particularly in education); called for an implementation of a tripartite,[1] directly democratic, decision-making process for the education system; and, finally, demanded 'that higher education be guided by education and cultural politics, not business, product development or commercial innovation' (Yliopistovaltaus, 2015). The last point was made a bit more crudely by the most (in)famous banner on display – one that was reincarnated in similar occupations at several other Finnish universities: 'shove innovations up your arse'.

In this chapter, we analyse the background of the occupations, namely austerity and neo-liberalism in Finnish education policy of recent years. The austerity measures reached – hopefully, that is – their climax in the major cuts to public funding introduced in 2015.[2] Our aim is to provide theoretical tools for understanding and

---

[1] Finnish public universities have traditionally followed a model in which the key decision-making bodies have a tripartite representation of professors (including associate/assistant professors), students (including graduate/PhD students) and other staff (including all instructors who are not professors and non-academic staff members). In the new 'foundation universities' (presently Aalto University and the Tampere University of Technology) this model is no longer legally sanctioned.

[2] As we write this (August 2016), it looks probable that the 2017 budget that is currently being prepared will introduce new cuts to the university sector.

assessing these developments critically, building mainly on the thinking of Arendt, seasoned with a Foucauldian understanding of neo-liberalism. Using these theoretical resources, we ask whether austerity is merely an economic measure, dictated by the necessities of the fiscal sector, or could it be interpreted as a political move, working in alliance with other political choices made in higher education policies in recent years? If so, what are the political backgrounds from which it draws, and what are its political consequences? We draw from two distinct, but intertwined, trains of thought.

The first train of thought concerns the role of higher education, and humanities in particular. Strictly speaking, an 'Arendtian theory of higher education' is an oxymoron. 'One cannot educate adults', Arendt wrote, arguing that whoever wants to do that 'really wants to act as their guardian and prevent them from political activity' (2006: 173). In addition, her mode of thinking was attuned to *theorizing* about experiences, not presenting ready-made theories of issues. It was this approach, rather than any results, that she wished to transmit to her own students, cultivating their ability to think critically.[3]

By 'critical' thinking, Arendt meant something like not letting oneself 'get away with repeating clichés of the public mood' (1979: 309), 'always taking sides for the world's sake, understanding and judging everything in terms of its position in the world at any given time' (1968: 7–8), where the world is understood as the in-between space in which issues become public and in which things appear and are seen from a plurality of perspectives. Even though it is an open possibility for all adults, the humanities (including social and political sciences in the sense of *politische Wissenschaft*) and humanism have a special relationship to such thinking. Because of the fact that they are – at least ideally – generalists, humanists embody an attitude that 'knows how to take care and preserve and admire the things of the world' (Arendt, 2006: 222). The humanities, for Arendt, aim at developing an ability to respond thoughtfully to the world we share with others and to the plurality of women and men who inhabit it. Such ability is crucial for democratically active citizenship. It fosters, first and foremost, a capacity to transcend the instrumental and self-centred attitude involved in most activities we engage in the society, and supplements them with one that attunes one to the worries of the 'common'.

The second strand of thought we take from Arendt relates to more general societal tendencies, explains why the kind of thinking championed by her is less and less engaged in today. In other words, we provide a reading of the recent austerity politics and the more general neo- and ordoliberal turn from the perspective of Arendt's critique of modern capitalist society. If austerity is seen as a form of fiscal policy, as a response to a sovereign debt crisis, it may seem as though Arendt has little to say about it. However, following Wendy Brown (2015) and several others, we argue that austerity is a particular operation within neo-liberalism, and hence integral to the neo-liberal reframing of all areas of human life in accordance to a particular notion of the economic sphere.[4] Broadly speaking, we understand neo-liberalism in 'ordoliberal' terms

---

[3] See, for example, the personal reflections on being Arendt's student, Young-Bruehl and Kohn, 2001.
[4] Our focus here is not in the question of economic effectiveness of austerity. Readers interested in economic criticism of austerity are suggested to consult, for example, Blyth, 2013.

most famously analysed by Michel Foucault, in other words, as an active intervention into the social fabric.

From Arendt's perspective, this tendency to frame life in its totality through economic terms relates to a particularly modern conception of societal existence, which emphasizes the 'undisturbed maintenance of the social life process' (2006: 149). Without ignoring some of the real novelties in neo-liberal logic, such thinking can easily be traced back to the previous stages of capitalism such as the imperial period analysed by Arendt in *The Origins of Totalitarianism*. What we find from these analyses is a notion of administrative processes that function by presenting public goods according to an accumulative logic of private interests, effectively presenting society as a constantly moving bio-socio-economic process.

In what follows, we argue that engaging with these trains of thought allows a better conceptual grasp of austerity in higher education. By locating austerity measures within the broader context of neo-liberal capitalism, we can better analyse their logic, history and reach. By the same token, this increase in analytic depth, we argue, is indispensable for understanding the power dynamics faced by activists who oppose the recent austerity measures.

In the first section, we discuss the ordoliberalist strand of neo-liberal capitalism, emphasizing the importance of active interventions to the social fabric – education institutions in particular – in the name of efficient markets and the creation of entrepreneurial subjects. The ordoliberal tradition, especially when located in the context of Arendt's analysis of capitalism that emphasizes the role of administering processes and their growth, sheds light on certain aspects of the neo-liberalization of universities – including the ethos of the 'entrepreneurial university' and the related strategies of privatization and the constant 'development' of institutional structures around higher education.

In the second and third sections, we use the Finnish case as illumination for the argument and, at the same time, as a window to broader tendencies in European higher education. We point out how austerity imposed upon the universities is part of the same movement in which entrepreneurial skills and know-how have almost completely replaced thinking and the quest for meaning (*Vernunft*).[5] We further analyse the detrimental consequences of such tendencies for democratic life. They tamper with the very idea of political freedom by clinging to the image of an ongoing socio-economic process, which makes it impossible to imagine real novelty or a properly functioning public sphere in politics. They also compromise certain capacities required for democratic citizenry, such as a willingness to look at the world as a shared space where different perspectives meet.

In the concluding section, finally, we once again assume a more general perspective, tentatively suggesting directions towards which – analytically as well as practically – we might move to look beyond the current austerity policies in higher education. Crucial to any attempt to see 'beyond', we suggest, is the ability to locate austerity measures in the broader context of neo-/ordoliberalism and ultimately to modern capitalism as

---

[5] For Arendt's distinction between knowledge/cognition (*Verstand*) and thought/understanding (*Vernunft*), see below and Arendt, 1978: I, 13–16.

such. Two further implications follow. First, a political critique of austerity needs to be able to question the whole ethico-political framework in which austerity makes sense, instead of simply opposing cuts. And second, single policy areas, such as higher education, must be seen together, building on an intersectional solidarity. The humanities, finally, being particularly experienced in operating in the kind of constant crisis now being imposed on all areas of the university and society at large, could potentially play a role in which this experience is channelled into the ability to respond in an autonomous fashion to external pressures, allowing us not only to see beyond austerity but also to grasp the severe humane problems facing our politics in the present.

The politics of austerity: ordoliberalism and the production of an entrepreneurial framework for society

The recent introduction of an entrepreneurial ethos and politics of austerity within the field of education should be understood, we argue, against the backgrounds provided, first, by the ordoliberalist version of neo-liberal thinking analysed by Foucault, and, second, by certain general ways of framing the human world that have existed since the inception of capitalism and that were analysed by Arendt. It is worth emphasizing, however, that these theoretical arguments are emphatically the *backgrounds* against which the novel features of the entrepreneurial university should be understood. It is exactly the new kind of amalgam between these different (most pre-existing) elements that makes them worth pondering in the present.

In his Collège de France (1978–79) lectures entitled 'Naissance de la biopolitique' Foucault (2008) distinguishes between two main strands of neo-liberalism. First is the American version, which culminated in the emergence of neoclassical economic theory, especially in the concept of *human capital* developed by Gary Becker, and second is the genealogy of neo-liberalism that, Foucault argues, also harks back to the ordoliberalist tradition in post-war Germany, which – unlike the American tradition – manifests itself first and foremost as an ethico-societal framework (for education, civil society and so on) and as a new kind of model for governing subjectivities. Ordoliberalists, such as Wilhelm Röpke, stressed that the ethos of this subjectivity formation and societal framework is formed according to the model of *enterprise*.

For Foucault (2008: 129–59), the ordoliberalist tradition of neo-liberalism cannot be reduced to a political ideology that simply seeks to decrease governmental regulation of economic activities. On the contrary, for ordoliberalism, the optimal functioning of the market mechanisms and the whole capitalist regime requires active and attentive sociopolitical acts. These may imply legislation but also broader initiatives such as educational interventions. Thus, it is important to notice that in ordoliberalist rationality societal interventions may be as numerous as in Keynesian policies, but their nature is completely different (see also Graeber, 2015: 8–9). For the former these interventions are not be made *in the markets* but instead *for the markets* throughout the societal fabric and its various processes.

In studies focusing on the European politics of austerity in recent years, ordoliberalist framing has been detected in, for instance, such macroeconomic issues as

Germany's emphasis on price stability (Dullien and Guerót, 2012). Yet, following Foucault's notions of ordoliberalist rationality and especially Röpke's sociological thought, the recent politics of austerity can also be seen as an 'ethico-political' neo-liberal intervention in which the whole framework of society, for example, civil society and education systems, is constituted by the principles of entrepreneurial ethos (Harni, 2014).

In this sense, the ordoliberal tradition is a direct follower of the trend analysed by Arendt in the chapter called 'The Political Emancipation of the Bourgeoisie' in *The Origins*. There, she argues that when, in the beginning of the imperial era, the bourgeoisie were driven to politics by economic motivators, they imposed upon political matters a set of ideas the origin of which lay in business speculation (1973: 125–6). Such economization meant, first and foremost, that functionality, wealth and consumption became the yardsticks of judgement in all matters (Arendt, 1973: 145 and 336). Like the ordoliberals, imperial agents framed all aspects of life according to the model of entrepreneurship and subjected these other areas – foreign policy in particular – to the service of the economic process.

The imperial agents started to consider themselves as mere functions that serve to keep the economy-driven process in motion and eventually 'consider such functionality, such an incarnation of the dynamic trend, his highest possible achievement' (Arendt, 1973: 215). A new vocabulary of justification was adopted, one that seems ever more powerful today. Politicians, Arendt (1973: 138) argues, were only taken seriously if they talked the 'language of successful businessmen'.

Now, it is not our intention to make such an analysis a general explanation of modernity. These modes of thinking have taken many turns in response to different political events. Without downplaying these vicissitudes, it is nevertheless possible to argue that in the later stages of capitalist nation states, this kind of process-oriented, consumption-driven thinking developed into the idea mentioned before, according to which the main purpose of the political structures – and other public institutions, such as universities – is to foster the development of the 'life process of society', in other words, its economic activity, consumption power, health, wealth and reproduction (Arendt, 2006: 148. For further analysis, see Hyvönen, 2016). In early modern times, this fostering of the life process was still linked to the liberal idea of historical progress. Today, innovation has replaced the idea of progress. While both notions are tied to the processual imaginary articulated here, innovation differs from its predecessor by having lost the sense of direction, focusing instead on mere renewal of the process by injecting it with new ideas.

In this mode of thinking, economy is the *primus mobile* that drives all other areas of societal existence – that is, when it is administered by the state in the right way. Accordingly, other areas, such as education, should support the economic realm, making sure its wheels keep turning. It is *particularly* in times of economic crisis that higher education, for instance, should scale down its other – not directly economically justifiable – activities in the spirit of austerity and focus on producing economically productive results that help keep the economic process in motion. Especially areas of academic life that seem superfluous to the functioning of economy are under enormous pressure to reinvent themselves so that they can prove to be important for the 'innovation economy'. In order to justify one's academic existence – to be taken seriously – in times of austerity, then, one needs to start talking the language of successful businessmen. Or better yet, become one.

The entrepreneurial university: the case of Finland

In this section, we describe how the ethos of entrepreneurialism has entered the field of Finnish higher education, especially in universities in the form of entrepreneurship education and the ideals of entrepreneurial culture. We also discuss how this is connected to the trajectories of ordoliberal capitalism described above and to the austerity measures implemented recently.

In the last two decades, the Finnish university has experienced some of the biggest changes in its history. Until the 1980s, it was developed and managed mostly under the protection of the state. In the spirit of the Humboldtian tradition, it was by characterized by relatively broad autonomy and academic freedom. Against this background, probably the most prominent change in recent years has been the commercialization of research and teaching, along with organizational intensification. Although this process of commercialization has been slowly developing over the last decades, the 2000s and 2010s have been decisive on this score. An encompassing term for describing these tendencies has been an *academic capitalism* (Rinne et al., 2012).

The two most eminent forms of academic capitalism in Finland are entrepreneurship education and entrepreneurial culture, which have at least since 2004 been brought into national education policy, into curricula and into every university as a compulsory part of teaching and the whole organizational culture (Ministry of Education, 2004). In accordance with the ordoliberalist mode of thinking, this has largely been a state-led project. The background for these tendencies has been the Organization for Economic Cooperation and Development's (OECD's) and the European Union's (EU's) political programmes, mainly the Lisbon Strategy, which states,

> The Lisbon European Council in 2000 set the aim to develop the Union into the most competitive and dynamic knowledge-based economy in the world, which is capable of maintaining economic growth, generating new and better jobs and creating social coherence. (Ministry of Education, 2004)
>
> What is the most crucial way for achieving these aims is the promotion of entrepreneurship in all education levels. For example, European Commission's 'Green Paper Entrepreneurship in Europe' proposes that education should contribute to encouraging entrepreneurship by fostering the right mindset, entrepreneurship skills and awareness of career opportunities as an entrepreneur. (European Commission, 2003)

As such statements make clear – and this pivotal for our argument – the ethos of entrepreneurialism in the Finnish university system is not limited to the juridical or commercial sense of the word. Rather entrepreneurship is a term that has, rephrasing Foucault's well-known notion, 'tactical polyvalence', that is, it can be used for numerous political aims, for example, in the context of an active citizenship or humanities in university (see Harni 2014; Pyykkönen, 2014). In fact, in the policy documents dealing with the entrepreneurial culture in Finnish higher education, two forms of entrepreneurship are apparent: (1) *entrepreneurship* in the sense of concretely running a business, and (2) an *entrepreneurial way of acting and thinking*, that is, an all-encompassing entrepreneurial attitude, creativity, initiative and mindset, in short: a whole way of living (Ministry of Education, 2015).

In accordance with the latter interpretation, the aim of entrepreneurship education in the universities is not so much – not primarily at least – to raise the number of jur-idical enterprises but rather to foster entrepreneurial mindsets, skills and behaviours in all aspects of education and human life. Therefore, entrepreneurship education and entrepreneurial culture in universities are much more than just one aspect of univer-sities' organizational culture. From the website of the University of Turku, which in fact explicitly calls itself an 'Enterprising University', a few representative examples can be found:

> University of Turku has drawn up 'the strategy of entrepreneurship education and entrepreneurship' which aims to boost entrepreneurial attitude and organizational culture supporting entrepreneurship.

Moreover,

> the purpose of entrepreneurship education is to increase the spirit of entrepre-neurialism in every aspect of the society … and to boost entrepreneurial culture and attitude in every aspect of the university.[6]

The latter passage makes explicit that the ethos of entrepreneurialism touches every aspect of society. It is not just one aspect or competence but an ethical-political inter-vention that seeks to change the whole framework of society. As the ordoliberalist tradition also suggests, this framework derives its shape from the model of entrepre-neurship. The education system, in this case an entrepreneurship education in univer-sities, has a pivotal role in promoting this aim, as we have shown.

Part and parcel of the entrepreneurial ideology is the fact that the university itself is increasingly seen according to the model of enterprise. Again, this is a European-wide tendency. Universities, as Willem Halffman and Hans Radder (2015) argue, increas-ingly conform to the image of the managerial processes of a company with a set num-ber of 'production targets' (degrees, publications) and with professional administrators overseeing the process and rendering academic professionals into mere technicions.

As many academics know from experience, emphasis on entrepreneurship rarely makes universities, as suggested by the proponents of this kind of thinking, more dynamic. On the contrary, the more universities and other public institutions are

---

[6] Both quotations come from http://www.yrittajyysyliopisto.fi/, a University of Turku website adver-tising its entrepreneurial qualities (the domain name translates as 'entrepreneur university').

viewed analogously to firms, the more bureaucratic they seem to become. As David Graeber has recently pointed out, contemporary bureaucratic practices and their lingua franca originate in financial and corporate sectors, from which they are expanded to other areas of life. The whole procedure is naturally guided by the bureaucratic lingua franca: stakeholders, leadership, excellence, innovation, vision, strategic goals, and so forth – terms mostly conceived from the marriage of the financial sector and 'self-actualization' movements (Graeber, 2015: 21). Finally, '*What is important is "the process", not the objectives. The objectives are, after all, obvious: output, quality, efficiency, excellence*' (Halffman and Radder, 2015: 170–1; emphasis ours).

Such internal processes are of course directly connected to the broader societal processes. Indeed, the adoption of a managerial, administrative point of view can be easily understood from the perspective of Arendt's analysis of modern capitalist societies discussed above (see also Owens, 2015; Hyvönen, 2016). The university is seen as a subcontractor contributing to the economic well-being of the social body as a whole, primarily by producing innovations and an entrepreneurially oriented labour force. In concordance with ordoliberal presuppositions, the university is seen as a target of political interventions setting the proper goals for its production process – not in terms of laissez-faire but as a kind of 'company' setting its own goals autonomously. Indeed, if it *were* seen as a business model in its own right, the argument could be made – as Dominic LaCapra has pointed out in the US context – that the university is actually among the most successful businesses on the market (2004: 205–6). In other words, the university has traditionally been rather effective in implementing its endogenous goals. As we have seen, however, this is of little importance from the ordoliberal perspective, which views the university from the perspective of the market functions of the society as whole.

Before moving on, it is worth pondering what – in terms of substance – is being replaced by the entrepreneurial ethos. The short answer is, learning in the proper sense of the word, thinking and curiosity for knowledge for its own sake (even though this is tied up with the discourse on a 'knowledge-based society'). The ethos springing from the academic activity itself – whether research, teaching or attending classes – is increasingly replaced by the acquisition of skills and (entrepreneurial) mindsets that are supposed to be valued by non-academic areas of life. As the novelist J. M. Coetzee puts it (in the South African context), 'universities have been coming under pressure to turn themselves into training schools equipping young people with the skills required by a modern economy' (2013: xi) – except it is not just skills but rather particular (entrepreneurial) mindsets and *attitudes* that a university education is supposed to provide.

In the next section, we discuss the implications of the entrepreneurial spirit from the perspective of a broadly conceived humanities. This is not to belittle their implications for other fields. First, as was just noted, the new entrepreneurial ethos impacts on the way in which the university as a whole is run, which naturally impacts on all disciplines in one way or another. Secondly, the demand for marketable innovations is no less opposed to the modus operandi of basic research in the sciences than it is to the humanities. However, we focus on the humanities and the social and political sciences since, we argue, it is in these fields of inquiry that the *political* implications of entrepreneurial modes of thinking have the greatest impact. In this context, it is also interesting to note that despite its strong Humboldtian tradition, Finland trains significantly fewer humanists and social science majors than both the OECD average and the EU21 average, and remarkably more engineers and people with practice-oriented business economics degrees (see, e.g., OECD, 2011: 83).[7] This fact is related to the nature of the Finnish job market, which differs from many other countries in that the mere possession of any university degree is not seen as a proper qualification for a job in the private sector.

From thinkers to innovators: reshaping the humanities through austerity

Public political discussion in Finland seems to support the argument that it is reasonable to see austerity as a tool for implementing the broader neo-liberal entrepreneurial agenda in the university. At the same time as the universities are forced to reduce their budgets, leading politicians have emphasized the need to reorganize the remaining resources so that new capitalizable innovations are created. Prime Minister Juha Sipilä even suggested in the opening ceremony of the academic year 2015–2016 at the University of Helsinki that 'scarcity may also bring about creativity' (2015).

There has been a clear attempt to redefine words such as 'knowledge' and 'thinking' so that they can be integrated into an entrepreneurial modus operandi. Sipilä's speech is an indication of this trend: 'The universities must continue to encourage critical thinking and creativity,' he said, continuing, 'University-based start-up activity and increased academic entrepreneurship are examples of this' (2015).

The prime minister's idiosyncratic definition of critical thinking can be seen as a continuation of a long trend, in which thinking (*Vernunft*), properly understood as a quest for meaning, has been questioned. In a two-phased process, thinking has been replaced first by an exclusive focus on knowing (or intellect, *Verstand*), a kind of law-guided use of our cognitive capabilities that leads to knowing (Arendt, 1978: I, 13–15). Arendt saw, justifiably, grave dangers in such a development, worrying that our technological know-how is increasingly emancipating itself from any reflective guidance – as illuminated most clearly by the threat of nuclear warfare:

> If it should turn out to be true that knowledge (in the modern sense of know-how) and thought have parted company for good, then we would indeed become the helpless slaves, not so much of our machines as of our know-how, thoughtless creatures at the mercy of every gadget which is technically possible, no matter how murderous it is. (Arendt, 1998: 3)

[7] The authors would like to thank Petri Koikkalainen for pointing us to this information.

In the second phase, the process, and even the curiosity and thirst for knowledge that are innately connected to the use of intellect, have been challenged by the entrepreneurial mentality that strives for immediately usable results (Harni, 2015). There are some genuinely novel features involved in the second phase – features we are only starting to comprehend. In its extreme forms, the new entrepreneurial ethos means that the university's *main* function is no longer even the production of new scientific knowledge but rather the development of commercial applications based on existing knowledge and know-how. In other words, universities are supposed to take over some of the functions that have been traditionally associated with the research and development departments in industry.

While such developments have implications for all fields, they are particularly consequential for the so-called liberal arts and, even more, the traditional humanities and social/political sciences. In fields whose focus is the human world as such, or particular objects (such as artworks) that appear in it, such an attitude cannot mean anything but fundamental disorientation towards its proper subject. Thinking, consequently, finds itself under an attack that has doubled in strength: critical, creative use of our mental faculties is reduced to the ability to innovate.

Our point is not that we should train more 'thinkers', if this is taken to mean a professional class specializing in this activity alone. The key point is that thinking is a civic activity that can and should be required of everyone. Hence, it is not limited to the university. But the university should play a key role in cultivating the ability to 'think things through' in society at large and beyond the boundaries of the campus – contributing to public debate, generating genuinely different viewpoints and developing people capable of taking surprising, new perspectives to the common and shared world. Thus, as Jon Nixon puts it, 'to understand why the university matters is to understand why thinking matters' (in press).

Arendt pondered the importance of thought throughout her career, from the 'unpremeditated, attentive facing up to, and resisting of, reality – whatever it may be' in *The Origins of Totalitarianism* (1973: xiii), to 'thinking what we are doing' in *The Human Condition* (1998: 5), to the lengthy discussions in *The Life of the Mind*. In the latter, Arendt argues that if human beings happened to 'lose the appetite for meaning we call thinking and cease to ask unanswerable questions, [they] would lose not only the ability to produce those thought-things that we call works of art but also the capacity to ask all the answerable questions upon which every civilization is founded' (1978: I, 62).

Such answerable questions include, but are not reducible to, the ability to tell right from wrong, to judge events politically. Thinking, in other words, may function as a bulwark against evildoing (Arendt, 1978: I, 13). If university studies really provoke critical thinking, this manifests itself primarily in this kind of ability to think *for oneself*, without repeating clichés of the public mood. Elsewhere Arendt names this kind of critical thinking as 'seeing politically' (2010: 96). Often, such thinking produces truths that are uncomfortable for the powers that be, checking the power of political actors. And it is this bulwark we are in danger of losing if university education is forced into a mould where critical thinking means the ability to come-up with ideas for start-ups.

It is not without warrant to call critical thinking a mode of seeing politically, as Arendt does. For what such thought implies is that one exposes one's own thoughts to the perspectives of others, either in an actual debate or by training one's imagination to 'go visiting' (Arendt, 1982: 42–3). The university classroom is a paradigmatic space where such thinking can be learned. The classroom can function as a sort of minipublic – a civic space where issues are looked at from a plurality of perspectives. What Arendt calls 'representative' and imaginative thinking is the central activity here, ideally leading to a better capacity to judge public issues, allowing us to stop and think, to imagine how things might be different, to challenge the dominant opinions – or rather prejudices – circulating in society. It is paramount for the democratic system in general that universities be capable of fostering the capacities of their students to engage in productive, factual, perspectival public debate – even to function as the Socratic 'electric eels', 'gadflies', or 'midwives' in it.

Instead of such democratic citizenry, however, the ethos of the entrepreneurial university encourages an attitude of *adaptation* vis-à-vis society as a whole (Harni, 2015). Instead of questioning the prevalent modes of seeing things, students are required to be able to respond to the trends of the day. Creativity is needed, but only the right kind of creativity: the kind that devises innovative products, services and techniques – solutions to given problems (see Deresiewicz, 2015: 31). In relation to the aims and goals of the political system as a whole, this can only mean endless flexibility and elasticity, instead of questioning and analysing. Entrepreneurs are not by definition primarily attuned to the common world as a space of multiple political perspectives. Rather, their viewpoint is one that sees the world as a network of changing consumption interests, in which one should find one's own niche, something one can offer to the markets.

Concluding remarks: austerity and beyond

In this chapter, we have analysed the links between austerity and the adoption of an entrepreneurial ethos in Finnish higher education. We have argued that austerity is best understood, at least in the Finnish context, as a new phase in the broader process of neo-liberalization. We further related the neo-liberal mindset to the ordoliberal tradition analysed by Foucault and others, and ultimately to the characteristics of modern capitalist states as presented by Arendt. From the viewpoint of the ordoliberal tradition, the entrepreneurial ethos in the Finnish university system can be understood as a sociopolitical intervention whose aim is to produce citizens who understand themselves, their attitudes and thinking, through the principles of enterprise. In this sense, entrepreneurship education in the university can be understood as an ordoliberalist intervention for the market par excellence, working hand in hand with austerity policies like two complementary tactics within a single strategy.

This argument has several implications that transcend the limited focus of the current chapter. First and foremost, we suggest that austerity – in education, or anywhere else in society – cannot be understood separately from neo-liberalism, or, at the end of the day, from capitalism. In analytic terms, this means that our studies of austerity policies ought to be integrated within a broader conceptual and historical framework of the kind we have tentatively outlined here. The dynamics and the novelties of contemporary austerity measures can only be grasped – especially in political terms – against their historical background. This move also prevents us from falling into a simple-minded trap, which falsely presents the past as a bygone golden age. Furthermore, it is only through such analytical and interpretive frameworks that we can start to seriously think about ways of politically going beyond the predicament of 'no options' austerity. Political opposition cannot be based on a simple 'no cuts' argumentation but must be able to question the whole ethico-political framework from which neo-/ordoliberal austerity draws its strength.

The problem that any political opposition and resistance to austerity needs to face is that the developments described in our chapter and throughout the present volume effectively amount to a loss of space in which political freedom can be exercised. The more we view the world exclusively as entrepreneurs, the more difficult it becomes to take a moment to proverbially stop and think, and question the general outlines of the process in which we are embedded. The more difficult it becomes, accordingly, to imagine that things might move in an entirely new direction. That is, the space for making a new beginning – an act of political freedom par excellence – dwindles into non-existence. Our temporal horizon shrinks, wrenching history from its meaningfulness and reducing the future to a kind of Today+, where the current state of things is improved by minor technological and commercial innovations. The university as an institute and the humanities in particular, however, also contain considerable promise as possible platforms of thinking and acting otherwise. The long tradition of critical thought within the universities is still alive, albeit currently on the defensive. What is more, the humanities are always in crisis, in one way or another (see, e.g., LaCapra, 2004: 230). Rightly channelled, this experience of being in crisis could be read as a promise for engaging the present crisis of higher education and finding ways to stop and question the orientation of the process in which we find ourselves.

While we have mainly focused on the political implications of such intervention, it is also worth noting that this kind of refashioning of life does not only affect the public aspects of our existence. It also it purposely meddles with all possible distinctions between different spheres of life. This is the phenomenon identified by Arendt in her notion of 'the social', replacing both public and private. Similarly, in his *Minima Moralia*, Theodor Adorno (2005: 23) notes how 'the entire private domain is being engulfed by a mysterious activity that bears all the features of commercial life without there being actually any business to transact'. Given that academic freedom – freedom to think – is dependent both on a rich private existence and public activity, we ought to engage both aspects in any attempts go 'beyond' austerity.

Living as we are in an age faced with immense political problems, from the human catastrophes related to the Mediterranean refugee crisis to the fact that the Earth as a life-sustaining environment is acutely endangered, the need for critical thought and political new beginnings is perhaps bigger than ever. The university as an institution could be a fertile soil in which the activities of thinking and acting could grow, as the occupations we mentioned in the beginning of the chapter also show. However, in order to seize this promise, higher education policies would need to refocus away from entrepreneurship and innovation and towards the core activities of the university. As Arendt (1962) puts it in a letter, 'from innovation as such, I am afraid, no one will ever be able to deduce any human objectives or any standards for the world we live in'. Not only are thinking and the thirst for knowledge the true sources of novelty in our world, but they are also the only bulwarks we have against the runaway processes that threaten to wash over us.

References

Adorno, T. (2005). *Minima Moralia: Reflections from Damaged Life*. London: Verso.
Arendt, H. (1962). Letter to Mr. Dexter, August 15, 1962. *Library of Congress, Arendt archive*.
Arendt, H. (1968). *Men in Dark Times*. New York: Harcourt Brace.
Arendt, H. (1973). *The Origins of Totalitarianism*. New York: Houghton Mifflin Harcourt.
Arendt, H. (1978). *The Life of the Mind. vol. 1; Thinking; vol. 2: Willing*. New York: Harcourt Brace Jovanovich.
Arendt, H. (1979). Hannah Arendt on Hannah Arendt, in M. A. Hill (ed.), *Hannah Arendt: The Recovery of the Public World*. New York: St. Martin's.
Arendt, H. (1982). *Lectures on Kant's Political Philosophy*. Chicago: University of Chicago Press.
Arendt, H. (1998). *The Human Condition*. Chicago: University of Chicago Press.
Arendt, H. (2006). *Between Past and Future: Eight Exercises in Political Thought*. London: Penguin.
Arendt, H. (2010). *Was ist Politik?* Munich: Piper.
Arendt, H., and K. Jaspers (1992). *Correspondence, 1926–1969*. New York: Harcourt & Brace.
Blyth, M. (2013). *Austerity: The History of a Dangerous Idea*. New York: Oxford University Press.
Brown, W. (2015). *Undoing the Demos: Neoliberalism's Stealth Revolution*. New York: Zone Books.
Coetzee, J. M. (2014). Foreword, in J. Higgins, *Academic Freedom in a Democratic South Africa: Essays and Interviews on Higher Education and the Humanities*. London: Bucknell University Press.
Deresiewicz, W. (2015). The neoliberal arts: How college sold its soul to the market, *Harper's Magazine*, September, 25–32.
Dullien, S., and U. Gurot. (2012). The long shadow of ordoliberalism. European Council on Foreign Relations, http://www.ecfr.eu/article/commentary_the_long_shadow_of_ordoliberalism.
Foucault, M. (2008). *The Birth of Biopolitics: Lectures at the Collège de France, 1978—1979*. New York: Palgrave Macmillan.
Graeber, D. (2015). *The Utopia of Rules: On Technology, Stupidity, and the Secret Joys of Bureaucracy*. London: Melville House.
Halffman, W., and H. Radder. (2015). The academic manifesto: from an occupied to a public university, *Minerva* 53(2): 165–87.
Harni, E. (2014). Yrittäjyys: ja kansalaiskasvatuksen uusliberalistiset tendenssit ordoliberalismin näkökulmasta, *Kansalaisyhteiskunta* 1: 71–90.
Harni, E. (2015). *Mielivaltaista kasvatusta, yrittäjyyskasvatusta*. in K. Brunila, J. Onnismaa and H. Pasanen (eds), *Koko elämä töihin*. Tampere: Vastapaino. 102–23.
Hyvönen, A.-E. (2016). Invisible streams: Process-thinking in Arendt, *European Journal of Social Theory*. Published online before print 22 February 2016. doi:10.1177/1368431016633572.

LaCapra, D. (2004). *History in Transit: Experience, Identity, Critical Theory*. Ithaca, NY: Cornell University Press.

Ministry of Education. (2004). Yrittäjyyskasvatuksen linjaukset ja toimenpideohjelma. http://www.minedu.fi/export/sites/default/OPM/Julkaisut/2004/liitteet/opm_169_opm18.pdf.

Ministry of Education. (2015). Yrittäjyyden ja yrittäjämäisen asenteen tukeminen suomalaisissa korkeakouluissa. http://www.minedu.fi/OPM/Julkaisut/2015/yrittajyys.html?lang=fi.

Nixon, J. (in press). Universities as civic spaces: Learning to think together, in R. Barnett and M. Peters (eds), *The Global University, vol. 2: Going Global*. New York: Peter Lang.

OECD. (2011). *Education at a Glance 2011: OECD Indicators*. Paris: OECD Publishing, http://dx.doi.org/10.1787/eag-2011-en.

Pyykkönen, M. (2014). *Ylistetty Yrittäjyys*. Jyväskylä: Sophi.

Rinne, R., R. Jauhiainen, H. Simola, R. Lehto, A. Jauhiainen and A. Laiho. (2012). *Valta, uusi yliopistopolitiikka ja yliopistotyö Suomessa*. Jyväskylä: Suomen kasvatustieteellinen seura Ry.

Sipilä, J. (2015). Address on behalf of the Government at the University of Helsinki opening of the academic year on 31 August 2015. Helsinki: Finnish Government, Government Communications Department. http://valtioneuvosto.fi/artikkeli/-/asset_publisher/valtioneuvoston-tervehdys-helsingin-yliopiston-lukuvuoden-2015-2016-avajaisissa-31-8-2015?_101_INSTANCE_3wyslLo1Z0ni_groupId=10616&_101_INSTANCE_3wyslLo1Z0ni_languageId=en_US.

Virtanen, A. (2006). *Biopoliittisen talouden kritiikki*. Helsinki: Tutkijaliitto.

Yliopistovaltaus. (2015). Press Release, 22 September 2015. https://www.facebook.com/yliopistovaltaus/posts/1390574864583611.

Young-Bruehl, E., and J. Kohn (2001). What and how we learned from Hannah Arendt: An exchange of letters, in M. Gordon (ed.), *Hannah Arendt and Education: Renewing Our Common World*. Boulder, CO: Westview Press. 225–56.

10

Advocating for Excellence: Stepping Beyond Austerity

Nicole Rege Colet

In 2011, under Nicolas Sarkozy's presidency, the French government launched an ambitious programme called *Investissements d'avenir* (Investing in the future) in order to support economic growth and innovation, and to help the nation meet the challenges it is now facing, among which are austerity and chronic long-term unemployment. A total of 35 billion euros was raised, through a public loan, of which 22 billion have been allocated to higher education and research. Several programmes were then designed for building up niches of excellence in research and research-based teaching. The programme with the highest financial notation is *Initiatives d'excellence* (Initiating excellence), and it focuses on the organizational development of a small number of leading higher education institutions that can compete efficiently with the best universities in the world.

In the years preceding *Investissements d'avenir*, the French government was not yet coping with scarcity or having to implement budgetary cuts, although austerity was looming. Sarkozy's neo-liberal administration wanted to make a statement about how to deal with austerity and keep it at a distance. Rather than focus on the lack of resources and on scarcity, thereby creating a sense of hopelessness and despair when the country was facing hardship, the proposed alternative was to focus on the resources available and on producing wealth. If the government could raise huge amounts of money and invest massively in innovation and cutting-edge projects, this would also imply that they could keep austerity away. Is this an economic form of 'looking at the bright side of things'? A twist on the idea of the law of attraction whereby we attract what we pay attention to? 'If you don't want austerity to come into your reality, don't look at it! Focus on wealth!' In France, there is also an underlying assumption that the French are more prone to looking at the half-empty glass rather than the half-full one. Restoring the deficit in optimism was also seen as a means of holding off austerity and its consequences for public services and economic growth. In other words, the response of the Sarkozy government to austerity was to strengthen optimism and a positive mindset that would help engage people in producing wealth and warding off scarcity. But do people and systems respond to such an agenda? Will allocating massive funding truly empower people and institutions to take responsibility for their contributions in building up well-being?

This chapter tells the story of the University of Strasbourg, one of the first three universities to be granted an *Initiatives d'excellence*, from 2012 to 2015. It describes the choices made and the projects implemented to support research, teaching and learning capacities in the regional context of Alsace, the strip of land east of France which borders Germany and Switzerland. Striving for excellence led to the designing of innovative programmes and the taking of tough decisions. The challenge has been to let go of traditional limitations and to explore beyond disciplinary and national boundaries, gradually making things possible in an environment more inclined to believe that change is impossible (the optimism deficit).

As the first cycle comes to an end, it is time to look back on the experience and get a deeper understanding of the lessons learned during this four-year period dedicated to transformation and innovation. Has it helped us deal with austerity and become a competitive higher education institution? If so, how? What are the skills that have made this possible? How did the people involved cope with severe cuts in the ordinary budget whilst managing the huge amount of funding? How did they balance out scarcity and uncertainties, while promoting innovation and creativity?

Capturing the story behind the case

I currently work at the University of Strasbourg where I was asked, in 2013, to implement one of the tools of the *Initiatives d'excellence* programme, an innovative teaching and learning centre. Taking part in the programme has given me a privileged standpoint from which I have been able to observe how the programme has unfolded and how the academic community is responding to what often appears as a paradox with, on the one side, massive budget cuts for recurrent research and teaching activities and, on the other side, the securing of a huge amount of money and the need to decide how to target the funds.

As an insider and recipient of the programme, I needed to consider carefully how I was going set up my work. What perspective should I take in order to relate the story so it could be told and heard? As a social scientist I carry out a lot of action research, and I am familiar with how to observe systems in order to understand how they operate and their underlying dynamics. I therefore decided to espouse a quasi-ethnological method grounded in appreciative inquiry using stakeholder interviews. This requires crafting a narrative and checking assumptions, implicit theories and observations against what other people experience or observe. The technique aims at the carrying out of interviews with an open mind so as not to confirm the beliefs and assumptions of the interviewer. The main challenge was to be able to see the inevitable blind spots within the system and to look at them with curiosity, suspending any judgement that might arise. Nobody sets off on such a journey without an appropriate framework for examining the unfolding reality. In my case, I took onboard my long-term interests in paradigm shifts, the principles of system thinking (Senge, 2007) and the framework I am exploring and experimenting with, Otto Scharmer's Theory U (2009, 2013).

The stakeholders' interviews led to my meeting all the key players of the University of Strasbourg *Initiatives d'excellence*: the internal consultant who drew up the original project, the administrative team who manage the programme, the president of the university, the vice president for research, the vice president for teaching and learning, the vice president in charge of running the programme. I chose to meet them at precise moments along my journey as I gathered information. Each time I met someone, I would tell them what I had sensed so far, asking them to share their insights and weaving more details into the narrative. My main interest was to capture how the key players were appraising the change process unfolding before our eyes and, in particular, the metaphors that capture the storyline. What story are we writing, inventing and experiencing? What do this experience and narrative reveal and highlight? What do they tell us about deep transformation and change?

Autonomy and austerity

What are the challenges for the French higher education system? And how does austerity show up in this landscape? Like most European countries, the main paradox for the French system is how to provide mass higher education when at the same time resources and, in particular, public funding, are diminishing. A recent governmental report (Béjean and Monthubert, 2015) confirms the target for higher education provision: 80 per cent of a class should achieve the baccalaureate (upper secondary level certificate) and 50 per cent should obtain a first degree. In order to deal with chronic massive unemployment (the first estimates for early 2016 are around 10 per cent), the French government has just put out a proposal to implement continuous education in order to support professional development and employability. This will most likely increase the number of adult students signing up for university programmes, who will then join the ever-growing flow of upper secondary school leavers wanting to get their first degree. Institutions are concerned about how they are going to cope with the increase in students when resources are vanishing and space for accommodating all these new students is already lacking.

The French higher education system contains both a vertical and a horizontal divide. The vertical divide separates the institutions, with a historical division between the prestigious *Grandes Écoles*, the universities, the universities of applied sciences and the private universities. The French government strongly believes in equal access to higher education and prides itself that all baccalaureate holders will eventually be admitted to a higher education institution. Also, grants are generously handed out to those in need to cover the costs. Nonetheless, the smarter students get into the more prestigious establishments and, because the universities are very crowded, students from wealthier families are more likely to apply to private universities. The French higher education system is not as egalitarian as it claims to be, and there are many voices – of students, parents and teachers – suggesting that the overcrowded universities offer poor education.

The horizontal divide is a result of the massive increase in students and the three-tiered European higher education structure (bachelor, master and doctoral studies). The request to take 50 per cent of a class of age up to a first level university degree has put a huge pressure on bachelor studies, where the focus is more on selecting and redirecting students with an attrition rate, at the end of the first year, grossly estimated at 40 per cent. The consequences are inevitably a decrease in academic standards and, although the debate has been going on for several years, there is some evidence that research-based teaching is more likely to start in master courses where the number of students is satisfactory. The French government has also devised a programme called '-3;+3' that covers the last three years of secondary education and the first three of higher education in order to promote a successful transition from secondary to higher education, thereby emphasizing the horizontal divide with an ever bigger gap between undergraduate and graduate studies.

France is governed according to what Scharmer (2013: 13) would call a 1.0 framework: a state-centric model characterized by coordination through hierarchy and control in a single-sector society. The description fits the higher education system where everything is decided by the ministries and passed on to the institutions for implementation. Added to this is the highly centralized organization of public services and mechanisms for training and hiring civil servants, including teachers, university professors and researchers. For the past years, as a result of recurrent economic crises, the need for deep structural and institutional reforms has been on the agenda. Steps have been taken, in particular under Sarkozy's presidency, to move into a 2.0 model, a free-market model, based on the mechanisms of market and competition.

For higher education institutions this took the form, in 2007, of a new act giving more responsibility to the universities, the *Loi relative aux libertés et responsabilités des universités* (LRU). The purpose of the act is to give more autonomy to the universities regarding the management of their budget and resources, and ownership of their buildings. The intention behind this push towards institutional autonomy is to make higher education more attractive and competitive at an international level, with a higher rating, for instance, on the Shanghai ranking. The act that came into force in 2013 has been much disputed, with student and teacher unions being afraid that the government is backing out of its financial responsibilities, while university presidents welcome the possibility to have more leverage for creating a vision and strategy. The LRU act has been a big step towards shifting the higher education system from a 1.0 model and stepping out of the inertia that was preventing the system from growing and meeting societal demands. Moving away from the state-centric model is important in order for a university not to be powerless in the face of austerity and to be able to move forward. Survival and growth require agility, agency and virtuosity for the system to make the best decisions in order to shift paradigms. Can the *Initiatives d'excellence* foster this?

Another important feature of the French higher education system is that the original traditional universities were split into disciplinary faculties after the disruption of May 1968. Many see in this decision a way for the centralized state to gain power over disruptive universities and to stifle their claims for more autonomy. At the University of Strasbourg, for instance, the original German established university was divided into three establishments, each named after a local scientist: University Louis Pasteur, University Marc Bloc, University Robert Schumann. Why is this feature important? Because *Initiatives d'excellence* is also about getting back the original research-led universities. Rationalizing costs is often suggested as a reason for promoting mergers, but there might also be a hint of trying the 'too big to fail' tactic to prevent higher education institutions from collapsing.

Austerity in French higher education means important cuts in state funding when, at the same time, the amount needed to pay salaries is getting dangerously too high. This requires more self-funding in a system that has not anticipated this situation. It is now necessary for staff to able essential to operate in highly competitive markets in order to gain external funding. As a result staff are facing a heavier workload and feeling the bureaucratic burden as they take on more work in answering calls for proposals or in paperwork related to accountability for funding secured.

Building capacities for innovation

The *Initiatives d'excellence* is part of an overarching drive (*Investissements d'avenir*) to reinforce scientific and technological innovation that will benefit economic growth in France in the next twenty years. Provisions have been made to support higher education and professional development and to invest in sustainable development in promising areas such as digital innovation, nanotechnology and nuclear energy, the purpose of all this being to encourage research and innovation and thereby making France a leader in the knowledge economy and society. A total of 22 billion euros was set aside for higher education and research for a trial period of four years from 2012 to 2015. Out of this, a slice of 15.35 billion euros has been allocated to building up niches of excellence for reforming higher education and research, improving governance of institutions and distinguishing leading campuses competing on an international level. The remaining 3.05 billion euros, the second portion, have been assigned to thematic projects and, in particular, for acquiring scientific equipment and supporting prospective domains (space, health and biotechnologies, aeronautical research, tomorrow's nuclear energy, non-fossil carbon energies).

Initiatives d'excellence is one of the six work packages that comprise the first portion and it amounts to 7.7 billion euros. A strong emphasis has been put on integrating the numerous establishments that comprise the fragmented landscape of French higher education and research. The first goal is to advocate for French excellence and to gain international recognition to attract the best researchers, teachers and students. The second goal is to build up a strong partnership between institutions and the economic world through the transfer of technology. And finally, the selected institutions are expected to be leaders in transforming and reforming the landscape of scientific education.

For the trial period three projects were selected amongst the seven first candidates: the IdEx Bordeaux, which brings together six higher education institutions in the Bordeaux region; the University of Strasbourg, which had already merged the three existing institutions based in Strasbourg; and Paris Sorbonne Cité, which involves thirteen partners in all. The University of Strasbourg received from the project 750 million euros for a four-year period in order to implement its proposal. The common features of all projects selected are outstanding research outcomes that receive international recognition, innovative teaching and learning practices, strong partnerships with local industries and businesses and strong leadership guiding reforms in governance and management, which can support organizational development through a clear vision and a sound strategic plan.

The main purpose of *Initiatives d'excellence* is to establish eight or ten leading research universities in France. All the same, this political choice might be difficult to sustain over the long term as universities now have to fight to get their hands on additional resources. Many will probably want to get a cut of whatever is available within the bulk of the *Investissements d'avenir*, claiming that they should benefit from it according to the principle that resources should be equally shared. This attitude reflects a strong tradition in France, where equality, a Republican value, takes precedence over singling out and acknowledging excellence. However, *Investissements d'avenir* does not intend to give to everyone, only to support excellent research and teaching. For many, the focus on excellence conflicts with the idea of egalitarianism.

This conflict explains why several actors see *Initiatives d'excellence* as a neo-liberal right-wing project that will lead to severe disruption and separation between the winners and the losers in the competition for limited and selective resources. The philosopher André Comte-Sponville (2015) recently commented that, in France, many actions are immediately classified as being either right- or left wing. Anything that involves large sums of money will most likely be classified as neo-liberal. He then added that this is a typical French outlook, a dualistic perspective that also reveals a deep confusion about goals and means. As a result, actions will be rejected because of their so-called political complexion rather than examining the nature and desirability of goals which are established and whether the actions are likely to achieve these goals. He suggests questioning our assumptions about economic growth and competitive financing, and how investing in innovation might meet these challenges.

Nevertheless, the intuition that fostering innovation will support deep changes inducing the much-needed reforms for an economic recovery plan pushing back austerity is so strong that, not surprisingly, François Hollande's socialist government took on the *Investissement d'avenir* programme as it had been designed by its predecessors in the Sarkozy administration without changing a single element. Could this constitute focusing on the target rather than on the means? Will the plan be carried out as initially designed? There are people voicing concerns that a socialist government might want to equally share the 35 billion euros. It is too early to tell what the outcome will be. It is, however, interesting to observe how the tension between equally sharing resources versus supporting excellence plays out, and to keep this tension in mind when observing the case study of the University of Strasbourg.

Advocating for an inclusive approach

The University of Strasbourg did extremely well in bidding for funds within *Investissement d'avenir*. The portfolio includes *Initiatives d'excellence* and also sixteen laboratories, eleven projects for sharing scientific resources and equipment, five research platforms, four advanced research projects and three research institutes.

The *Initiatives d'excellence* project bears the title 'Beyond frontiers, the University of Strasbourg', which tells of the university's ambition to be amongst the top research universities in the world, to provide innovative and attractive education, to play a major part in developing a knowledge society and to insure that the university will be of service in addressing economic and social issues in a regional context comprising Alsace and nearby Germany and Switzerland. The strategy is grounded in five components: (a) pushing back the boundaries of research, (b) shifting the boundaries of teaching and learning, (c) bringing together the academic and economic worlds, (d) blending science, culture and society, (e) conquering new territories in governance and administration of higher education. The proposal is built on three pillars: (1) innovation in research, (2) innovation in teaching and learning, (3) innovation in organizational development.

The strong link between research and teaching is considered a key feature of Strasbourg's proposal embodying the research-teaching nexus promoted by the League of European Research Universities (LERU) of which the University of Strasbourg is a founding partner. Seventy per cent of the funds obtained have been allocated to further support the research projects that contributed to building up research capacities, thereby securing the *Initiatives d'excellence*. The remaining 30 per cent were set aside for supporting teaching and learning capacities through nurturing a strong connection between excellence in research and in research-oriented teaching. Most often excellence is associated with the outputs of research labs and teams. Nonetheless the University of Strasbourg felt that is was also important to support the dissemination of knowledge and the different forms of scholarship that define academia (Boyer, 1990). *Initiatives d'excellence* endorses the belief that the quality of courses and programmes comes from their interdependence with research and the fact that teaching explicitly targets learning outcomes that increase students' employability in knowledge society. Receiving a degree from a university recognized for its excellence both in research and in teaching definitely holds an added value that should be acknowledged and promoted.

The Strasbourg proposal also calls attention to organizational development since the merging of the three former universities was achieved in 2009. There was – and still is – a lot of work to be carried out in strengthening the sense of belonging to a university and in shifting professional and institutional identity. It is well known that academics' identity is more often related to their discipline and to their department or faculty. Here the goal was to nurture a sense of belonging to an academic community – with no disciplinary or organizational divides – and to develop a shared organizational culture.

The rationale for Strasbourg's *Initiatives d'excellence* is to select high-potential projects and to provide incentives so that scholars can try out new ideas, experiment and step out of the inertia induced by heavy bureaucracy and a lack of financial resources. Allocation of the 750 million of euros was based on a call for proposals, which were then subject to peer review and external evaluation. This process clearly involves a definition of the criteria of excellence used in judging the proposals. A strong emphasis was placed on adopting an inclusive approach to excellence as opposed to an exclusive approach that would be more likely to have a divisive effect on the sector as a whole. An inclusive approach aims at nurturing excellence in all members of the community so as to reinforce creative ideas that would not be followed up without additional resources, in the hope that should these ideas mature, they will then benefit all the community. In other words fostering creative thinking will eventually benefit a larger circle of researchers, teachers and students.

Altogether eleven schemes were set up for developing innovative research including reinforcing labs and research institutes, providing quality scientific equipment and infrastructure, developing doctoral education, putting out a call for research proposals and providing incentives to attract top researchers. Fostering innovative teaching and learning led to five schemes comprising calls for proposals for innovative programmes and teaching practices, for the establishment of a teaching and learning centre and for several programmes focusing on lifelong learning, employability and student achievement. Organizational development focused on career management and the restructuring of internal governance in order to achieve the strategic goals that would place the University of Strasbourg among the leading research universities of the world.

The range of projects subsidized within *Initiatives d'excellence* is huge as well as the number of people who benefit from it. In all, the programme comprises sixteen targets including 275 research projects, 20 scientific and 12 teaching awards, 100 fellowships, a foreign doctoral programme with 58 students, 128 patents filled, the creation of 14 start-ups, internships for 3,500 trainees each year, the creation of 50 medical businesses, scientific awareness programmes involving 2,450 secondary pupils each year, 7 artist residencies, 60 cultural events, 390 mobility grants, 15 summer schools, 19 Franco-German courses, 40 innovative courses involving 15,000 students and the professional development of 200 teachers.

Embodying a collegial approach

Distributing 750 million euros according to the blueprint of the programme while honouring its underlying values was a challenge. It required a great amount of courage for the leaders to stick to their vision and to carry out the plan, sometimes taking difficult decisions as they had to face severe cuts in the university's state-funded budget. Their first concern was to avoid having people treat the additional funds as a means of compensating for overall cuts in expenditure . The intention was to nurture innovative ideas and allow curiosity to take over from fear so as to go beyond the boundaries and the limitations (including budget cuts), and help people and teams to achieve their highest aspirations.

The years 2013, the year *Initiatives d'excellence* really began, was a year of big changes. The president was elected for his third mandate, at the end of 2012, and formed his new office in early 2013 with the explicit purpose of carrying out all forty-two of the selected *Investissements d'avenir* programmes. This was also the year that the LRU act, giving more responsibilities and autonomy to the universities, was enforced. A direct consequence was that the internal structures (governing board, administrative and scientific boards) were reviewed, bringing in new members and representatives with new roles.

The new internal organization and the need to manage a huge additional amount of money offered an opportunity for the president's office to encourage the academic community to take ownership of the programme and responsibility for its management. Fostering collective learning through doing and advocating for a collegial approach became guiding principles. This showed up in several ways, for instance, the general supervision of the programme, the mechanisms for allocating money and internal communication.

A steering committee supervised the implementation of the numerous tools and actions, and the allocation of resources. The steering committee was also called upon to monitor how the programme helped achieve the goals of the university's strategic plan. In particular it was looking at the effects of managing the programme on the general organization and management of the university. A team of five people (one academic and four administrative positions) was appointed for running the programme.

Allocation of resources was always based on calls for proposals, which meant that candidates needed to put forward a proposal, stating their goals and how they intended to achieve them. They also had to present a clear action plan. Submitting a project is one way of beginning to inquire into an innovative idea and taking a step towards making something of it. The review process was carried out according to international standards which drew on peer review. It also meant that transparency was required and could be attained through explicit and clear criteria for selecting projects. All the calls were carefully designed, focusing on the criteria, and support was offered to help individuals or teams transform their innovative idea into a prototype. Most calls valued team work over the individual, paying attention to building collective awareness rather than to individual achievements.

Peer review was both internal and external. The University of Strasbourg is composed of thirty-seven departments that are then united into seven collegiums which act as an intermediary level between the president's office and the departments. Collegiums are a new structure that needed to find its purpose within the reorganization of the university. They rapidly became an important party for evaluating prospective projects – taking ownership of the scientific growth of the community – and for reviewing them against frameworks and criteria. The first level of evaluation of projects submitted was carried out by the collegiums, and external evaluation was handed over to international experts.

Communication about how the programme was organized and run was crucial in overcoming applicants' fears that striving for excellence would go against the principle of equality. The team running the programme embraced the idea that excellence can inspire a virtuous circle rather than cultivate a vicious circle. Frequent internal and external communication through the website and communiqués, and regular reporting facilitated an inclusive approach to excellence.

Excellence and equity

As with all innovative projects, the destination is not always what we think it is going to be when we start out. The lessons we learn along the way might diverge from what we were expecting to pick up. As I write, the Strasbourg *Initiatives d'excellence* is coming to the end of the first trial period. Now is the perfect time to look back on the experience and to take stock of the outcomes that surfaced during the stakeholders' interviews.

Performing in competitive research

The vice president for research suggests that *Initiatives d'excellence* has boosted morale. It helped the higher education sector remain competitive on an international level and support dynamics that yield results and push back the boundaries of knowledge. The extra money was like an oxygen mask that maintained the driving force essential for standing out in blue-sky or frontier research. Nevertheless, the programme was compared to receiving a wonderful first-class Porsche without the allowance to run it, which in time could cause frustration.

The first noticeable signs of austerity hit the university badly in 2014 with a 20 per cent cut in research expenditures, with the amount of money allocated to each researcher per year dropping from 1,000 euros to 800. The additional 7 million euros allocated to research could not go to everyone. It could only go to promising projects demonstrating peer-reviewed high scientific quality. The lab directors felt the pressure of managing the cuts while bidding for additional resources. Therefore a new unit was put together to assist teams in drafting their proposals and finding their way through the administrative labyrinth. One of the outcomes of working with the restriction-profusion paradox has been the empowering of research communities where individuals can contribute to the benefit of the whole through their excellence.

A large share of the research allocation was assigned to early-stage researchers through doctoral and postdoctoral programmes. The intention was to attract promising and top researchers and help them set up their working conditions. As a result professional development of researchers and their needs in order to fulfil their highest aspirations came on the agenda. All in all, the *Initiatives d'excellence* has facilitated researchers coming together, stepping across disciplinary boundaries in order to design innovative research and to succeed in a highly competitive context through taking responsibility for the quality of their research.

Achieving teaching effectiveness

Excellence in teaching should reflect excellence in research, a principle upheld by most research-led universities. Quality teaching is also about preparing people for jobs that do not yet exist and remaining connected to the emerging international academic culture. According to the vice president in charge of teaching and learning, the *Initiatives d'excellence* helped mature projects that were gestating, in particular in the social sciences and humanities where research was not on the same international level as the experimental sciences. It provided a holding space for cultivating innovative ideas and trying them out. Academics applying for funds were encouraged be to explicit regarding their intentions and to build up an argumentative proposal explaining the goals of a particular course in terms of learning outcomes and the innovative teaching practices and learning environments that would frame these learning outcomes.

Prototyping an innovative idea and taking it through the peer-review process – and learning from it – contributed to fostering a quality culture and building up capacities in teaching and learning. The support offered by the teaching and learning centre was crucial for endorsing such ideas and introducing academics to innovative pedagogical approaches in higher education.

The calls for proposals enabled academics to take ownership of *Initiatives d'excellence* for teaching and to reap the benefits of an inclusive approach that does not separate people but brings them together either as teaching teams or in learning communities. The distinction between teacher and student becomes blurred, and genuine transformational learning can take place, thereby shifting teaching philosophy from teacher-centred, which focuses on content, to student-centred, which focuses on the learning experience.

The teaching award for excellence in teaching practices and curriculum development challenged academics' assumptions, since most consider awards in teaching to be inappropriate. Over time they did admit that acknowledging excellent teaching is just as important as recognizing excellent research because paying attention to teaching and learning requires the same skills as developing high-quality research. The growing awareness of the interdependence of teaching and research led to a broader and much richer view of academic identity, where the four forms of scholarship suggested by Boyer (1990) – discovery, integration, application and teaching – have become a reality.

Sustaining organizational development

Some stakeholders thought that organizational development was the weakest point of the programme, providing little evidence that things were changing. Perhaps hopes that implementing innovative projects would support organizational development were too high? It might simply be too early to make any statement on the impact on organizational development. Shifts require time, as people need to absorb the changes in their environment and find their place in the new setting. Quick-fix theories are not always the best way to think about shifts. The system always needs to reorganize itself around the actions carried out. Intuitive and down-to-earth approaches usually win over conceptual and theoretical approaches in organizational growth.

The projects financed within *Initiatives d'excellence* need to run their course before their impact within the system can be assessed. The first signs suggest that outcomes relate closely to the participant's professional development in terms of them becoming more competitive and gaining an increasing sense of belonging to a growing community. Nevertheless the programme did not explicitly aim to prepare people to operate in a competitive environment. Competition may be positive when it implies taking ownership and responsibilities for one's contributions to the growth of the system, or it can be negative when perceived as shallow and ego driven. The main purpose of *Initiatives d'excellence* has been to provide more flexibility and agency for overcoming organizational inertia. According to the president, organizational development requires sincerity and maturity, and staying aligned with the core values embedded in the philosophy of the programme. In the case of the University of

Strasbourg it was about rejecting an exclusive approach (having to choose between excellence and equality) in favour of an inclusive approach (matching up excellence and equality, and sustaining egalitarianism and fairness).

Professional development is often about empowering people, in particular in difficult contexts such as austerity. For this reason the key actors of *Initiatives d'excellence* recognize that a lot of work involved attending to the soil and nurturing enthusiasm for promising ideas. In many respects their views reflected the principles of Theory U (Scharmer, 2013) about paying attention to how people grow and what they need to do so. It is about allowing people to carry out their ideas, becoming experimental, building up their capacities through positive experience and being more agile. The goal remains fostering creativity, cultivating excellence in people and empowering them to follow their highest aspirations.

Dancing with austerity

Looking back on the lessons harvested from *Initiatives d'excellence*, how is the University of Strasbourg coping with austerity? On the whole, all the stakeholders interviewed agreed that academics are satisfied with the way the money has been spent. Efforts put into shifting from intuition to explicit intentions have seemed to effectively contribute to building up teaching and research capacities whilst respecting the deep-rooted principle of egalitarianism. The initial threats regarding the use of the extra amount of money dwindled as the community came together to discuss where funds should be targeted. The first outcomes are the projects themselves both in research and teaching, while the second outcomes concern professional development and academic identity. Implementing the programme has prevented decision makers from remaining blind to the long-lasting effects of austerity, defensively waiting for it to pass. Although *Initiatives d'excellence* started before austerity became critical for higher education, it has helped overcome the first high waves and prepare for further ripples as the French government hands over more responsibility to the universities.

Notwithstanding these positive outcomes, we need to question whether *Investissement d'avenir* (the overarching programme) is a viable response to austerity. The French government's expectations are that focusing on wealth and the distribution of incentives will reduce the deficit in optimism, which in time will empower people to engage in strengthening research capacities and innovation. The stakeholder interviews at the University of Strasbourg exemplify these assumptions. These individuals talked about boosting morale, cultivating innovative ideas, lighting sparks, experimenting and following up on a promising idea, learning by doing or cultivating a sense of belonging to a lively community. The underlying assumption as suggested by Scharmer (2013) is that experiencing something new and stepping out of the box helps people get to the edge of the system and understand how it operates. This transformational journey, through engagement in action and experimentation, enables a paradigmatic shift of the participants' mindset and the emergence of new frameworks from which to operate.

Nobel Prize winner in economics Daniel Kahneman (2011: 300–9) suggests that there is a big difference between allocating losses and gains. If the decision makers are managing the extra money with the thought of austerity and losses in the back of their mind, things will not go well, according to his theory of economic thought. It is only when we distribute gains that we step into a creative mindset and move into the realm of innovation. From this perspective, allocating the gains of *Initiatives d'excellence* has fulfilled the supporting of creativity and innovation, through fostering excellence. The psychologist Ilios Kotsou (2014: 195) points out that striving for excellence divides and separates people within communities. However, it can also help people relate to each other and bring more connectedness since being with others is essential in order to achieve something. What does scarcity bring out in each of us: ruthless competition for scarcer resources? Or a drive to connect and deal with reality in order to find new solutions and shift paradigms? The first readings of what has happened with *Initiatives d'excellence* indicate that excellence, due to the inclusive approach, has built up the capacities of the academic community.

The prospect of a long period of austerity raises the issue of institutional autonomy and the need to lead the university into the future. The first steps have been taken, although the road is still long. *Initiatives d'excellence* has provided an interesting learning context for exploring new venues and stepping out of the box. It has been a wonderful opportunity for the members of the community to carry out their work with passion and wholeheartedly, and to secure the resources to do so.

References

Béjean, S., and B. Monthubert. (2015), *Pour une société apprenante: Propositions pour une stratégie nationale de l'enseignement supérieur*. Paris: Ministère de l'éducation nationale de l'enseignement supérieur et de la recherche.

Boyer, E. (1990). *Scholarship Reconsidered: Priorities of the Professoriate*. New York: The Carnegie Foundation for the Advancement of Teaching.

Comte-Sponville, A. (2015). *C'est chose tendre que la vie: Entretiens avec François L'Yonnet*. Paris: Albin Michel.

Kahnemann, D. (2011). *Thinking, Fast and Slow*. London: Penguin Books.

Kotsou, I. (2014). *Eloge de la lucidité*. Paris: Robert Laffont.

Scharmer, C. O. (2009). *Theory U. Leading from the Future as It Emerges: The Social Technology of Presencing*. San Francisco: Berret-Koehler.

Scharmer, C. O., and K. Kaufer. (2013). *Leading from the Emerging Future: From Ego-System to Eco-system Economies: Applying Theory U To Transforming Business, Society, and Self*. San Francisco: Berret-Koehler.

Senge, P. M. (2006). *The Fifth Discipline: The Art and Practice of the Learning Organisation*. New York: Currency Doubleday.

11

Towards a New Epistemic Order: Higher Education after Neo-liberalism

Ourania Filippakou

The relationship between higher education and the society in which it exists is, at once, both stable and unstable: stable, in that it always reflects in some ways the meanings, values, needs, purposes, anxieties and aspirations of that society and its economy; unstable because the *tightness* of the links may vary, as does their 'usefulness'. When society is stable, universities – and higher education systems at large – are usually left to their own devices, and the relation becomes one of seeming autonomy for the universities. When there is societal instability, the links and their implicit promises are soon questioned, and demands multiply for higher education either to 'deliver' on its function or for its function to be reformulated, its promises fulfilled. In austerity Europe, this multiplication of demand is currently happening while significant changes in the relationship between higher education and society have been taking place. There is a shift in power from the state to the market, so that the ends of the state are giving way or have already given way to the ends of the market. So the question for higher education – posed initially by the Treaty of Maastricht in 1992– has not been 'What is higher education?', but rather is increasingly becoming 'What is higher education *for*?'

This chapter focuses on the relationships between the policy discourse and evolution of higher education studies, with an implicit foregrounding of the second question, that is, 'What is higher education *for*?' Higher education is not a single or unified field of specialized academic study. However, discursively, much of higher education (as an academic subject) has been shaped by the assumption that it should be based on 'evidence'; should be 'useful' and 'relevant'; and that its academic value is to influence policy. This view – often driven by economics and positivist structural-functionalist sociology (cf. Milam, 1991) – located the field of study of higher education politically, and has been of continuing influence epistemologically, or perhaps more precisely, ideologically.

In this chapter, I explore how we might think and theorize differently about higher education studies. First, I analyze some of the powerful sources of the current reading of higher education and show how they have framed the agenda of higher education studies. Second, the analysis locates historically the concept of a deductive rationality;

briefly illustrates its sociological power and legitimation motif; and asks whether and in what ways we can or should define a core intellectual problematic of higher education as an academic subject. Finally, I reflect on where the future might lie in relation to this field, what issues might emerge, what kinds of long-standing concerns might be re-examined productively.

The problem

There are important questions to be asked about the political position of higher education and its performative praxis. There are questions that raise important epistemological issues, such as the following: What is good higher education knowledge, and who says so? How did our current assumptions about higher education evolve? What is the contemporary political discourse within which higher education as an academic subject is being shaped? What at the present moment should be the agendas of academic attention in higher education studies?

Research, teaching and writing under the heading of higher education studies has been going on for maybe more than a century. 'Higher education' as such names a field of work, a domain for enquiry, and quite distinct positions exist within it. The label has gathered up a variety of work, in various parts of the humanities and social sciences: in part work that had been going on before and which had been in search of an apt name; in part work newly inspired by the possibility of a potentially more revealing theoretical lens. I start the analysis from three assumptions about higher education, as assumptions are also political positions – particularly as these political positions tend to be taken for granted by the economic–technocratic rationality of the European higher education research agenda.

The *first assumption* – deriving from the functionalist paradigm – is that social, economic and even pedagogic objectives agreed upon by governments and different interest groups can succeed through the manipulation of certain structural frames such as access, student financing and the reshaping of the curriculum and course structure. The *second assumption* is that similar manipulation such as educational technologies can have an impact on the internal workings of higher education or how students learn (cf. Filippakou, 2011). The *third assumption* has an impact on the research function of higher education. Research in the case of higher education studies is seen as providing a direct and important element in policy: higher education research, it is assumed, should act as a direct and effective instrument to monitor, to inform and thus to regulate the capacity of the higher education system to meet likely future demands that economic and social change might impose. (For example, within the context of the European Union higher education should be responsive to the needs of the knowledge economy.) In this context, therefore, higher education research is, or should be, in some self-evident axiomatic way, more 'useful' and more 'relevant', and has a 'cybernetic function' designed either to assist short-term reorganization within individual institutions or, if the scope of the reorganization exceeds such limits, to change administration at the national or even supranational level (cf. Neave, 2012).

Such assumptions are simplistic: for example, what does 'knowledge economy' mean? What does 'doing higher education' signify? The vocabularies of politics and higher education rapidly overlap. Globalization, internationalization, Europeanization, regionalization, harmonization, lifelong learning, social capital, quality, academic professionalism and skill formation are already major policy topics. Discursively (in the higher education journals, in books about higher education, in courses in our field of study) such themes are being presented as disciplinary topics, even as hot topics (cf. Kehm, 2015; Tight 2012, 2014) as if they are representing our paradigmatic intellectual 'supercomplexities' (cf. Barnett, 2000). As Kehm (2015: 60–1) observes, 'the specific problems on which higher education research tends to focus vary according to reform cycles and what is perceived or anticipated as a policy problem, e.g. the Bologna reforms, institutional governance and management, systems steering and structural developments, quality of teaching and learning, transition of graduates onto the labour market, funding of higher education, etc.'

These policy assumptions redefine the politics and sociology of knowledge in Europe and many other Western societies. The request, from government departments and major research-funding bodies, is for research that is 'robust and relevant' for policy formulation and policy delivery (Ozga et al., 2006). The pressures for research, including higher education research, to be helpful to national and supranational policy agendas seem rational within the present trend, marked in many places by the neo-liberal project itself and already legitimated in elections in Australia, Belgium, Canada, England and, to a lesser extent, across the whole of the United Kingdom, the Netherlands, until recently New Zealand and the United States (ibid.). In England, in particular, redefining and reorganizing what counts as good academic production has been successfully done as part of the state's national agenda, incorporating the quality agenda and research assessment exercises in the universities (Filippakou et al., 2010). This has lasted now for more than thirty years.

Thus higher education policy in the last two decades has been repositioned discursively (in many European societies): there are assumptions which suggest that it is very useful and relevant as a guide to higher education research and teaching agendas, and that higher education studies has a strong and obvious immediacy in terms of its ability to deal with hot policy topics such as the Bologna Process or skill formation or university league tables.

How did things change, so quickly? The answer is that, on the contrary, they have evolved steadily and slowly, since contemporary higher education studies began. The question that arises is, to what extent does higher education as an academic subject have the intellectual potential of a complex intellectual agenda that can also act wisely upon the world?

The genealogy of a field

Much of modern higher education in Europe has been shaped by the assumption that at the heart of higher education studies lies higher educational policy (cf. Teichler and Sadlak, 2000). Scott (2000: 145–6) has emphasized the problematic nature of the research, policy and practice triangle and identified two basic models for describing these three elements: the European and the American:

> The 'European model' of higher education research has a strong policy focus, in particular on developments at the macro level (national and system-wide policies). This model also tends to emphasize research contracts and consultancy, often on behalf of national policy-makers, rather than academic programmes which tend to be weakly developed. The masters and doctoral programmes that do exist are frequently secondary phenomena, mechanisms to provide research assistants. (2000: 146)

In contrast, the American model has a much stronger practice focus, particularly at the meso- (institutional improvement) and microlevel (academic practice). This model is also strongly oriented towards academic programmes. Large-scale master's and doctoral programmes are offered which serve as a form of 'staff college' for academic managers. Research is much less policy focused and is more scholarly in tone, providing more analytical (and rhetorical) accounts of higher education (ibid.). As Clark (1983) observes, institutional research *à l'américaine* served as a way of internal audit by which higher education institutions determined their own lot, in the absence of a strong top layer of national agencies of coordination.

The histories of higher education locate its genesis in 1893 in the work and words of Granville Stanley Hall at Clark University in the United States who asserted the possibilities of a 'science' of higher education pedagogy 'to educate a new generation of university administrators and education faculty' for the growing number of junior colleges (Goodchild, 1996: 70). Hall was a strong believer in the scientific method and its application to the study of human nature and perceived education as an area of applied psychology. He believed that 'science' would explore the meaning of higher pedagogy, describe college and university problems and include an international higher education perspective at all times. It would also need to collect data in systematic form that permitted exact descriptions of educational processes, such as classroom arrangements and pedagogic practices. Hall wrote frequent *Pedagogical Seminary* editorials explaining the purpose of studying higher education. It was, he said, 'training future leaders in the field of higher education to the same expert knowledge of efforts and achievements in other lands' through 'a wide survey in order to profit by experiences of success and failure elsewhere' (1891: 312). Hall's 'training' involved more than exposure to a survey course or two and, as he also explained, the president intended to implement his regional and national reform agendas through an extensive programme of studies.

This then was the moment of birth of the motif of 'science', and – although far less fuss has been made about it in our histories of the field of study – of the alliance of the science of higher education (and empirical fieldwork data) and political power. Politically, higher education studies would contribute to professional practice and the reform agenda of governments. By the 1960s – the golden years of higher education in the United States – more than 100 higher education programmes offered master's and doctoral degrees in higher education (Fulton, 1992). During this period a growing body of literature and research developed in this emerging field of study (Kellams,

1975). The Carnegie Commission of Higher Education (1967–73) and the Carnegie Council on Policy Studies (1974–80) generated a series of eminent publications on higher education. 'Prior to that', noted Fulton (1992: 1812) 'much of the literature was anecdotal and largely descriptive, providing numerical data about the structure of higher education institutions and systems.' The publication of the *Encyclopaedia of Higher Education*, edited by Burton Clark and Guy Neave (1992), was further evidence of the development and formalization of the field.

Epistemically, the field of higher education became further institutionalized with the development of the Society for Research into Higher Education (SRHE) in the United Kingdom in 1965 and the Association for the Study of Higher Education (ASHE) in the United States in 1983, and, at the same time, the social sciences were beginning to engage new research paradigms. One might assume that because the field became formalized in the beginning of these changes and was not heavily associated with a particular dominant approach, it might have been open to engaging these different epistemological debates as other fields that emerged at the time did, such as women's studies, critical 'race' theory or postcolonial studies. However, for the most part, higher education studies mostly followed the dominant scientific positivistic paradigm, especially those social sciences – such as economics and structural-functionalist sociology – clustered at the hard end of the evidence continuum which emphasized the apparent precision brought by numbers as evidence. Over the years, more scholars in this field began to use interpretive and critical paradigms, but humanities and philosophy in particular remained relatively marginalized (cf. MacFarlane, 2012). For example, it was just in the early 1990s when the ASHE *Reader on Qualitative Research* was published, while Pascarella and Terenzini (1991, 2005) write about the dominance of one paradigm in the field of higher education research, that of positivism.

Thus, arguably, there is still considerable political and ideological power in the long-running epistemological self-justifications of modern higher education which was born with the Granville Stanley Hall version of 'relevant research' and the aspiration to provide – by surveys – 'robust data'. Even now, it tends to be taken for granted – for example, by many higher educationists in the English-speaking world – that higher education policy talk and higher education policy action are the proper raw material of modern higher education and that probably the main purpose of higher education studies is to influence higher education policy (cf. Altbach, 2014; Axelrod et al., 2014).

Gradually, through institutionalization, the political economy of higher education knowledge shifted to a mode of industrial production – advanced diplomas, bibliographies, MBA degrees, PhDs and EdDs, and the formation of a class of qualified experts to work in the 'industry' (that is, to take up jobs in university departments primarily as professional staff), sometimes, with 'exports' of the newly trained to different parts of the world. The main form of understanding that was encouraged was the higher education policy analysis and improvements in the 'productivity' of the higher educational system, though, of course, that aspiration was expressed in terms of the 'reform' of curriculum, academic professionalism, the 'student experience' and so on – the sectors of higher education of interest to national governments.

Later, as an international knowledge economy evolved, the systematization, organization and finance of higher education research developed to include international higher education – and changed its shape. Recent higher education studies include university-based (often European) contract research and consultancies as well as more traditional forms of internally funded research. Increasingly, however, higher education is no longer in that old epistemical-political space: speaking in an academic voice from the university. A number of forms of higher education are in the epistemical-political space of the agent and speak in an agency voice.

The political space of and the political intentions of international or global higher education research has changed. The agency – the European Commission, the Organization for Economic Cooperation and Development (OECD), the World Bank – needs universalized and universalizing forms of higher education as solutions. Thus, it requires further measures, targets and rankings. The measures, targets and rankings might be targets for the Bologna Process (Benelux Bologna Secretariat, 2009), global indicators (Altbach and Salmi, 2011; World Bank, 2011) or outcomes (see, e.g., OECD's *Assessment of Higher Education Learning Outcomes* (AHELO), 2016). This knowledge transfer – in other words, the transfer of potential global solutions – is carried in rankings and objective measures: the political message is that there is no alternative to corrective action on the basis of an international language of numbers and economic-technocratic rationality.

One response to this message is that higher education works on the problem of performance and higher educational policy implementation, and that, since higher educationists are assumed to be familiar with higher education reforms, it does so under conditions of economic rationality. Higher educationists have always dealt with a set of routine policy issues, treated as 'normal-puzzle' higher education (cf. Kuhn 1970). Higher educationists know about quality assurance, governance, finance, lifelong learning, access and equity and so on, in increasingly marketized higher education systems. For example, during the 1990s, in higher education publications and conferences, higher education policy continued to be a central concern (cf. Teixeira 2013; Tight 2014), albeit with authors showing an increasing alertness to a changing inter-national, trans-national or even a supra-national world.

Within the shifting agendas of 'normal-puzzle' higher education, there are a few higher education motifs which help to define the core intellectual problematic of higher education as an academic subject. These include what we may call the 'unit ideas' (cf. Nisbet 1966) of higher education: autonomy, space, time, pedagogy, the state and so on. Within the frame of analysis of this chapter perhaps the two most historically visible of these motifs are (1) system and (2) knowledge. The motifs have not radically changed since Hall's in 1893. The two themes give three intellectual puzzles, creating what might look to be a fairly simple intellectual agenda:

(1) What ways are there of understanding the concept of knowledge?
(2) How can we understand the problematic of (higher education) system?
(3) In what ways should we try to understand the relation between knowledge and system?

In other words, any higher education research that attempts to respond to public and policy scepticism with regard to its practical value as well as its influence on the policy agenda has to deal with the themes of system and knowledge.

The significance of all of this 'history' is that it is not history. The three motifs – the relationship of higher education to local and international politics; the terms on which higher education may be defined as, or should aspire to be, a 'science'; and the question of what we see as knowledge in different higher educational systems – are not merely still with us in higher education. They define higher education studies.

Ways of understanding higher education

There are, then, continuities.

- The main overall theme of higher education studies remains 'system'. A vast body of literature on different higher education systems affirms the general point (cf. Becher and Kogan, 1980; Clark, 1983; Kogan, 1996; Rothblatt and Sheldon, 2012; Slaughter and Leslie, 1997). Higher education also continues with its agenda of finding a theoretical way of understanding 'system', and it is a problematic of continuing interest (cf. Bok, 2013; Filippakou et al., 2012; Marginson, 2016). This is a continuity in work agenda, which grows more complex as the political and economic and cultural spaces of the world system alter, sometimes in unpredictable ways.
- The field remains both multilingual and monolingual: it remains many voiced in the analytical languages of academe but relatively monolingual in a literal way. One version of this continuity in ambiguities is that there remains a sense that there may be a parent discipline, although so far no one has been able to find it (Clark 1987). Thus, what we still have in higher education is a continuing set of claims for the importance of different disciplinary perspectives such as anthropology, or history, or sociology, or feminist studies, or postmodern or postcolonial studies. At any given moment, there is an excitement for a specific method of exploration (example.g., social network analysis). The aspiration to influence policy also remains explicit.
- And, there is a continuity in the form of a paradigm war. Thomas Kuhn's idea of a paradigm shift was a way of labelling the methods wars: the struggle between the early historian–philosophers and the 'new scientists' in the 1960s. Almost sixty years later, there is another 'paradigm war' symbolized by the phrase 'world culture theory' and the word 'anthropology'. The literature is massive (cf. Well et al.). The 'war' is usually over different definitions of 'higher education' as presented by the first generation of 'neo-institutionalists' in higher education and in later demonstrations of their ideas (cf. Bastedo 2007) and by arguments from anthropologists (cf. Strathern 2000) (although clearly the tradition of anthropology is a long one within North American higher education studies). In other words, the war is over a particular version of 'a science' of higher education studies which theorizes, demonstrates and explains the spread of modern systems of higher education in world-space. But it does not explain adequately.

This paradigm war has been more visible in US higher education studies and to a lesser extent in Britain and Europe. The answer lies in a full break with the epistemological foundations of higher education studies that blocks ways to understand the field of study. It involves a changed politics of *space, number* and *knowledge* which have redefined the political location of higher education.

Systems and knowledge

Almost all persons writing in higher education studies struggle with the motifs of systems and knowledge. Within the classic canon of higher education, scholars differ in their approach to these motifs. There are, for example, those scholars who so heavily stressed a particular conceptual way of understanding system – through 'national character' – that they almost managed to make the problematic of knowledge disappear by making knowledge culturally impossible, while in the eighties, a new methodology was offered called 'Mode 2' or the problem-solving approach, whereby Gibbons et al. (1984) prioritized the problematic of knowledge so heavily that they neglected to re-think seriously the issue of system.

Probably Burton Clark offered the most coherent account of system as a problematic for higher education. Clark insisted on the importance of certain major 'forces and factors' which he argued constrained the shape of higher education systems everywhere and limited the options for higher educational reform. With a great deal of historical exemplification, he traced the importance of geographic and economic circumstance, history, religion, language and political philosophies, and how they work in various combinations to frame higher educational policy in countries such as Canada, France, Germany, Japan, Sweden, the United Kingdom, the United States and Yugoslavia. Clark did write on 'system' (e.g., he was also alert to the international flow of educational ideas and to the impact of European models of education on Latin America), but he ran his commentaries on 'system' through the concept of knowledge (Clark, 1983).

In many ways, contemporary writers are very alert to the problem of system, particularly with regard to the motif of knowledge. Ronald Barnett, for example, has carefully problematized both the state and culture as powerful contextualizers as well as giving a complex account of aspects of knowledge (Barnett 1990, 1994, 2000). Salter and Tapper (1994), Peters (1992) and Neave (2006) have explored and refined both the concepts of system and knowledge. Delanty (2001) and Marginson and Rhoades (2002) have offered some of the most complex current accounts of both motifs by rethinking the concept of space – both European space and 'the international'. And several more recent scholars in higher education have taken up the problematic of system and knowledge in a range of political spaces and different times. In other words, higher education as an academic subject through the work of different scholars has created a very interesting and complex intellectual agenda on 'system'.

The motif of knowledge, in contrast, is perhaps less developed. It is not that, currently, we are unaware of the significance of knowledge. Writing by scholars such as Becher (1989) has emphasized very strongly the necessity for an almost anthropological sense of knowledge. Despite its global development and shared significances, higher education studies have long been dominated by scholars from the developed and predominantly Anglophone world, notably Australia, the United States, Canada and the United Kingdom or the countries that are broadly categorized as 'the West'. Thus, higher education studies has been institutionalized, but often from Western or English-speaking perspectives (cf. Kehm, 2015; Musselin and Kehm, 2013; Teichler, 2014).

Institutionalized initiatives in higher education studies, whether they originate at the national or the international level, have established their own hierarchies of knowledge where certain kinds of knowledge claim higher standing and greater influence over other kinds (cf. Lyotard 1984). As Peters pointed out in 1992, the university as an idea has drawn critique from international agencies, from national governments and from several postmodernists: in particular, in the questioning of the kind of knowledge which universities construct, transmit to their students and diffuse outside of the university. One major contemporary public agency and public-political critique of the university begins in views of 'the international'. As Peters (1992) noted, the OECD report includes the proposition that the university should more carefully meet external expectations, and one emphasis in the international policy recommendations (written by the OECD) is to note that not all universities do basic research well and that basic research should perhaps be concentrated for financial reasons. A second emphasis is on the absolute need for applied research and development, effective technology transfer and knowledge diffusion, and the aggregation, synthesis and interpretation of information (Taylor, 1987: 100). Such tendencies relocate knowledge. In one sense it becomes 'international', but in a new form of performative internationalism.

The obvious outcome is that higher education got what it wished for. Hall and many higher educationists signed up to different versions of an ideology of science. The assertion of policymakers, that we needed to know the outcomes and performance of higher education systems and institutions, overlapping with the expectation of Hall that careful empirical data-gathering work would lead to a 'science of higher education', came to fruition in a specific form: institutional rankings together with the Bologna Process as key items in the quality agenda . The urgent insistence that the European Higher Education Area is not higher education is correct, but the Bologna Process certainly looks like what is routinely thought to be higher education. Higher education studies looks at higher education systems, the Bologna Process compares the outcomes and overall merits of higher education systems, and so the Bologna Process is 'higher education'.

However, it is being suggested that we are nowhere near having sorted out, intellectually, the problem of knowledge, and it is also being suggested that work on system is now interesting and particularly productive, but we are still nowhere near being able to define the conceptual grammars of higher education. Earlier, in this chapter, three questions were asked:

(1)   What ways are there of understanding the concept of knowledge?
(2)   How can we understand the problematic of (higher education) system?
(3)   In what ways should we try to understand the relation between knowledge and system?

These questions, it is suggested, remain unanswered in any sustained and intellectually coherent way by the theory of higher education. But if we do not understand the rules of relation between knowledge and systems, then how may we do higher education? Perhaps the correct answer is that we should not, or, more precisely, that we should not act upon the world in the name of higher education studies.

Is there, then, a crisis? No, but what is suddenly and newly significant are the great difficulties which Williams (2010) had in defining higher education studies. The difficulties were a reflection of a problem that had become structural and esoteric in our field of study. The field of study had grown in the post-war period. It acquired psychology, organizational studies and policy analysis, and its literature multiplied to include planning and economics of education, interesting sociological and historical writing and, later on, it drew new perspectives from anthropology and feminist thinking and postcolonialism and postfoundationalism. As a consequence, in 2017 the field of academic higher education and some of the theoretical ideas available to us are very attractive. However it is probably time for an intellectual tidy-up.

At the moment our theories of higher education, in whatever discipline, are founded on the late-nineteenth-century notion (as it afterwards appeared in the writings of Émile Durkheim) of positivism and stable social systems and their abstract reified formal appearance – treating the individual as a passive user and not as an active producer. This approach produces dispositions inclined towards an allegiance to and adherence to abstract, autonomous, authoritative systems and their roles. This may have been useful and even essential in the age of Fordist production. It will not be useful in an age in which Europe will need to construct new forms of societies founded on the productive resources of cultural difference, change and innovation. For that, a new mode of thinking about higher education will be essential, one in which the human being is placed in the centre. Higher education will have its part in that, but in dynamic interrelation with a web of social factors and a complex system of other modes of disciplinary enquiry. In that dynamic, higher education studies will undergo transformations which are not at the moment fully knowable.

Perhaps a change of paradigm is required and, with it, a higher education research agenda foreshadowing, in its constitutive principles, an era of post-austerity Europe?

Conclusion

The overall argument of this chapter has been that, first, we can construct the higher education narratives for a rapidly changing Europe under the impact of the importation of neo-liberal ideas and higher education practices, or for the export of a quality system between, the United States, Australia, New Zealand and the United Kingdom, or for a mobile lifelong learning system. The second overall argument of this chapter has been that it is quite difficult to interpret such narratives. There is a lack of a coherent conceptual apparatus which permits us to extend the existing work on 'system'. Higher educational systems can – and should – be read as compressed political messages and not just as products of recent political action by ministers and civil servants.

Thus, for the purposes of developing a better understanding of the intellectual complexity of the problem, one of our resources is the existing literature, rather than more research data. What do we already know but had not noticed we know? If, in the light of that question, we ask, 'What is higher education?' and 'What is higher education *for?*' we might answer something like this: in a society dominated by the demands of the market, by consumption, there is an absolute demand that higher education research and scholarship should question itself and its relations to policy and whether it has, as one of its central principles, a concern for the theoretical condition of higher education. Squaring up to that demand will require a reorientation towards the ethical – a reorientation that is an essential requirement of any *legitimate* higher education system in a market-dominated society and that opens up a huge future agenda for all those involved in the study of higher education. Mapping the emergent field – fashioning the theories, epistemologies and methodologies of higher education – will make for a huge task.

References

Altbach, P. (2014). The emergence of a field: Research and training in higher education, *Studies in Higher Education* 39(8): 1306–20.

Altbach, P. G., and J. Salmi (eds) (2011). *The Road to Academic Excellence: The Making of World-Class Research Universities*. Washington, DC: The World Bank.

Axelrod, P., R. Desai Trilokekar, T. Shanahan and R. Wellen (eds) (2014). *Making Policy in Turbulent Times: Challenges and Prospects for Higher Education*. Montreal: Queen's Policy Studies.

Barnett, R. (1990). *The Idea of Higher Education*. Buckingham: Society for Research into Higher Education and Open UP.

Barnett, R. (1994). *The Limits of Competence: Knowledge, Higher Education and Society*. Buckingham: Society for Research into Higher Education and Open UP.

Barnett, R. (2000). *Realizing the University in an Age of Supercomplexity*. Buckingham: Society for Research into Higher Education and Open UP.

Bastedo, M. N. (2007). Sociological frameworks for higher education policy research, in P. J. Gumport (ed.), *The Sociology of Higher Education: Contributions and Their Context*. Baltimore: Johns Hopkins University Press. 295–317.

Becher, A., and M. Kogan. (1980). *Process and Structure in Higher Education*. London: Heinemann Educational Books.

Becher, T. (1989). *Academic Tribes and Territories: Intellectual Enquiry and the Cultures Of Disciplines*. Milton Keynes: Society for Research into Higher Education and Open University Press.

Benelux Bologna Secretariat. (2009). *Bologna beyond 2010 Report on the Development of the European Higher Education Area*. Leuven/Louvain-la-Neuve Ministerial Conference, 28–29 April 2009.

Bok, D. (2013). *Higher Education in America*. Princeton: Princeton University Press.

Burton R. C., and G. R. Neave. (1992). *Encyclopaedia of Higher Education*. Oxford: Pergamon.

Clark, B. R. (1983). *The Higher Education System: Academic Organization in Cross-National Perspective*. Berkeley; Los Angeles: University of California Press.

Clark, B. R. (1984). *Perspectives on Higher Education: Eight Disciplinary and Comparative Views*. Los Angeles: University of California Press.

Delanty, G. (2001). *Challenging Knowledge: The University in the Knowledge Society*. Buckingham: Society for Research into Higher Education and Open UP.

Filippakou, O. (2011). Quality as ideology in higher education: A conceptual approach, *Discourse: Studies in the Cultural Politics of Education* 32(1): 15–28.

Filippakou, O., B. Salter and T. Tapper. (2010). Compliance, resistance and seduction: Reflections on 20 years of the Funding Council model of governance, *Higher Education* 60(5): 543–57.

Filippakou, O., B. Salter and T. Tapper. (2012). Higher education as a system: The English experience, *Higher Education Quarterly* 66(1): 106–22.

Fulton, O. (1992). Higher education studies, in B. R. Clark and G. Neave (eds), *The Encyclopaedia of Higher Education*, vol. 3. Oxford: Pergamon Press.

Gibbons, M., C. Limoges, H. Nowotny, S. Schwartzman, P. Scott and M. Trow. (1984). *The New Production of Knowledge: The Dynamics of Science and Research in Contemporary Societies*. London: Sage.

Goodchild. L. F. (1996). G. Stanley Hall and the study of higher education, *Review of Higher Education* 20(1): 69–99.

Hall, G. S. (1891). Editorial, *Pedagogical Seminary* 1(3): 310–26.

Kehm, B. (2015). Higher education as a field of study and research in Europe, *European Journal of Education* 50(1): 60–74.

Kellams, S. E. (1975). Research studies on higher education: A content analysis, *Research in Higher Education* 3(2): 139–54.

Kogan, M. (1996). Comparing higher education systems, *Higher Education* 32(4): 395–402.

Kuhn, T. S. (1970). *The Structure of Scientific Revolutions*. 2nd ed. enlarged. Chicago: University of Chicago Press.

Lyotard, J. F. (1984). *The Postmodern Condition*. Minneapolis: University of Minnesota Press.

Macfarlane, B. (2012). The higher education research archipelago, *Higher Education Research and Development* 31(1): 129–31.

Marginson, S. (2016). High participation systems of higher education, *Journal of Higher Education* 87(2): 243–71.

Marginson S., and G. Rhoades. (2002). Beyond national states, markets, and systems of higher education: A glonacal agency heuristic, *Higher Education* 43(3): 281–309.

Milam, J. H. (1991). The presence of paradigms in the core higher education journal literature, *Research in Higher Education* 32(6): 651–68.

Musselin, C., and B. Kehm. (eds) (2013). *The Development of Higher Education Research in Europe: 25 years of CHER*. Rotterdam; Boston; Taipei: Sense Publishers.

Neave, G. R. (2006). *Knowledge, Power and Dissent: Critical Perspectives on Higher Education and Research in Knowledge Society*. Paris: UNESCO.

Neave, G. R. (2012). *The Evaluative State, Institutional Autonomy and Re-Engineering Higher Education in Western Europe: The Prince and His Pleasure*. Basingstoke; New York: Palgrave Macmillan.

Nisbet, R. A. (1966). *The Sociological Tradition*. Piscataway, NJ: Transaction Publishers.

OECD (2016). *Testing Sudent and University Performance Globally: OECD's AHELO*, https://www.oecd.org/edu/skills-beyond-school/testingstudentanduniversityperformancegloballyoecdsahelo.htm#What_is_AHELO. Accessed on 15 April 2016.

Ozga, J., T. Seddon and T. S. Popkewitz (eds) (2006). *Education and Research Policy: Steering the Knowledge-Based Economy*. London: Routledge.

Pascarella, E. T., and P. T. Terenzini. (1991). *How College Affects Students: Findings and Insights from Twenty Years of Research*. San Francisco: Jossey-Bass.

Pascarella, E. T., and P. T. Terenzini. (2005). *How College Affects Students: A Third Decade of Research*, vol. 2. San Francisco: Jossey-Bass.

Peters, M. (1992). Performance and accountability in 'post-industrial society': The crisis of British universities, *Studies in Higher Education* 17: 123–38.

Rothblatt, S., and R. Sheldon (eds) (2012). *Clark Kerr's World of Higher Education Reaches the 21st Century: Chapters in a Special History*. Higher Education Dynamics, vol. 38. New York: Springer.

Salter, B., and T. Tapper. (1994). *The State and Higher Education*. London: Woburn P.

Scott, P. (2000). Higher education research in the light of dialogue between policy-makers and practitioners, in U. Teichler and J. Sadlak (eds), *Higher Education Research: Its Relationship to Policy and Practice*. Oxford: IAU/Elsevier.

Slaughter, S., and L. Leslie. (1997). *Academic Capitalism: Politics, Policies, and the Entrepreneurial University*. Baltimore, MD: Johns Hopkins University.

Strathern, M. (2000). *Audit Cultures: Anthropological Studies in Accountability, Ethics and the Academy*. London: Routledge.

Taylor, W. (1987). *Universities under Scrutiny*. Paris: OECD.

Teichler, U. (2005). Research on higher education in Europe, *European Journal of Education* 40(4): 447–69.

Teichler, U., and J. Sadlak (eds) (2000). *Higher Education Research: Its Relationship to Policy and Practice*. Oxford: IAU/Elsevier.

Teixeira, P. (2013). Reflecting about current trends in higher education research, in B. M. Kehm and C. Musselin (eds), *The Development of Higher Education Research in Europe: 25 years of CHER*. Rotterdam; Boston; Taipei; Sense Publishers. 103–22.

Tight, M. (2012). Higher education research 2000–2010: Changing journal publication patterns, *Higher Education Research and Development* 31(5): 723–40.

Tight, M. (2014). Discipline and theory in higher education research, *Research Papers in Education* 29(1): 93–110.

Wells, R. S., E. A. Kolek, E. A. Williams and D. B. Saunders. (2015). 'How we know what we know': A systematic comparison of research methods employed in higher education journals, 1996–2000 v. 2006–2010, *Journal of Higher Education* 86(2): 171–98.

Williams, G. (2010). Perspectives on higher education after a quarter of a century, *London Review of Education* 8(3): 239–49.

World Bank (2011). *Learning for All: Investing in People's Knowledge and Skills to Promote Development – World Bank Group Education Strategy 2020*. Washington, DC: World Bank.

12

Reflections: From the Outside Looking In

Tanya Fitzgerald, Manja Klemenčič and Jae Park

Three scholars with an interest in European higher education but located outside Europe were invited to reflect on early drafts of the chapters and add their own perspectives. The following accounts not only add to the debate but broaden its horizons and, hopefully, point to the continuing global interconnectivity of European higher education and the need to keep open the frontiers of thinking and communication. So, while the accounts are from the outside looking in – and represent very different frames of reference and intellectual positions – they also invite us, by way of conclusion, to look outward and enlarge our European mentality.

* * *

An Australian Perspective

Tanya Fitzgerald

Australia, situated on the global periphery, has not been immune to the cascade of reform and transformation of higher education.[1] A key starting point was the reintroduction of university fees in 1989 that redefined higher education as a commodity in the global marketplace. The powerful effect of this policy change was that higher education was reshaped by a market agenda in which numbers count. In similar ways to other public institutions such as hospitals, schools and the military, higher education is governed by numbers (Lynch, 2015; Ozga, 2008). Whether research metrics, teaching evaluations, student enrolment and demographics, student retention and satisfaction, or workforce data or myriad other data, the division and differentiation of numbers are used to define academic worth and measure effectiveness and productivity. Two immediate effects from these levels of measurement and monitoring are evident. First, academics invest in their work and productivity to enhance performance and outputs. Second, institutions use numbers to drive up their position on international and regional rankings of universities (Ball, 2012; Connell, 2013; Fitzgerald, White and Gunter, 2012).

Across the past two decades there has been considerable economic and political pressure on institutions of higher education. Terms such as 'productivity', 'efficiency' and 'cost' draw attention to the political and policy changes impacting on universities and academic work. This has included the introduction of the tenets of new public management (Deem, Hillyard and Reed, 2007), which has given rise to new forms of governance and audit (Blackmore, Brennan and Zipin, 2010; Lewis, 2013; Power, 1997) and the consequent reshaping of higher education to meet new global rankings and performance benchmarks (Hazelkorn, 2011; Marginson, 2007). These reforms further stimulated the development and proliferation of formal mechanisms for the measurement and evaluation of university performance and the distribution of funding based on predefined outputs (Cardak and Ryan, 2009). More significantly, what has occurred in Australia is the adoption of governance by numbers approaches as well as a template approach that one size does indeed fit all. There is little or no attention to the diversity

---

[1] In terms of nomenclature, 'higher education' is used in Australia to refer to universities and the term 'tertiary education' refers to all forms of post-secondary education. This includes universities, polytechnics, dual sector universities and technical and further education (TAFE).

of institutions across the states and territories of Australia, or mindfulness of the distorting and damaging effects of such approaches.

I begin this section with an overview of the Australian higher education sector. Then, I examine the influence of global pressures of modernization, productivity and performance that have impacted on universities in Australia as well as elsewhere as the chapters in this book highlight. Although there is a broader argument here with regards to the overall effect of governance by numbers on academic work (Shore, 2008), the knowledge economy (Lauder et al., 2012), equity and widening participation (Chesters and Watson, 2013; Peacock, Sellar and Lingard, 2014; Teese, 2000), gender regimes (Fitzgerald, 2014; Morley, and Crossouard, 2013) and the student body (Savage, 2011; Sellar and Gale, 2011), my attention is on the cumulative effect of these global ebbs and flows.

The introduction of managerialism and managerialist practices has not been a neutral strategy. Ostensibly the express intention is to institutionalize market principles, values and practices into the organization, governance and regulation of public services. Accordingly there has been an emphasis on outputs measured by performance indicators, and the inculcation of the language of choice, efficiency, competition, accountability, quality and audit (Clarke and Newman, 1997; Deem et al., 2007). Higher education in Australia is an instructive example of the quantitative expansion of the sector and the impact of governance-by-numbers approaches.

In addition to the forty public universities in Australia, there is one specialist university (University of Divinity, founded in 1910 as the Melbourne College of Divinity), two private universities (Torrens University, enrolled its first students in 2014 and is owned by an American for-profit group, Laureate Universities International; Bond University in Queensland which opened in 1989 is a not-for-profit institution funded via a joint venture between Bond Corporation in Australia and the Japanese entity, EIE International), and two overseas universities (Carnegie Mellon and University College, London). Australian universities have also opened up campuses in offshore locations such as Vietnam (RMIT University), Singapore (Curtin University), Dubai (University of Wollongong) and Monash University (Malaysia and South Africa). In total there are thirty-one offshore university campuses and a further 821 programmes delivered offshore (Universities Australia, 2014).

Polytechnics, dual-sector universities (such as Victoria University in Melbourne) and tertiary and further education institutions (TAFEs) predominantly offer vocational qualifications, although they do offer associate degrees and a range of bachelor degrees (e.g., applied management, creative industries, teacher education). The Tertiary Education Quality and Standards Agency (TEQSA) is the national regulator of the higher education sector, and since 1995 all qualifications are required to meet standards set by the Australian Qualifications Framework (AQF).

In 2013 domestic and international student numbers exceeded 1.3 million (Norton and Cherastidtham, 2014: 20). One in five students is an international student, with one-quarter of this group coming from China (Norton and Cherastidtham, 2014: 24). Higher education is a significant export industry. Public universities earned AUD $4.3 billion in 2013 (Norton and Cherastidtham, 2014: 41) from international student income. What has occurred in a relatively short period of time is a focus on extracting income from international students rather than educating a citizenry in developing countries.

The market agenda has prompted a reliance on an insecure workforce. In 2014 Australian universities employed 118,000 people on fixed-term or permanent positions, and academics comprised 52,600 of this workforce (Department of Education, 2014). However, the proportion of casual academics has grown steadily since the 1990s, and in 2014 comprised 20 per cent of the full-time equivalent academic workforce (Norton and Cherastidtham, 2014: 34). This emphasis on labour market flexibility rebounds to the benefit of institutions and their quest to control costs (wages) and employ a flexible workforce. Less recognized is that the casualization of the academic workforce has also produced a privileged workforce: those with secure and tenured employment. But it is the tenured workforce that are further required to act as managers of their colleagues, control departmental budgets, attract external funding, market their products (degrees and fields of expertise), participate in audits of teaching and research and contribute to institutional targets and successes (Blackmore et al., 2010).

Australian higher education is grounded in two particular policy discourses. The first, embedded in the rhetoric of access and equity, transformed the sector from an elite and binary system to a mass unitary system and is linked with the Dawkins reforms of the late 1980s. It was in 1988 that the then-labour education minister, John Dawkins, introduced a comprehensive system of performance-based funding for Australian universities. This change was underpinned by a view that the current system was inefficient and that funds linked with 'a range of output, quality and performance measures' (Dawkins, 1988: 85) would both broaden and expand higher education. Although strongly committed to expanding higher education the Labour government (1983–96) was equally determined to implement managerial and bureaucratic control of universities through budgetary devolution and quality assurance mechanisms that included external audit and funding based on outcomes-based performance.

The second policy discourse is strongly influenced by economic imperatives and managerialism. In addition to the abolition of a binary system, the Dawkins reforms of 1997–1998 introduced minimum enrolment levels for universities, established the Australian Research Council (ARC) to administer nationally competitive research grants, stimulated the amalgamation of institutions (e.g., Colleges of Advanced Education were amalgamated with local universities), students were required to contribute to their fees, university governance and management was subject to predetermined output measures and a complex array of funding mechanisms was implemented. Different fees are now charged for different courses (Medicine, e.g., is more expensive than teacher education), and although students can receive support through student loans, the proportion of students from low socio-economic backgrounds remains low (Chesters and Watson, 2013; Teese, 2000).

In effect, what has occurred over the past two decades is a level of homogenization through amalgamation, yet at the same time the global pressures for modernization, performance and productivity have led to a diversification among universities. Accordingly, universities are now grouped according to 'type'. There are the eight research-intensive universities known as the Group of Eight, the six Innovative

Research Universities (or IRU), the five Australian Technology Network (ATN) universities, the six Regional Universities Network, and then the remaining eighteen universities (Norton and Cherastidtham, 2014). While this may highlight a level of institutional diversity, it is the case that growth is necessary for institutions to survive. That is, bigger is better.

Despite differences of size, geography, institutional mission, student and staff demographics or teaching and research strengths, the bureaucratic structures and academic hierarchies are remarkably similar (Fitzgerald et al., 2012). A striking feature of Australian higher education is the strong emphasis on performance-based measurements and the relentless quest for expansion. Increasingly, university rankings and league tables are used to secure market position (Dill and Soo, 2005; Hazelkorn, 2011) as well as offer a mechanism for differentiation between universities. Competitiveness and attractiveness in the global marketplace secure advantage in terms of increasing domestic and international students, the ensuring rapid desirability of qualifications from world-class universities and guaranteeing the ability to secure the best researchers, resources, benefactors and sponsorship (Lynch, 2015; Marginson, 2007).

Competitiveness and funding are common themes. The rankings of universities are used to create both vertical (reputational) and horizontal (functional) differentiation. Reputation, visibility and brand contribute to the strategic positioning of Australian universities as well as their attractiveness in the marketplace. A cursory glance at any one of the web pages of research-intensive universities (the Group of 8) highlights the extent to which rankings are used for publicity purposes. The benefit is twofold: first, rankings attract the attention of those in the market keen to purchase the best product (degree) and the best institution and, second, highly ranked institutions can be selective about the students they attract. Increased commercial opportunities include offering degrees offshore or establishing campuses in international locations. This commodification and commercialization has created new forms of trade. Degree programmes are exported to offshore locations as well as imported into local sites as franchise arrangements. There appears to be little or no recognition of local context and custom as homogenized degrees are traded and English is increasingly situated as the global academic language. While there is the potential here to promote a fusion and hybridization of cultures, I have deep concerns that these cross-border flows will lead to increased inequities. Access to these opportunities are for those who can afford to be mobile and travel, or for those who speak English or for those who can afford international tuition fees, whether they stay at home or travel abroad. Higher education has become a tradable service and commodity (Lynch, 2015).

Evident across the contributions in this book are the economic and social transformations that universities have undergone as a result of global pressures for competitive advantage, fiscal efficiency, commodification of goods and services, audit and regulation (Enders, Boer and Weyer, 2013). Policy changes in Australia in particular have served to secure commitment to market logics. Universities compete for students, budget funds, research funds and with each other for status and prestige (Marginson, 2007).

Universities have variously responded to the challenges presented by the global knowledge economy and have fused new understandings of what it means to be a university in the twenty-first century. The logic of the market ensures that 'numbers count'. Numbers in the form of rankings determine the status and standing of a university, academic work is measured through research productivity and teaching performance data, numbers of students contribute to financial health and institutions, academic staff and students are incited to invest in their performance and improvement (Blackmore et al., 2010; Lynch, 2015; Ozga, 2008).

It is easy to engage in a level of despair about recent policy trends and the erosion of the ideal of the university. Rational alternatives do not seem possible. What has survived, however, is the notion of a public sector. And it is the public that has the capacity to re-form and agitate for what is important. In the current climate of market logic it is difficult to hear competing voices. However, these do exist. What is apparent from the chapters of this book is that the possibility exists for coalitions or groups to come together to create the spaces to disrupt. What is significant to remember is that universities have a history that spans 800 years. This is not a history that can be undone in little more than two decades. What is needed then is a global coalition of resistance. The present economic crises are an indication and reminder of the failure of the market system. This book is timely, therefore, as it casts an opportunity for us to think beyond the market. The challenge before us is to return to the origins and purposes of education more generally and higher education more specifically. The outlook does not have to be bleak.

There can be little question that the world of higher education has changed. Three decades ago no one could have imagined changes such as new governance and management structures, the commodification and commercialization of higher education, international students as integral to the 'business' of the university, performance management of academics, the institutional focus on external rankings and the countless strategic plans to ensure strategic positioning in a global marketplace. This is the new unequal world of higher education in which new inequalities have emerged.

References

Ball, S. J. (2012). Performativity, commodification and commitment: An I-spy guide to the neoliberal university, *British Journal of Educational Studies* 60(1): 17–28.

Blackmore, J., M. Brennan and L. Zipin (eds) (2010). *Re-positioning University Governance and Academic Work*, Rotterdam: Sense Publishers.

Cardak, B., and C. Ryan. (2009). Participation in higher education in Australia: Equity and access, *The Economic Record*, 85(271): 433–48.

Chesters, J., and L. Watson. (2013). Understanding the persistence of inequality in higher education: Evidence from Australia, *Journal of Education Policy* 28(2): 198–215.

Clarke, J., and J. Newman. (1997). *The Managerial State*, London: Sage.

Connell, R. (2013). The neoliberal cascade and education: An essay on the market agenda and its consequences, *Critical Studies in Education* 54(2): 99–112.

Deem, R., S. Hillyard and M. Reed. (2007). *Knowledge, Higher Education, and the New Managerialism*, Oxford: Oxford University Press.

Department of Education (2014). *Staff: Selected Higher Education Statistics 2014*. Canberra: Department of Education.

Dill, D., and M. Soo (2005). Academic quality, league tables, and public policy: A cross-national analysis of universities ranking system, *Higher Education* 49: 495–533.

Enders, J., H. Boer and E. Weyer (2013). Regulatory autonomy and performance: The reform of higher education revisited, *Higher Education* 65(1): 5–23.

Fitzgerald, T. (2014), *Women Leaders in Higher Education: Shattering the Myths*. Abingdon: Routledge.

Fitzgerald, T., J. White and H. M. Gunter. (2012). *Hard Labour? Academic Work and the Changing Landscape of Higher Education,* Bingley, UK: Emerald.

Hazelkorn, E. (2011). *Rankings and the Reshaping of Higher Education: The Battle for World-class Excellence,* New York: Palgrave Macmillan.

Lauder, H., M. Young, H. Daniels, M. Balarin and J. Lowe (eds) (2012). *Educating for the Knowledge Economy? Critical Perspectives*. London: Routledge.

Lewis, J. (2013). *Academic Governance: Disciplines and Policy*. New York: Routledge.

Lynch, K. (2015). Control by numbers: New managerialism and ranking in higher education, *Critical Studies in Education* 56(2): 190–207.

Marginson, S. (2007). Global positioning and position taking: The case of Australia, *Journal of Studies in International Education* 11(1): 5–32.

Morley, L., and B. Crossouard. (2016). Gender in the neoliberalised global academy: The affective economy of women and leadership in South Asia, *British Journal of Sociology of Education* 37 (1): 149–68.

Norton, A., and I. Cherastidtham. (2014). *Mapping Australian Higher Education 2014–15*. Melbourne: Grattan Institute.

Ozga, J. (2008). Governing knowledge: Research steering and research quality, *European Educational Research Journal* 7(3): 261–72.

Peacock, D., S. Sellar and B. Lingard. (2014). The activation, appropriation and practices of student-equity policy in Australian higher education, *Journal of Education Policy* 29(3): 377–96.

Power, M. (1997). *The Audit Society*. Oxford: Oxford University Press.

Savage, G. C. (2011). When worlds collide: Excellent and equitable learning communities? Australia's 'social capitalist' paradox?, *Journal of Education Policy* 26(1): 33–59.

Sellar, S., and T. Gale (2011). Mobility, aspiration, voice: a new structure of feeling for student equity in higher education, *Critical Studies in Education* 52(2): 115–34.

Shore, C. (2008). Audit culture and illiberal governance: Universities and the politics of accountability, *Anthropological Theory* 8(3): 278–98.

Teese, R. (2000), *Academic Success and Social Power: Examinations and Inequality*. Melbourne: Melbourne University Press.

Universities Australia (2014) *Offshore Programs of Australian Universities 2014*. Canberra: Universities Australia.

* * *

A View from the United States

Manja Klemenčič

In the canonical work within our field, *The Uses of the University,* Clark Kerr (2001, ix) describes the beginning of an age of austerity in US higher education: 'The federal government has exhausted its vast post-WWII enthusiasm for higher education as shown in support for research and development and student grants and loans ... An economic depression was reducing state support for higher education'. Until the 1990s, the higher education system in the United States was experiencing rapid expansion both in terms of student enrolment and the opening of new public universities and colleges, among them the prominent federal grant universities. State funding was flowing into public universities and institutions to support increases in enrolment, and federal funds complemented this by making available student grants. This was also a period of significant growth of federal funding for research – the bulk of it motivated by the Cold War arms race. As Kerr (2001, 141) puts it, this was 'a largely golden age for the research university in the United States'.

The brief economic recession of 1990/91 brought about the end of the contiguous growth in the public funding of higher education. It was the beginning of the long-term withdrawal of public funding for higher education; indeed, a trend that continues into the present time. The global economic recession that began in 2007/ 08 has only aggravated this trend, and political support for public funding of higher education continues to wither. In the foreword to the *2015–2016 Financial Report of Harvard University*, President Drew Faust writes:

> American higher education is entering an era of constrained financial circumstances. Colleges and universities across the country are facing challenging endowment returns and intense pressures on both federal research funding and tuition revenue. Long-anticipated shifts across the sector have arrived, and they have the potential to alter fundamentally the ways in which teaching, learning, and research are accomplished.[1]

---

[1] Harvard University. 2016. *Financial Report – Fiscal Year 2016*. Message from the President: Drew Gilpin Faust, President. Cambridge, MA: Harvard University, 1 November 2016, p. 2, http://finance. harvard.edu/files/fad/files/message_from_the_president_2016_ar.pdf.

Across Harvard and the entire higher education sector the outlook for the traditional sources of revenue for higher education in the United States in the next few years are fairly bleak. Harvard's vice president for finance and treasurer in their joint letter preceding the report make the following prediction: 'Tuition revenue growth will continue to be limited by affordability pressures, federal research funding faces an increasingly uncertain political climate, and most financial market experts agree that investment results for endowments will be modest due to low interest rates, low risk premiums and muted worldwide economic growth'.[2] When a university with the largest endowment in the world and amidst a highly successful capital campaign emphasizes the need for 'prudent financial management' and to 'carefully analyse our expense ledger for any opportunities for improvement', this sends an alarm across the system. Those that should worry even more are the public colleges and universities.

The withdrawal of public funding for higher education in the United States has most strongly manifested itself in two occurrences. First, there has been a significant reduction of state funding for public colleges and universities. Within the federal system, the states are responsible for financing student places at public institutions, and these rely heavily on state and local appropriations. In 2015, these appropriations constituted 54 per cent of the funds public institutions used directly for teaching and instruction (Mitchell, Leachman, and Masterson, 2016). Public colleges and universities educate 68 per cent of the nation's post-secondary students (Pew Charitable Trust, 2015). Ninety-eight per cent of state and 73 per cent of federal higher education funding flows to these institutions (ibid.). Revenue from federal and state sources made up 37 per cent of total revenue at public colleges and universities in 2013 (ibid.).

When state tax revenues fall either due to economic recession or tax-cut policies favoured by the Republican party, the competition among public service institutions for their share of the funding intensifies. The higher education sector competes against K–12 schools, preschools, medical care institutions, infrastructure and so forth … and tends to lose out. In the United States, higher education is widely regarded as a private good, and this conception has been evoked repeatedly in present times when public intellectuals are making 'the case for college'. The arguments in favour of seeking a college education inevitably highlight the private benefits that a college degree affords to graduates: higher earnings, more job security and likelier marriage. Public funding of higher education has long been justified on the grounds of affordability to make way for meritocratic social mobility. Federal student support by way of grants, such as the Federal Pell Grant programme and government-backed loans, fits into this picture.

The implications of this development for public higher education institutions are manifold. On the revenue side, institutions are raising tuition fees to compensate for declining state funding and rising costs. The competition for paying students is severe, and universities spend a lot of effort and resources to market themselves and

---

[2] Harvard University. 2016. *Financial Report – Fiscal Year 2016*. Financial Overview From the Vice President for Finance and the Treasurer: Thomas J. Hollister, Vice President for Finance and Paul J. Finnegan, Treasurer. Cambridge, MA: Harvard University, 1 November 2016, pp. 3–4, http:// finance.harvard.edu/files/fad/files/vpf_letter_ar_2016.pdf.

to develop amenities that will attract students. Not all amenities are necessarily linked to raising the quality of teaching and research. As the CNN documentary *The Ivory Tower*[3] captures and as studies such as Armstrong and Hamilton's (2013) *Paying for the Party* describe, some institutions purposefully invest in luxury student housing and state-of-the-art facilities as one of their key selling points. Fundraising from private donors is a common phenomenon in the United States and has only intensified. All institutions try to cut costs in one way or another: by freezing faculty searches, cutting course offerings, closing campuses and reducing student support services. And they try to strengthen revenue-making areas of teaching, such as in the case of Harvard, the continuing education (Harvard Extension School) and executive education programmes offered by the professional schools.

Second, federal funding for research has declined. Data gathered by the American Association for Advancement of Science shows a continuous decline in federal spending on research and development, stabilizing at about 2.9 per cent of the nation's gross domestic product (GDP) in 2012.[4] The rate of investment in research and development is directly associated with research intensity: data shows that research intensity in Organization of Economic Cooperation and Development (OECD) countries has outpaced that of the United States.[5] Furthermore, there is also evidence of a decrease in the share of federal research spending directed to basic research (MIT, 2015), which is typically funded through public rather than private sources and is widely considered as a driver of innovation.

With decrease in federal spending, research universities are required to turn to industry and private donors. In fact, they are forced to come closer to the ideal of the entrepreneurial university, a model that originated in the United States. According to Etzkowitz (forthcoming), the entrepreneurial university includes the following elements:

(1) the organization of group research, (2) the creation of a research base with commercial potential, (3) the development of organizational mechanisms to move research out of the university as protected intellectual property, (4) the capacity to organize firms within the university and (5) integration of academic and business elements into new formats such as university-industry research centers.

Waning federal research funds push universities to build relationships with foundations, individual donors and corporations and set up institutional structures which work on the commercialization of research through the creation of ventures and licensing royalties. While proponents of these measures argue that 'universities assume an entrepreneurial role and identity due to perception of opportunity, civic duty and external pressures' and that this sort of strategic thinking and positioning ultimately strengthens universities (Etzkovicz, forthcoming), there are also ample opposing voices that point

---

[3] Rossi, Andrew. 2014. *The Ivory Tower*. CNN Documentary, http://www.cnn.com/shows/ivory-tower.
[4] http://www.aaas.org/sites/default/files/Budget%3B.jpg.
[5] http://www.nytimes.com/2015/05/20/business/economy/american-innovation-rests-on-weak-foundation.html?_r=0.

to permanent changes in the types and areas of research towards those that are more suitable for commercialization and to the commercialization of research becoming the primary focus of universities (Bok, 2003; Slaughter and Leslie, 1997).

These well-rehearsed US developments have a familiar resonance – albeit with some time delay – in Europe. European higher education embarked on its age of austerity following the global economic recession that started in 2007/08. Public revenues have decreased due to the economic downturn. There is fierce competition over public resources from a number of public services, all of which are essential to the idea of the welfare state. The higher education sector is losing out. Significantly, in Europe also the notions of higher education as a public good and therefore as primarily funded by the state are being contested. As Nixon (forthcoming) suggests, 'the debate on higher education and the public good is shifting significantly from the need to maintain a system of publically funded higher education towards the need to develop a system whereby the state exercises public responsibility for higher education through a variety of funding mechanisms'.

A major driver of this shift in emphasis has been the need to reconcile the funding of higher education with the austerity measures that have, rightly or wrongly, followed the 2007/08 economic crisis and its continuing aftermath. In turn it is becoming more plausible also in the context of European welfare societies that students will have to assume greater responsibility for paying for public higher education. Within such a normative framework, the rationale for cost sharing between the state and students and their families – and (in the case of research) industry – becomes much more plausible. Some types of tuition fee – if not for native students then at least for foreign students – are on the table in most European higher education systems. Closer ties between higher education and industry are encouraged and often also supported through public research funding initiatives. At least a portion of funding for university research is expected to come from private sources through service contracts and the commercialization of research. European universities have had little or no tradition of philanthropy, and states have not supported it through tax breaks. In countries where there are at least some enabling conditions for philanthropic giving to higher education, such as Ireland, universities are now actively developing their fundraising efforts. The conception of the entrepreneurial university is embraced by policymakers unable or unwilling to maintain the same levels of public funding.

Yet several notable differences relating to austerity measures exist between the United States and the European higher education systems. First, the European cuts in public spending have a shorter life span and thus lower accumulated value (and milder social consequences) than those in the United States. In the United States, higher education has not been able to correct for the rising inequality, and perhaps even perpetuates social inequality. As Marginson (2016) suggests, the problem lies in socially unequal entry into tier-one institutions and the great positional differences between different institutions as well as affordability, default in repayments and the rising total cost of student debt. Federal student aid available to individual students and tax breaks have increased over the past years, but not enough to balance out the increases in tuition fees.

Then there are federal student loans, which have quadrupled since early 2000 and which in 2016 amounted to around $1.3 trillion in outstanding loan balances, which is more than any other type of household debt except mortgages. The student debt crisis is associated not only with the sheer amount of such loans but also with the rate of default, which is particularly high among borrowers attending for-profit schools but which also affects (though to a lesser extent) those in community colleges and other non-selective institutions (Looney and Yannelis, 2015). Marginson (2016) contends that the United States could mitigate some of the challenges associated with student debt by following the example of countries such as the United Kingdom and Australia, which introduced income-contingent loans. But even with possible changes in the loan mechanism, the increases in tuition fees are not sustainable and cannot continue to rise faster than the growth in median income, and, as Marginson (2016) points out, should necessarily be capped by the federal government.

By comparison, in Europe tuition fees in public higher education are much less frequently required, and where these exist are much more recent and significantly lower than in the United States. Jongbloed (2008) found that government appropriations were the dominant source of revenues in all countries except the United Kingdom, exceeding two-thirds in all countries except the United Kingdom. Over the period 1995–2003, there was a slight decrease in the share of government appropriations, no change at all in the share of tuition fees and a general increase in the share of competitive grants and contracts (ibid.).

Second, European universities have gained a significant degree of autonomy vis-à-vis the state, which increases the opportunities for generating external funds from business and industry or private donors as well as from tuition fees, especially from students in continuing and/or adult education. Yet, unlike the United States where a university administration decides without input from faculty and student representatives on the strategic direction of the institution, in most parts of Europe such decisions are still monitored and often voted upon by representatives of faculty and students. These internal constituencies at least in principle might hamper the university managers from a market orientation. Hence, the speed and extent of institutional reforms towards market-driven behaviour could be buffered by the interests of these two groups. The interests of academics and students still carry more formal decision-making power within the governance of European institutions than is the case in the corporate governance of US institutions where these two constituencies most typically hold only the right to be consulted.

The austerity measures in European higher education play out differently across different European countries. Each country's government has come up with its own formula. And even if the political discourse at the state level prescribes cost reduction as the main policy measure, higher education institutions are actively seeking new sources of revenue. Cost cuts are painful and more difficult to achieve in democratic collegial systems of governance – which are still prevalent in Europe, although with modifications – which require consent from the representatives of academic staff and often also from students. With the existence of strong and well-connected student unions nationally and through the European Students' Union across Europe, significant rises in tuition fees or the introduction of significant fees in countries where none existed is a difficult policy outcome to achieve.

In conclusion, systems of European and US higher education in 'austerity Europe' are subject to similar trends despite the differences in the historical context of state–higher education relations and university governance. The common overtones to these developments lie in the more explicit link between higher education policy and economic policy; indeed, the former is a subset of the other within the neo-liberal conception of higher education (Slaughter and Rhoades, 2009). Given these isomorphic tendencies, Europeans ought to take note of the proliferation of books recently published in the United States pointing in one way or another to the demise of US higher education: *Our Underachieving Colleges* (Bok, 2006); *How Colleges Are Wasting Our Money and Failing Our Kids – and What We Can Do About It* (Hacker and Dreifus, 2010); *American Higher Education in Crisis?: What Everyone Needs to Know* (Blumenstyk, 2015); *Fail U: The False Promise of Higher Education* (Sykes, 2016), to mention just a few.

One book resonates particularly strongly with an outside-in perspective on higher education in austerity Europe. *Austerity Blues: Fighting for the Soul of Public Higher Education* (Fabricant and Brier, 2016) speaks of the harmful effects that public disinvestment had on public universities' ability to enable access while retaining quality education provision. Universities have increasingly turned to privatization and technology to remain financially afloat. As tuition hikes for domestic students become unsustainable, the possibility of moving education branches to other parts of the world to generate fresh overseas revenue is becoming an increasingly desirable business proposition. In the meantime concerns mount regarding underinvestment in faculty and the future of the academic profession, which is losing out on salaries and job security with more and more academic positions becoming adjunct.

References

Armstrong, E. A., and L. T. Hamilton (2013). *Paying for the Party: How College Maintains Inequality*. Cambridge, MA: Harvard University Press.

Blumenstyk, G. (2015). *American Higher Education in Crisis?: What Everyone Needs to Know*. Oxford and New York: Oxford University Press.

Bok, D. (2003). *Universities in the Marketplace*. Cambridge, MA: Harvard University Press

Bok, D. (2006). *Our Underachieving Colleges*. Princeton and Oxford: Princeton University Press.

Etzkowitz, H. (forthcoming). The entrepreneurial university, in J. C. Shin and P. N. Teixeira (eds), *International Encyclopedia of Higher Education Systems and Institutions* (Section: 'Mass Elite Higher Education in the 21st Century', ed. M. Klemenčič). Dordrecht: Springer.

Fabricant, M., and S. Brier. (2016). *Austerity Blues: Fighting for the Soul of Public Higher Education*. Baltimore: John Hopkins University Press.

Hacker, A., and C. Dreifus. (2010). *How Colleges Are Wasting Our Money and Failing Our Kids – and What We Can Do about It*. New York: St. Martin's Press.

Jongbloed, B. (2008). Funding higher education: a view from Europe. Paper prepared for the seminar Funding Higher Education: A Comparative Overview organised by the National Trade Confederation of Goods, Services and Tourism (CNC) Brasilia, October 13, 2008, Netherlands: Center for Higher Education Policy Studies (CHEPS).

Kerr, C. (2001). *The Uses of the University, 5th ed*. Cambridge, MA: Harvard University Press.

Looney, A., and C. Yannelis. (2015). A crisis in student loans? How changes in the characteristics of borrowers and in the institutions they attended contributed to rising loan defaults. A Brookings Paper on Academic Activity, https://www.brookings. edu/bpea-articles/a-crisis-in-student-loans-how-changes-in-the-characteristics-of-borrowers-and-in-the-institutions-they-attended-contributed-to-rising-loan-defaults/#recent/

Marginson, S. (2016). *The Dream Is Over: The Crisis of Clark Kerr's California Idea of Higher Education.* Berkeley: University of California Press. doi:http://dx.doi. org/10.1525/luminos.17.

MIT. (2015). *The Future Postponed: Why Declining Investment in Basic Research Threatens a U.S. Innovation Deficit.* A Report by the MIT Committee to Evaluate the Innovation Deficit. Cambridge: Massachusetts Institute of Technology (MIT), April 2015, http:// dc.mit.edu/sites/default/files/Future%20Postponed.pdf

Mitchell, M., M. Leachman and K. Masterson. (2016). *Funding Down, Tuition Up: State Cuts to Higher Education Threaten Quality and Affordability at Public Colleges.* Center on Budget and Policy, Washington, DC. Center on Budget Policy Priorities, http:// www.cbpp.org/research/state-budget-and-tax/funding-down-tuition-up#_ftn9.

Nixon, J. (forthcoming). Higher education and the public good, in M. Klemencic (ed.), *Elite and Universal Higher Education in the Twenty-First Century: International Encyclopedia of Higher Education.* Dordrecht: Springer.

Pew Charitable Trust. (2015). Federal and state funding of higher education: A changing landscape. Issue Brief, http://www.pewtrusts.org/en/research-and-analysis/ issue-briefs/2015/06/federal-and-state-funding-of-higher-education.

Slaughter, S., and L. Leslie, (1997), *Academic Capitalism.* Baltimore: Johns Hopkins University Press.

Slaughter, S., and G. Rhoades, (2009), *Academic Capitalism and the New Economy: Markets, State, and Higher Education.* Baltimore: Johns Hopkins University Press.

Sykes, C. (2016), *Fail U: The False Promise of Higher Education.* New York: St. Martin's Press.

* * *

Through Asian Eyes

Jae Park

European austerity appears to my Asian eyes as someting intriguing afforded to the wealthy. We Asian countries had our own financial predicaments and austerity measures during downturns such as the 1997 financial crisis and the 'dot-com bubble blast'. Asian countries greatly suffered and came under austerity measures from within, in addition to those from international monetary authorities. Asian nations demonstrated how well they learnt the 1997 lesson a decade later when the 2004 global financial crisis which reached its peak in 2007/08. Perhaps we will manage well again, and soon, as global financial downturns seem to follow a ten-year cycle of human greed and need.

A global financial crisis does not hit a limited number of local industries and people but triggers a domino effect, knocking down many industries and social institutions. One of the social institutions most affected is the university. European austerity measures have been uniform neither in modality nor in the scale of their repercussions. Unlike Asia, where austerity measures were 'dictated', the European ones seem more politically negotiated, self-imposed and uneven. For example, the European University Association reported budget cuts of up to 10 per cent across Europe in May 2010. Latvia, arguably a part of the 'lesser-off EU', had a 48 per cent cut in state funding for public universities in 2009, followed by a further 18 per cent reduction in 2010 (Altbach, 2012: 207). The way Europe as a whole sees itself can run counter to its diversity and heterogeneity.

Why of all social institutions is time-honoured higher education the usual target of state-backed austerity measures? First, already for more than a decade, there has been very rapid growth in higher student enrolment, with more student capacity and academic staff (Altbach, 2012). Second, the same phenomenal growth rate resulted in a huge amount of expansion in infrastructure with corresponding policies. Third, higher education administration and management have become increasingly dependent on subsidies and corresponding regulations by the state and by public–private partnerships under the banner of 'global practices' such as marketization, privatization and decentralization. Neo-liberal states are no longer haunted by the liberal delusion of the old laissez-faire policy, and instead now openly promote a system of competition for internal markets or quasi markets in which students and teachers are human capital if not 'commodities'. Governments in Europe and Asia have, therefore, rapidly changed their higher education identity from that of a primarily hierarchical public agent into that of a market-based 'commodified' agent.

Managerialism in higher education is rampant (Ginsberg, 2011), where authorities are subjected to market principles encouraging competition among institutions. The dictum by Deng Xiaoping, who launched Communist China into a free-market system: 'Whether white or black, a cat is a good cat so long as it catches the rat' (Evans, 1995: 164), was prophetic also for other Asian institutions of higher education. Today, neo-liberal political and economic discourses in Asia have further eroded traditional public safety net systems which provide support for weaker and less competitive institutions. Now, even public institutions of higher education are held responsible for their success or failure, and funded accordingly based on research performance under the new nomenclature of excellence hierarchy. In my view, it is a now only a matter of time until the brand new British Research Excellence Framework (REF) and similar higher education assessment mechanisms become entrenched in former British colonial territories such as Hong Kong and Singapore.

The intertwined neo-liberal discourses of competitiveness, efficiency and accountability are intensifying in Asia. For this vast region, where Woodrow Wilson's 1905 declaration of the principle of national self-determination had such a huge impact on the local politics of countercolonialism and independence, these Western-born neo-liberal discourses could be

> capital-driven forces which seek to penetrate and colonize all spaces on the earth with unchecked freedom, and that in so doing have eroded national frontiers and integrated previously unconnected zones. In this ongoing process of globalization, unequal power relations become intensified, and imperialism expresses itself in a new form. (Chen, 2010: 4)

In other words, Asian states' self-imposed neo-liberal paradigms relating to – and policies on – higher education could not only be the cause but also a justification of their own political manoeuvrings. This is the reason that there is a need to look at higher education austerity measures more critically, that is, to consider austerity not as a social virtue or salvific remedy for catastrophes but as an immoral means of instrumentalizing it, of inflicting upon institutions of higher education what the incumbent power structure with all its parasites want to achieve through higher education by reifying their social and political agenda.

In my view, the main and ultimate victims of some ongoing changes in higher education, at least here in Asia, are the humanities and social sciences. Two cases in Far East Asia are showcased here to support this point – Japan and Korea – both with a unique process of modernization which was hijacked by colonization (Park, 2016) coupled with the import of Western-style higher education institutions and which are now euthanizing the social sciences and humanities.

In Asia, austerity is choking institutions of higher education but is doing so selectively within the social sciences and humanities, in which the 'field' of education is usually categorized. An overview of the history of the social sciences is needed if we are to look into this subject, that is, the rise of the social sciences and how they have now come under siege in the name of capital-driven urges. While Asia was founding new institutions of higher education amidst the presence of colonial powers at the turn of the nineteenth to the twentieth century, European modernists were in quest of certainty in the social sciences (Wagner, 2001). By then, intellectuals had become disenchanted with Auguste Comte's positivistic social science and its anti-philosophical stance. In its stead, political speculation – political sociology which could decipher 'social questions' – dominated the social concerns and speculation of the fin de siècle. This 'political sociology', according to Peter Wagner and his metatheory of modernity,[1] was dethroned by the modern social sciences of the 1960s under the patronage of novel philosophical speculations on politics and language, which provided thinkers with an 'epistemic optimism', or a feeling that social science could, indeed, be a real, fruitful and 'pure' scientific endeavour (2001).

The social sciences flourished in Asia during this period, for about three decades. But by the 1990s, a new wave of uncertainty in sociological circles emerged. Once optimists, social theorists again became suspicious of neatly structured discourses on social realities and their naively fixed conceptual categories. They devoted their energy to shaking the tree of extant sociological concepts and to debunking modernity with fresh incredulity, criticism and even cynicism (Lyotard, 1984; Rorty, 1989).

I contend that Asia had been engaged in 'business as usual', soaking up all these pulls and pushes of Western-born sociology and its metatheories, from Comte to Max Weber through Anthony Giddens. It cannot be otherwise because Asian institutions of higher education have as yet not been able to entirely decolonize themselves intellectually (Chen, 2010; Park, 2016), while the existing social structure herded Asian intellectuals and the creative class into the higher education system (inextricably neoliberal by now) and its associated labs and research centres. It is in this current state of affairs that Asian social sciences and humanities are being supressed in the name of austerity.

Japan's Ministry of Education's early policies were aligned with an ideal of imperialistic regional hegemony and pursuit of the Western model of modernization (Takeuchi, 2005 [1961]). When the Ministry was merged with the former Science and Technology Agency to become the Ministry of Education, Culture, Sports, Science and Technology (MEXT) in 2001, it signalled the national priority of science and technology, with which education would be aligned. No sooner had this occurred than new policies on Japanese institutions of higher education were implemented. For MEXT, Japanese institutions of higher education have to respond to market pressures by introducing the idea of rank-tabled excellence, competition, higher managerial autonomy, reduced costs and, in short, organizational reform as 'agencification' (Yamamoto, 2004). The move also included changes in the management of both publicly and privately funded Japanese higher education institutions in the form of a profit-oriented business model (Parker, 2012).

---

[1] Wagner never mentions, not even once, any alternative understanding or perception of modernity other than his universalistic and homogenizing Western modernity.

In 2015, Takamitsu Sawa, the president of Shiga University, expressed concern over MEXT's ad hoc policy on the humanities and social sciences in higher education (2015):

> On June 8 [2015], all presidents of national universities received a notice from the education minister telling them to either abolish their undergraduate departments and graduate schools devoted to the humanities and social sciences or shift their curricula to fields with greater utilitarian values.

Sawa had previously alerted the Japanese public that Japan's national universities were being forced to implement unprecedented reforms following a business model (Grove, 2015; Nakata Steffensen, 2015; Sawa, 2014). MEXT's (2015: 3) response was unflinching:

> At teacher training universities and faculties, we are meanwhile working to raise teacher quality while reducing student quotas, based on factors such as expected demographic dynamics and teacher demand. To that end, we already have a policy to 'abolish' courses in the teacher training universities and faculties which do not focus on acquisition of a teacher certificate. From now on emphasis will be placed on teacher training courses and the issue is to raise teacher quality.

The impact of this heavy-handed policy is expected also to affect private universities in Japan. Indeed, Japanese private universities have been receiving government subsidies based on Article 89 of the constitution (1946)[2] and have become increasingly dependent on government aid. Kyoko Anegawa (2015) empirically demonstrates that government subsidies for private universities have an impact on university management, study and research.

Coincidentally, the Korean Ministry of Education announced in 2015 a similar policy when, after professional but no public consultation, the government announced its official and final decisions on the Program for Industrial Needs Matched Education (PRIME) (Lee, 2015). In May 2016, the policy started being piloted in twenty-one universities representing about 10 per cent of all Korean universities. The condition for state funding was that every piloted university had to commit itself to reducing its enrolment of humanities students by 2,500 while increasing science, technology, engineering and mathematics (STEM) students by 4,500, creating a one-time numerical gap of 7,000 students per university (An, 2016). The aim is to raise the average employment rate of graduates by 7.7 per cent between 2015 and 2023 (An, 2016). The policy has already been criticized for its arbitrary manipulation of choice of school or major (Kim, 2016), but the current conservative government under the leadership of Park Geun-hye is adamant.

The core of the related controversies in Japan and Korea is, first, whether there is a need and even right for the government to forcefully scale down the humanities/STEM ratio in educational institutions and, second, the fate of academic and intellectual

---

[2] No public money or other property shall be expended or appropriated for the use, benefit or maintenance of any religious institution or association, or for any charitable, educational or benevolent enterprises not under the control of public authority.

freedom. The policies in the two countries are also comparable in that their policy justification is based on functionalist assumptions with neo-liberal seasoning.

The sociopolitical engineering of the social sciences and humanities in higher education is, indeed, a global phenomenon (Eagleton, 2015), where the humanities and social sciences are not shut down upfront but their student enrolment is given a ceiling figure and preferential majors and programmes are silently depopulated. The only glaring difference in the Korean and Japanese cases is the sudden attack, à la a swordsman, which is unlike the case of many global 'all-administrative universities' (Ginsberg, 2011) where the social sciences and humanities have been subtly and gradually choked over the years.

Salaries and wages for faculty and support staff involved in instruction, research, public affairs and student and other institutional services constitute a major item of average university expenditure (e.g. 85 per cent in Argentina; Altbach, 2012: 42) (See NCES, 2014). Higher education austerity measures particularly affect instructors. Frozen salaries have a greater impact on teaching than research staff because the latter can have access to alternative funding sources (see the Italian case explained by Capanao, in Altbach, 2012: 177). A corollary is that higher education instructors tend to be hired as part-timers, while their chances at tenure and promotion become slower and rarer. Additionally, academics in less prestigious institutions might earn up to 70 per cent less than at a prestigious one (see discussion on the case of Armenia by Ohanyan, in Altbach, 2012: 55).

Consequently, the dominant higher education mission statement exults knowledge production. Almost all higher education institutions worldwide are almost exclusively gauged and funded by their research output. In Hong Kong, for example, universities established by the local government as technical or professional training institutions (frequently offering twilight or evening courses) were turned into research universities within less than two decades after their founding. As the budget allocation and curriculum of public universities are determined almost solely by the university grant committee of the state in tandem with a few opportunistic industries, all further incentive to every university is to frantically increase research productivity. University teaching is no longer considered as knowledge transfer or any meaningful service to the community. Rather, university teaching is now an institution's second mission, whereas knowledge transfer and community extension are normally bundled together as the third.

Meanwhile, STEM-centred education policies dictate a course of action that includes redistribution of budget allocation, preferential selection of programmes and related staff hiring. On the surface, such policies aim at immediate effects, including job placement rate, salary level upon graduation and the essentially flawed idea that all skill-demanding jobs are better performed by engineers and mathematicians. For Asia, the very ideology of STEM-oriented policies across primary, secondary and tertiary education is not original but once again imported from Europe and North America (Curriculum Development Council, 2015; Office of the Chief Scientist, 2013; Stephens and Richey, 2011).

Higher education institutions are increasingly recognized for their commitment to contributing to human and social development (Global University Network for Innovation, 2008, 2014). In this view, scant community–university engagement indicates ghetto-like intellectual endeavours producing knowledge irrelevant to social need. Less naively interpreted, however, it could also indicate that people outside the campus green belt are unable to constitute a *public* in a Deweyan sense[3] to whom knowledge produced and taught in universities becomes the driving power to solve their own problems with their own hands.

The suppression of the social sciences and humanities cannot and should not be lineally attributed to the 'ivory tower higher education institutions' in Europe. Europe seems to be not only tired of modernity, as Jean-François Lyotard (1984) announced, but also bored with the modern humanities and sociological enquiry and even postmodern deconstruction. This 'European weariness' – together with the deep skepticism of modernity and the clashing voices of post-modernity – has arrived on our Asian shores. For the weary minds of Asian politicians, perhaps, the ultimate practical action appears to be a pragmatic dismissal of the humanities and social sciences. Here in Asia, and probably elsewhere within the ongoing globalization buzz, the recent policies against universities and their *scientia et humanitas* could be a rather accurate reflection of a brave new condition of knowledge: a condition which places institutions of higher education back on the positivist ground zero of Comte, with his profound rejection of the humanities and his vision of a society encoded with the STEM-knowledge construct of his time.

Acknowledgement

This work was sponsored by the Committee on Research and Development of the Education University of Hong Kong [RG 97/2014-2015R].

References

Altbach, P. G. (2012). *Paying the Professoriate: A Global Comparison of Compensation and Contracts*. New York: Routledge.

An, J. W. (2016). 프라임사업 확정…대학가 구조조정 본격 막 올랐다 [Prime industries decided: main university regulations unveiled]. *Yonhapnews*, 3 May. Retrieved from http://www.yonhapnews.co.kr/bulletin/2016/05/02/0200000000 AKR20160502111800004.HTML

Anegawa, K. (2015). 'Government subsidy impact on private university management in Japan', *The Keizai Ronkyu* 151(1): 1–16. doi:10.15017/1498373.

Chen, K.-H. (2010). *Asia as Method: Toward Deimperialization*. Durham, NC: Duke University Press.

Constitution of Japan. (1946). *The Constitution of Japan 1946*. Tokyo: Prime Minister of Japan and His Cabinet.

Curriculum Development Council. (2015). *Promotion of STEM Education-Unleashing Potential in Innovation*. Hong Kong: Education Bureau HKSAR Government.

---

[3] According to Dewey, the public is 'brought ... into existence' by the 'harm wrought' on it. For Dewey, the public does not emerge until it is faced with adversity and when it has risen, it proactively self-organizes: 'Recognition of evil consequences brought about a common interest which required for its maintenance certain measures and rules, together with the selection of certain persons as their guardians, interpreters, and, if need be, their executors' (1954 [1927]: 17).

Retrieved from http://www.edb.gov.hk/attachment/en/curriculum-development/renewal/Brief%20on%20STEM%20%28Overview%29_eng_20151105.pdf.

Dewey, J. (1954 [1927]). *The Public and Its Problems*. Athens, OH: Swallow Press.

Eagleton, T. (2015). The slow death of the university, *The Chronicle Review*, 6 April. Retrieved from http://chronicle.com/article/The-Slow-Death-of-the/228991/.

Evans, R. (1995). *Deng Xiaoping and the Making of Modern China*. London; New York: Penguin Books.

Ginsberg, B. (2011). *The Fall of the Faculty: The Rise of the All-Administrative University and Why It Matters*. Oxford: Oxford University Press.

Global University Network for Innovation. (2008). *Higher Education: New Challenges and Emerging Roles for Human and Social Development*. Basingstoke: Palgrave Macmillan.

Global University Network for Innovation. (2014). *Higher Education in the World 5: Knowledge, Engagement and Higher Education: Contributing to Social Change*. Basingstoke: Palgrave Macmillan.

Grove, J. (2015). Social sciences and humanities faculties 'to close' in Japan after ministerial intervention: Universities to scale back liberal arts and social science courses, *Times Higher Education*, 14 September. Retrieved from https://www.timeshighereducation.com/news/social-sciences-and-humanities-faculties-close-japan-after-ministerial-intervention.

Kim, S. J. (2016). 프라임 사업, 왜 문제이고 뭐가 문제일까 [Prime industries: why and what are its problems?]. 회대알리 [Hwyedaeali], 21 March. Retrieved from http://univalli.com/alliskhu/view.php?idx=74&ckattempt=1

Lee, M. H. (2015). 프라임사업의 주요 내용과 쟁점 [The content and controversies of the prime industries]. 대학교육 [Higher Education], 9 December, 190.

Lyotard, J.-F. (1984). *The Postmodern Condition: A Report on Knowledge*. Manchester: Manchester University Press.

MEXT. (2015). *National University Reform for the Coming Era*. Tokyo: Higher Education Bureau, Ministry of Education, Culture, Sports, Science and Technology-Japan. Retrieved from www.mext.go.jp/english/highered/__icsFiles/.../10/.../1362381_1_1.pdf.

Nakata Steffensen, K. (2015). Japan and the social sciences: Behind the headlines: Kenn Nakata Steffensen takes an in-depth look at the challenges facing Japan's public universities, *Times Higher Education*, 30 September. Retrieved from https://www.timeshighereducation.com/blog/japan-and-social-sciences-behind-headlines

NCES. (2014). The National Center for Education Statistics. Retrieved from https://nces.ed.gov/ipeds/datacenter/Default.aspx

Office of the Chief Scientist. (2013). *Science, Technology, Engineering and Mathematics in the National Interest: A Strategic Approach*. Canberra: Australian Government Retrieved from http://www.chiefscientist.gov.au/wp-content/uploads/STEMstrategy290713FINALweb.pdf.

Owens, P. (2015) *Economy of Force: Counterinsurgency and the Historical Rise of the Social*. Cambridge: Cambridge

Park, J. (2016). Asian Education and Asia as method, in C. M. Lam and J. Park (eds), *Sociological and Philosophical Perspectives on Education in the Asia-Pacific Region*, New York; London: Springer. 205–25.

Parker, L. D. (2012). From privatised to hybrid corporatised higher education: A global financial management discourse, *Financial Accountability & Management* 28(3): 247–68. doi:10.1111/j.1468-0408.2012.00544.

Rorty, R. (1989). *Contingency, Irony, and Solidarity*. Cambridge: Cambridge University Press.

Sawa, T. (2014). University is not a business, *Japan Times*, 22 June. Retrieved from http://www.japantimes.co.jp/opinion/2014/06/22/commentary/japan-commentary/university-business/#.VrW6Tk-BpdA.

Sawa, T. (2015). Humanities under attack, *Japan Times*, 23 August. Retrieved from http://www.japantimes.co.jp/opinion/2015/08/23/commentary/japan-commentary/humanities-attack/#.VihJ9W5N_AH

Stephens, R., and M. Richey. (2011). Accelerating STEM capacity: A complex adaptive system perspective, *Journal of Engineering Education* 100(3): 417–23.

Takeuchi, Y. (2005 [1961]). Asia as method [Hoho to shite no Ajia], in R. F. Calichman (ed.), *What Is Modernity? Writings of Takeuchi Yoshimi*. New York: Columbia University Press. 149–65.

Wagner, P. (2001). *Theorizing Modernity: Inescapability and Attainability in Social Theory*. London: SAGE.

Yamamoto, K. (2004). Corporatization of national universities in Japan: Revolution for governance or rhetoric for downsizing?, *Financial Accountability & Management* 20(2): 153–81. doi:10.1111/j.1468-0408.20.

Coda: Where Do We Go from Here?

Jon Nixon

We are entering, I suspect, upon a time of troubles. (Judt, 2010: 207)

The European project emerged from the horrors of World War II. It was an attempt to build a lasting political settlement based on cultural and institutional interchange, a commitment to state 'welfarism', the agreement to trade freely across national boundaries and the acknowledgement of the need for a united front within the context of the polarizing Cold War. These various aspects of the post–World War II 'settlement' never quite added up to an ideal. They were based on compromise, accommodation and realpolitik. But at their heart was an important idea: the need for the nation states of Europe – in the aftermath of an appalling and bloody 'short twentieth century' – to work together for the common good and in the interests of a fairer and more socially cohesive society. It was an idea that, as we now know, may – tragically – never be realized. But it was an idea that – for a while – had the kind of tough and unsentimental hopefulness that is now almost entirely lacking from the cultural landscape of Europe.

Three major occurrences – the decision by the United Kingdom to exit the European Union (EU), the election of Donald Trump to the US presidency and the electoral success of far right parties – are now shaping the economic, political and social dimensions of that landscape.[1] They are, of course, disparate events. Each has its own causality. But they do share one common element: they were each, in part at least, an expression of the alienation felt by some of the most economically vulnerable groups in society. There is no doubt that some of the more affluent and upwardly mobile sections of society bought into what was presented as a radical agenda for change. But had it not been for the support of those who feel 'left behind' – those whose standard of living has declined over the past ten years, whose traditional skills are no longer valued in an increasingly technologized labour market and whose sense of fairness is constantly challenged by rising levels of inequality – the result of the UK EU membership referendum and of the US presidential election may well have been very different. Both were in large measure a rejection of a political class which was seen to be increasingly out of touch and elitist.

---

[1] As noted in the introduction, these events occurred after most of the contributions to this volume had been finalized.

That rejection was fuelled by a deep sense of unfairness which the austerity meas-ures pursued by successive governments since the 2007/08 financial crisis undoubt-edly helped engender. When particular sections of society bear the brunt of economic decline, population loss and urban decay, a deep sense of unfairness will inevitably result. Moreover, when that sense of unfairness becomes a chronic condition through the failure of successive governments to address the social inequalities resulting from their economic policies, outrage becomes a rational response. Since 'exit' is not an option and one's 'voice' is repeatedly ignored, the only option is what Albert O. Hirschman (1970: 33–6) termed '*voice* as a residual of exit': the residue of one's agency expressed as emphatic and uncompromising acts of rejection (original emphasis). Such acts are driven primarily by the impulse towards negative freedom: *freedom from* constraint, and may have little purchase on the positive freedoms that may then open up: *freedom to* imagine new political trajectories and build new pathways into the future.

Nevertheless, that impulse can give rise to progressive grass-roots movements that are effective in drawing attention to the gross inequalities within society. Moreover, these movements – even if they do not have a direct impact on policy – may have an indirect impact on the general climate of opinion. But that same impulse may also open the door to individuals who by claiming to represent the interests of the most vulnerable in society are able to channel popular outrage to their own advantage. Such individuals may be excessively wealthy beyond the wildest dreams of those they claim to represent. They may be inextricably entwined in the global elites against which they vent their rhetorical ire. Indeed, their policies may, after close scrutiny, be seen to privilege those elites. None of these factors would seem to have a bearing on their credibility which resides solely in their perceived claim to be the 'voice of the people'. When that cred-ibility achieves legitimacy through the ballot box we have entered the age of the dema-gogues: an age in which the rhetoric of populism dominates the political discourse.

'Populism' is a slippery, catch-all term. What does it mean? Jan-Werner Müller (2016) addresses this question by suggesting that the notion of populism involves two related claims. First, populists claim that 'the voice of the people' takes precedent over all other sources of legitimate political authority: the judiciary, parliament and local government. The complexity of democratic sovereignty is thereby collapsed into a notion of 'the sovereignty of the people' – a notion that licenses populists to decry any attempt by the courts to pursue their constitutional function, to demand that elected members adhere to a popular mandate rather than exercise their independent judge-ments and to inveigh against any sections of the free press that are critical of the sup-posed 'will of the people'. The separation of powers, the constitutional cornerstone of liberal democracy, is thereby put at risk.

Second, populists claim to know what constitutes 'the people'. Within the current pol-itical discourse 'the people' are variously defined as 'ordinary people', 'decent people' and even 'real people'. 'The people', in other words, are invariably defined against 'other people', who by implication are not 'ordinary', not 'decent' and not 'real'. It is these 'other people' who then become the targets – the scapegoats – of populist outrage: immigrants, refu-gees, religious minorities, recipients of state benefit, the unemployed … the list of poten-tial scapegoats is endless. The point is to define 'the people' against some available 'other'.

Pluralism – the cultural heartbeat of liberal democracy – is thereby not only put at risk but denied.

To those two claims, a third claim should be added. Populists claim a monopoly on the truth regardless of its factual accuracy. The traditional distinction between deception and self-deception is not particularly helpful in this context. To tell an untruth with a view to deceiving others is one thing. To tell an untruth that we have wrongly persuaded ourselves is true is another. But to state an untruth that neither seeks to deceive others nor is a consequence of self-deception is something different again. It is an expression of power and control, demanding unconditional assent. It assumes that assent matters more than truth, that to unite around an untruth is justifiable and that – in the moral wasteland of populism – truth-telling no longer matters. What matter are so-called 'alternative facts', the rubbishing of serious investigative journalism as 'fake news' and the incessant barrage of half-truths, untruths and downright lies. In the age of the demagogues, post-truth politics reigns supreme.

So, where do we go from here? Higher education, I would argue, has four crucial functions to fulfil within this new age of populist dogma. First it has an historic duty to insist on the distinction between truth and untruth, verifiable belief and wishful thinking, fact and fantasy. 'Our concern', as Bernard Williams (2002: 133) put it, 'is with the virtues of truth'.[2] Those virtues cannot be discovered ready made within a single method. As Hans-Georg Gadamer (2001: 42) insisted, truth resides in our commitment to 'the questionableness of something and what this requires of us'. Methods matter, but they cannot provide us with a ladder of perfection that inevitably leads us to 'the truth'. The quest for truth is always a messy and muddled affair characterized by false starts, blind alleys, occasional insights, provisional resolutions and leaps of 'the hermeneutical imagination' (see Nixon, 2017). Higher education exists to provide us with the resources necessary to engage in this lifelong process of truthfulness.

Second, higher education is, as the term 'university' suggests, universal. It reaches out and is by definition inclusive. 'Universal' means much more than – and, indeed, is something very different from – the international marketization of higher education with a view to the recruitment of overseas students. It means developing what Feng Su and Margaret Wood (2017) call a 'cosmopolitan outlook': an outlook that circumscribes both the local and the global and perceives the interplay between the two.[3] This is what Kwame Anthony Appiah (2005: 213–71) terms 'rooted cosmopolitanism' or 'a tenable cosmopolitanism': a cosmopolitanism that one can hold on to and that is grounded in the here and now. It resists insularity and any form of institutional belongingness that relies on exclusivity. It is committed to the extension – and fusion – of our horizons of understanding.

Third, institutions of higher education are, within the broader framework of civil society, the upholders of certain values. Paramount among these values is the recognition of – and respect for – others. Without this core value, there can be neither mutuality nor reciprocity, and without mutuality and reciprocity there can be no rational discourse – and, without rational discourse, we sink into the thick sedge of platitude,

---

[2] See the discussion of truthfulness in Chapter 4 of my *Towards the Virtuous University* (Nixon, 2008: 47–65).

[3] See the discussion of 'cosmopolitan imaginaries' in Chapter 4 my *Higher Education and the Public Good* (Nixon, 2011: 51–65).

of unsubstantiated claim and counterclaim, that is the defining feature of our sound-bite culture. Rational discourse is impossible in the absence of mutual respect and the willingness to listen. It may be true that all civilizations are built on bloodshed, but it is also true that unless they go on to construct an institutional framework that values and protects mutuality and reciprocity then they will collapse back into bloodshed. Institutions of higher education – as exemplars of what Axel Honneth (2014: 49) calls 'institutions of recognition' – remind us that our individual freedoms rely crucially upon our capacity to live together and reason together (see also Honneth, 1995).

Finally, institutions of higher education provide us with a distinctive idiom: explorative, nuanced, self-questioning, tentative, uncertain and forever in search of fine distinctions. It is an idiom – and a cast of mind – that has little or no place in a populist discourse in which the major protagonists are not only assured of certain certainties but assured of their right to assert those certainties. That idiom – the idiom of Socrates – has always fallen foul of regimes and political cultures that, even when democratic in name, obstruct the free interplay of ideas and arguments. Higher education exists in part to encourage and support this idiom, to ensure that it retains a presence in social and political discourse and to provide it with the wherewithal for present and future generations to speak truth to power. Higher education exists not only to remind us that uncertainty is intrinsic to the human condition but to provide us with the wherewithal to dwell in uncertainty.

We live in an increasingly uncertain world. For the last seventy years Europe has, for Europeans at least, provided some measure of economic, political and social stability. Ten years ago a global financial crisis exposed the fault lines in the European project. As the previous chapters show, the nation states of Europe responded in different ways according to their histories and political trajectories. But the centralizing tendencies of the European bureaucracy in pushing through austerity measures – and of the more powerful nation states in following suit – has meant that we are, as Tony Judt (2010: 207) suggested in his final work, entering upon 'a time of troubles'. How well or ill we fare in the troubled times ahead will depend crucially on how we defend our institutions of higher education: the values they represent and the practices of disinterested but passionate inquiry that they sustain.

References

Appiah, K. A. (2005). *The Ethics of Identity*. Princeton and Woodstock: Princeton University Press.

Gadamer, H.-G. (2001). *Gadamer in Conversation: Reflections and Commentary*. Edited and Translated by R. E. Palmer. New Haven and London: Yale University Press.

Hirschman, A. O. (1970). *Exit, Voice, and Loyalty: Responses to Decline in Firms, Organizations, and States*. Cambridge, MA, and London: Harvard University Press.

Honneth, A. (1995). *The Struggle for Recognition: The Moral Grammar of Social Conflicts*. Cambridge: Polity.

Honneth, A. (2014). *Freedom's Right: The Social Foundations of Democratic Life*. Translated by J. Ganahl. Cambridge: Polity.

Judt, T. (2010). *The Memory Chalet*. London: William Heinemann.

Müller, J-W. (2016). *What Is Populism?* Philadelphia: University of Pennsylvania Press.
Nixon, J. (2008). *Towards the Virtuous University: The Moral Bases of Academic Practice.* London and New York: Routledge.
Nixon, J. (2011). *Higher Education and the Public Good: Imagining the University.* London and New York: Continuum.
Nixon, J. (2017). *Gadamer: The Hermeneutical Imagination.* Dordrecht: Springer.
Su, F., and M. Wood (eds) (2017). *Cosmopolitan Perspectives on Academic Leadership in Higher Education.* London and New York: Bloomsbury.
Williams, B. (2002). *Truth and Truthfulness: An Essay in Genealogy.* Princeton and Oxford: Princeton University Press.

Index